CIMA EXAMINATION KIT

Intermediate Level

Paper 4

Finance

ISBN 1 84390 118 8

British Library Cataloguing-in-Publication data

A catalogue record for this book is available from the British Library.

We are grateful to the Chartered Institute of Management Accountants for permission to reproduce past examination questions. The solutions have been prepared by The Financial Training Company.

Published by

The Financial Training Company
22J Wincombe Business Park
Shaftesbury
Dorset
SP7 9QJ

Contents

Questions and Answers

Syllabus

Syllabus overview

This is an introduction to financial management. It builds on the Foundation units of Economics for Business, Business Mathematics and Financial Accounting Fundamentals.

This syllabus deals with the evaluation of short and long term financing and requires an appreciation of the relevant theories underpinning this together with an understanding of working capital management.

The Finance paper underpins the Financial Strategy paper at the Final level.

Aims

This syllabus aims to test the student's ability to:

♦   Explain the role and purpose of financial management

♦   Identify and evaluate sources of finance

♦   Calculate cost of capital

♦   Analyse the overall management of working capital

♦   Evaluate debtor and creditor management policies.

Assessment

There will be a written paper of 3 hours. The paper will comprise two sections.

Section A :   40% Objective testing. All questions will be compulsory.

Section B :   3 questions will be answered out of a choice of 5.

All learning outcomes may be tested in either section.

Formulae will be given as required.

Learning outcomes and syllabus content

4(i)   The finance function – 10%

Learning outcomes

On completion of their studies students should be able to:

♦   Explain the interrelationships between decisions concerning investment, financing and dividends.

♦   Describe and explain the operation of the securities markets.

♦   Describe and explain the role and management of the treasury function.

♦   Compare and contrast the services provided by financial institutions and recommend appropriate providers in different scenarios.

Syllabus content

♦ The financial objectives of different organisations eg value for money, maximising shareholder wealth, providing a surplus.

♦ The three key decisions of financial management (ie investment, financing, dividend) and their links.

♦ The operation of securities markets (stock exchanges) ie how share prices are determined and what causes share prices to rise or fall. (No detailed knowledge of any specific country's stock exchange will be tested.) Financial institutions eg stock brokers, institutional investors, merchant banks, venture capitalists, money brokers.

♦ The efficient market hypothesis (EMH).

♦ The role of the treasury function in terms of setting corporate objectives, liquidity management, funding management, currency management.

♦ The benefits and shortcomings of establishing treasury departments as profit centres or cost centres.

♦ The control of treasury departments when established as cost centres or profit centres.

4(ii) Sources of long term finance – 30%

Learning outcomes

On completion of their studies students should be able to:

♦ Recommend the sources of capital most appropriate for an organisation.

♦ Evaluate the most appropriate method of funding an asset.

♦ Calculate investor ratios and demonstrate the impact of changing capital structures on these ratios.

♦ Calculate the cost of capital and demonstrate the impact of changing capital structures.

♦ Explain the impact of interest rate changes on the cost of capital.

Syllabus content

♦ Types of share capital ie ordinary, preference, deferred, warrants.

♦ Equity issues; new and rights issues.

♦ Long term debt finance (ie secured, unsecured, redeemable, irredeemable, convertibles and debt with warrants).

♦ Methods of issuing securities eg rights, placing, offer for sale.

♦ Fraud related to sources of finance (eg advance fee fraud and pyramid schemes).

♦ Operating and finance leases (one year lagged tax savings will be tested with leases and comparisons of the cost of a lease with the cost of buying).

♦ The calculation of the cost of equity using the capital asset pricing model (CAPM) and the dividend growth model (knowledge of methods of calculating and estimating dividend growth will be expected).

♦ An introduction to the relationship between risk, uncertainty and reward eg use of CAPM (Beta, R_m and R_f will be given and a simple understanding of the CAPM is all that will be tested. Gearing and ungearing betas will not be tested).

♦ The ideas of diversifiable risk (unsystematic risk) and systematic risk (use of the two asset portfolio formula will not be tested).

♦ The cost of redeemable and irredeemable debt including the tax shield on debt (numerical questions on the cost of convertible debt will not be tested).

♦ The weighted average cost of capital (Modigliani and Miller will not be tested).

♦ Investor ratios ie EPS, Price/Earnings (P/E) ratio, dividend cover, dividend yield, interest yield, earnings yield, redemption yield.

♦ Gearing ratios (market and book values) and interest cover.

4(iii)   Sources of short term finance – 20%

Learning outcomes

On completion of their studies students should be able to:

♦ Identify alternatives for investment of short term cash surpluses.

♦ Identify sources of short term funding.

♦ Calculate and explain rates of interest.

♦ Explain the yield curve and its practical use.

♦ Analyse an organisation's creditworthiness from a lender's viewpoint.

♦ Identify appropriate methods of finance for trading internationally.

Syllabus content

♦ Interest rate arithmetic (compound, simple, annual, quarterly, monthly).

♦ The yield curve and theories concerning normal and inverse yield curves.

♦ The principles of investing short term ie maturity, return, security, liquidity and diversification.

♦ Types of investments eg interest bearing bank accounts, negotiable instruments (including certificates of deposit, short term treasury bills), securities.

♦ The difference between the coupon on debt and the yield to maturity.

♦ Types of borrowing eg overdrafts, short term loans, invoice discounting.

♦ The effect of short term debt on the measurement of gearing.

♦ Use and abuse of trade creditors as a source of finance.

♦ The lender's assessment of creditworthiness.

♦ Export finance ie documentary credits, bills of exchange, export factoring, forfeiting.

4(iv)   Working capital management – 40%

Learning outcomes

On completion of their studies students should be able to:

♦ Calculate and interpret working capital ratios for business sectors.

♦ Prepare and analyse cash flow forecasts over a 12 month period.

♦ Identify measures to improve a cash forecast situation.

♦ Compare and contrast the use and limitations of cash management models and identify when each model is most appropriate.

♦ State and illustrate the main issues in group cash flow management.

♦ Identify appropriate bank services to assist in cash management.

♦ Identify debtor management policies and procedures for an organisation.

♦ Interpret the creditworthiness of a customer.

♦ Analyse trade debtor information.

♦ Evaluate debtor and creditor policies.

♦ Evaluate appropriate methods of stock management.

Syllabus content

♦ Working capital ratios ie debtor days, stock days, creditor days, current ratio, quick ratio and the working capital cycle.

♦ The working capital characteristics of different businesses (eg supermarkets being heavily funded by creditors) and the importance of industry comparisons.

♦ Cash flow forecasts, use of spreadsheets to assist in this in terms of changing variables (eg interest rates or inflation) and in consolidating forecasts.

♦ Which variables are most easily changed, delayed or brought forward in a forecast.

♦ The link between cash, profit and the balance sheet.

♦ The Baumol and Miller Orr cash management models.

♦ Group cash flow management eg netting.

♦ Bank services available to organisations in order to help them manage cash eg investing overnight, Bankers' Automated Clearing Services (BACS), automated matching, minimising service charges.

♦ Bank services and facilities and their impact on organisational activities and costs.

♦ The credit cycle from receipt of customer order to cash receipt.

♦ Payment terms.

♦ Assessing a customer's creditworthiness eg sources of credit status information (eg bank references, trade references, internal credit rating information).

♦ Evaluating settlement discounts.

♦ Methods of payment eg cash, BACS, cheque, banker's draft, standing order, direct debit, credit card, debit card.

♦ Present and interpret an age analysis of debtors.

♦ The stages in debt collection eg reminder, statement, telephone call, personal visit, legal action, debt collection agency, interest on overdue debts.

♦ Establishing collection targets on an appropriate basis eg motivational issues in managing credit control.

♦ Factoring and invoice discounting.

♦ Remedies for bad debts eg credit insurance, debt collection agencies, specialist solicitors, guidance in taking legal action, negotiated settlements, an outline of the differences between bankruptcy and insolvency (no legal aspects to be examined).

♦ The payment cycle from agreeing the order to making payment.

♦ Payment terms as part of the order.

♦ Centralised versus decentralised purchasing.

♦ Present and interpret an age analysis of creditors.

♦ The link between purchasing and the budget for cost centres.

♦ The relationship between purchasing and stock control.

♦ The Economic Order Quantity (EOQ) model (ie reorder levels, reorder quantities, safety stocks and evaluating whether bulk order discounts should be accepted).

MATHEMATICAL TABLES AND FORMULAE

PRESENT VALUE TABLE

Present value of £1 ie $(1 + r)^{-n}$ where r = interest rate, n = number of periods until payment or receipt.

Periods (n)	1%	2%	3%	4%	5%	6%	7%	8%	9%	10%	11%	12%	13%	14%	15%	16%	17%	18%	19%	20%
1	.990	.980	.971	.962	.952	.943	.935	.926	.917	.909	.901	.893	.885	.877	.870	.862	.855	.847	.840	.833
2	.980	.961	.943	.925	.907	.890	.873	.857	.842	.826	.812	.797	.783	.769	.756	.743	.731	.718	.706	.694
3	.971	.942	.915	.889	.864	.840	.816	.794	.772	.751	.731	.712	.693	.675	.658	.641	.624	.609	.593	.579
4	.961	.924	.888	.855	.823	.792	.763	.735	.708	.683	.659	.636	.613	.592	.572	.552	.534	.516	.499	.482
5	.951	.906	.863	.822	.784	.747	.713	.681	.650	.621	.593	.567	.543	.519	.497	.476	.456	.437	.419	.402
6	.942	.888	.837	.790	.746	.705	.666	.630	.596	.564	.535	.507	.480	.456	.432	.410	.390	.370	.352	.335
7	.933	.871	.813	.760	.711	.665	.623	.583	.547	.513	.482	.452	.425	.400	.376	.354	.333	.314	.296	.279
8	.923	.853	.789	.731	.677	.627	.582	.540	.502	.467	.434	.404	.376	.351	.327	.305	.285	.266	.249	.233
9	.914	.837	.766	.703	.645	.592	.544	.500	.460	.424	.391	.361	.333	.308	.284	.263	.243	.225	.209	.194
10	.905	.820	.744	.676	.614	.558	.508	.463	.422	.386	.352	.322	.295	.270	.247	.227	.208	.191	.176	.162
11	.896	.804	.722	.650	.585	.527	.475	.429	.388	.350	.317	.287	.261	.237	.215	.195	.178	.162	.148	.135
12	.887	.788	.701	.625	.557	.497	.444	.397	.356	.319	.286	.257	.231	.208	.187	.168	.152	.137	.124	.112
13	.879	.773	.681	.601	.530	.469	.415	.368	.326	.290	.258	.229	.204	.182	.163	.145	.130	.116	.104	.093
14	.870	.758	.661	.577	.505	.442	.388	.340	.299	.263	.232	.205	.181	.160	.141	.125	.111	.099	.088	.078
15	.861	.743	.642	.555	.481	.417	.362	.315	.275	.239	.209	.183	.160	.140	.123	.108	.095	.084	.074	.065
16	.853	.728	.623	.534	.458	.394	.339	.292	.252	.218	.188	.163	.141	.123	.107	.093	.081	.071	.062	.054
17	.844	.714	.605	.513	.436	.371	.317	.270	.231	.198	.170	.146	.125	.108	.093	.080	.069	.060	.052	.045
18	.836	.700	.587	.494	.416	.350	.296	.250	.212	.180	.153	.130	.111	.095	.081	.069	.059	.051	.044	.038
19	.828	.686	.570	.475	.396	.331	.277	.232	.194	.164	.138	.116	.098	.083	.070	.060	.051	.043	.037	.031
20	.820	.673	.554	.456	.377	.312	.258	.215	.178	.149	.124	.104	.087	.073	.061	.051	.043	.037	.031	.026

CUMULATIVE PRESENT VALUE OF £1

This table shows the Present Value of £1 per annum, receivable or payable at the end of each year for n years $\dfrac{1-(1+r)^{-n}}{r}$.

Periods (n)	Interest rates (r)																			
	1%	2%	3%	4%	5%	6%	7%	8%	9%	10%	11%	12%	13%	14%	15%	16%	17%	18%	19%	20%
1	.990	.980	.971	.962	.952	.943	.935	.926	.917	.909	.901	.893	.885	.877	.870	.862	.855	.847	.840	.833
2	1.970	1.942	1.913	1.886	1.859	1.833	1.808	1.783	1.759	1.736	1.713	1.690	1.668	1.647	1.626	1.605	1.585	1.566	1.547	1.528
3	2.941	2.884	2.829	2.775	2.723	2.673	2.624	2.577	2.531	2.487	2.444	2.402	2.361	2.322	2.283	2.246	2.210	2.174	2.140	2.106
4	3.902	3.808	3.717	3.630	3.546	3.465	3.387	3.312	3.240	3.170	3.102	3.037	2.974	2.914	2.855	2.798	2.743	2.690	2.639	2.589
5	4.853	4.713	4.580	4.452	4.329	4.212	4.100	3.993	3.890	3.791	3.696	3.605	3.517	3.433	3.352	3.274	3.199	3.127	3.058	2.991
6	5.795	5.601	5.417	5.242	5.076	4.917	4.767	4.623	4.486	4.355	4.231	4.111	3.998	3.889	3.784	3.685	3.589	3.498	3.410	3.326
7	6.728	6.472	6.230	6.002	5.786	5.582	5.389	5.206	5.033	4.868	4.712	4.564	4.423	4.288	4.160	4.039	3.922	3.812	3.706	3.605
8	7.652	7.325	7.020	6.733	6.463	6.210	5.971	5.747	5.535	5.335	5.146	4.968	4.799	4.639	4.487	4.344	4.207	4.078	3.954	3.837
9	8.566	8.162	7.786	7.435	7.108	6.802	6.515	6.247	5.995	5.759	5.537	5.328	5.132	4.946	4.772	4.607	4.451	4.303	4.163	4.031
10	9.471	8.983	8.530	8.111	7.722	7.360	7.024	6.710	6.418	6.145	5.889	5.650	5.426	5.216	5.019	4.833	4.659	4.494	4.339	4.192
11	10.368	9.787	9.253	8.760	8.306	7.887	7.499	7.139	6.805	6.495	6.207	5.938	5.687	5.453	5.234	5.029	4.836	4.656	4.486	4.327
12	11.255	10.575	9.954	9.385	8.863	8.384	7.943	7.536	7.161	6.814	6.492	6.194	5.918	5.660	5.421	5.197	4.988	4.793	4.611	4.439
13	12.134	11.348	10.635	9.986	9.394	8.853	8.358	7.904	7.487	7.103	6.750	6.424	6.122	5.842	5.583	5.342	5.118	4.910	4.715	4.533
14	13.004	12.106	11.296	10.563	9.899	9.295	8.745	8.244	7.786	7.367	6.982	6.628	6.302	6.002	5.724	5.468	5.229	5.008	4.802	4.611
15	13.865	12.849	11.938	11.118	10.380	9.712	9.108	8.559	8.061	7.606	7.191	6.811	6.462	6.142	5.847	5.575	5.324	5.092	4.876	4.675
16	14.718	13.578	12.561	11.652	10.838	10.106	9.447	8.851	8.313	7.824	7.379	6.974	6.604	6.265	5.954	5.668	5.405	5.162	4.938	4.730
17	15.562	14.292	13.166	12.166	11.274	10.477	9.763	9.122	8.544	8.022	7.549	7.120	6.729	6.373	6.047	5.749	5.475	5.222	4.990	4.775
18	16.398	14.992	13.754	12.659	11.690	10.828	10.059	9.372	8.756	8.201	7.702	7.250	6.840	6.467	6.128	5.818	5.534	5.273	5.033	4.812
19	17.226	15.679	14.324	13.134	12.085	11.158	10.336	9.604	8.950	8.365	7.839	7.366	6.938	6.550	6.198	5.877	5.584	5.316	5.070	4.843
20	18.046	16.351	14.878	13.590	12.462	11.470	10.594	9.818	9.129	8.514	7.963	7.469	7.025	6.623	6.259	5.929	5.628	5.353	5.101	4.870

FORMULAE

Valuation Models

(i)   Irredeemable preference share, paying a constant annual dividend, d, in perpetuity, where P_0 is the ex-div value:

$$P_0 = \frac{d}{k_{pref}}$$

(ii)   Ordinary (Equity) share, paying a constant annual dividend, d, in perpetuity, where P_0 is the ex-div value:

$$P_0 = \frac{d}{k_e}$$

(iii)   Ordinary (Equity) share, paying an annual dividend, d, growing in perpetuity at a constant rate, g, where P_0 is the ex-div value:

$$P_0 = \frac{d_1}{k_e - g} \text{ or } P_0 = \frac{d_0[1+g]}{k_e - g}$$

(iv)   Irredeemable (Undated) debt, paying annual after tax interest, i(1 - t), in perpetuity, where P_0 is the ex-interest value:

$$P_0 = \frac{i[1-t]}{k_{d\,net}}$$

or, without tax:

$$P_0 = \frac{i}{k_d}$$

(v)   Future value of S, of a sum X, invested for n periods, compounded at r% interest:

$$S = X[1 + r]^n$$

(vi)   Present value of £1 payable or receivable in n years, discounted at r% per annum:

$$PV = \frac{1}{[1+r]^n}$$

(vii)   Present value of an annuity of £1 per annum, receivable or payable for n years, commencing in one year, discounted at r% per annum:

$$PV = \frac{1}{r}\left[1 - \frac{1}{[1+r]^n}\right]$$

(viii) Present value of £1 per annum, payable or receivable in perpetuity, commencing in one year, discounted at r% per annum:

$$PV = \frac{1}{r}$$

(ix)   Present value of £1 per annum, receivable or payable, commencing in one year, growing in perpetuity at a constant rate of g% per annum, discounted at r% per annum:

$$PV = \frac{1}{r - g}$$

Cost of Capital

(i)   Cost of irredeemable preference capital, paying an annual dividend, d, in perpetuity, and having a current ex-div price P_0:

$$k_{pref} = \frac{d}{P_0}$$

(ii)   Cost of irredeemable debt capital, paying annual net interest i(1 – t), and having a current ex-interest price P_0:

$$k_{d\ net} = \frac{i[1-t]}{P_0}$$

(iii) Cost of ordinary (Equity) share capital, paying an annual dividend, d, in perpetuity, and having a current ex-div price P_0:

$$k_e = \frac{d}{P_0}$$

(iv)   Cost of ordinary (Equity) share capital, having a current ex-div price, P_0, having just paid a dividend, d_0, with the dividend growing in perpetuity by a constant g% per annum:

$$k_e = \frac{d_1}{P_0} + g \quad \text{or} \quad k_e = \frac{d_0[1+g]}{P_0} + g$$

(v)   Cost of ordinary (Equity) share capital, using the CAPM:

$$k_e = R_f + [R_m - R_f]\beta$$

(vi)   Weighted average cost of capital, k_0:

$$k_0 = k_e \left[\frac{V_E}{V_E + V_D} \right] + k_d \left[\frac{V_D}{V_E + V_D} \right]$$

Stock Management

(i)   Economic Order Quantity

$$EOQ = \sqrt{\frac{2C_0 D}{C_h}}$$

Where C_0 = cost of placing an order

C_h = stockcarrying cost

D = annual demand

Cash Management

(i)   Optimal sale of securities, Baumol model:

$$\text{Optimal sale} = \sqrt{\frac{2 \times \text{Annual cash disbursements} \times \text{Cost per sale of securities}}{\text{Interest rate}}}$$

(ii)   Spread between upper and lower cash balance limits, Miller-Orr model:

$$\text{Spread} = 3\left[\frac{\frac{3}{4} \times \text{transaction cost} \times \text{variance of cash flows}}{\text{Interest rate}}\right]^{1/3}$$

Meaning of CIMA's examination requirements

CIMA use precise words in the requirements of their questions. In the schedule below we reproduce the precise meanings of these words from the CIMA syllabus. You must learn these definitions and make sure that in the exam you do precisely what CIMA requires you to do.

Learning objective	Verbs used	Definition
1 Knowledge		
What you are expected to know	List	Make a list of
	State	Express, fully or clearly, the details of/facts of
	Define	Give the exact meaning of
2 Comprehension		
What you are expected to understand	Describe	Communicate the key features of
	Distinguish	Highlight the differences between
	Explain	Make clear or intelligible/state the meaning of
	Identify	Recognise, establish or select after consideration
	Illustrate	Use an example to describe or explain something
3 Application		
Can you apply your knowledge?	Apply	To put to practical use
	Calculate/compute	To ascertain or reckon mathematically
	Demonstrate	To prove with certainty or to exhibit by practical means
	Prepare	To make or get ready for use
	Reconcile	To make or prove consistent/compatible
	Solve	Find an answer to
	Tabulate	Arrange in a table
4 Analysis		
Can you analyse the detail of what you have learned?	Analyse	Examine in detail the structure of
	Categorise	Place into a defined class or division
	Compare and contrast	Show the similarities and/or differences between
	Construct	To build up or compile
	Discuss	To examine in detail by argument
	Interpret	To translate into intelligible or familiar terms
	Produce	To create or bring into existence
5 Evaluation		
Can you use your learning to evaluate, make decisions or recommendations?	Advise	To counsel, inform or notify
	Evaluate	To appraise or assess the value of
	Recommend	To advise on a course of action

Objective test questions

The objective test questions will comprise a question with four possible answers. For example,

1   What is the world's tallest mountain?

    A   Ben Nevis

    B   K2

    C   Mount Everest

    D   Mount Snowdon

You have to select the correct answer (which in the above example is of course **C**).

In the examination, however, the incorrect answers, called distractors, may be quite plausible and are sometimes designed if not exactly to mislead you, they may nevertheless be the result of fairly common mistakes.

The following is a suggested technique for answering these questions, but as you practise for the examination you have to work out a method which suits you.

Step 1

Read all the questions, but not necessarily the answers. Select the ones which you think are the most straightforward and do them first.

Step 2

For more awkward questions, some people prefer to work the question without reference to the answers which increases your confidence if your answer then matches one of the options. However some people prefer to view the question with the four answers as this may assist them in formulating their answer.

This is a matter of personal preference and you should perhaps practise each to see which you find most effective.

Step 3

If your answer does not match one of the options you must:

(a)   Re-read the question carefully to make sure you have not missed some important point.

(b)   Re-work your solution eliminating any mistakes.

(c)   Beware the plausible distractors but do not become paranoid. The examiner is not trying to trip you up and the answer should be a straightforward calculation from the question.

Step 4

Time allocation. As with all questions you must not overrun your time. The questions are technically worth only two marks each which is about three to four minutes per question. It is very easy to get bogged down. If you cannot get one of the right answers then move on to the next question.

Step 5

When you have finished all the questions go back to the ones you have not answered.

Keep an eye on the clock – don't overrun the time allocation.

If you really cannot do it, **have a guess**. You are not penalised for wrong answers. **Never leave any questions unanswered.**

Objective test questions

1 Shareholder wealth maximisation is most likely to be achieved by which of the following:

    A   maximising the rate of growth of sales?

    B   maximising the net profit margin?

    C   maximising share price year-by-year?

    D   maximising long-term net cash flows?

---

2 Total Shareholder Return (TSR) is:

    A   dividends gross–of-tax relative to share price?

    B   the increase in share price over a given period?

    C   the total dividends received over a given period?

    D   the average annual return received by shareholders, including both dividends and capital appreciation?

---

3 The functions of a securities market are best explained by which of the following:

    A   to enable information flows to be reflected in share prices?

    B   to allow people to quickly and easily realise their wealth?

    C   to allocate new supplies of finance in the most productive directions and to facilitate the sale of existing securities?

    D   to enable entrepreneurs to realise their wealth via IPOs?

---

4 Which of the following institutions is likely to have the lowest proportion of its investments in ordinary shares:

    A   Venture Capital Trusts?

    B   Investment Trusts?

    C   Insurance Companies?

    D   Building Societies?

---

5   Which of the following institutions is most likely to assist in organising a new issue of shares:

    A   Investment Trusts?

    B   Merchant Banks?

    C   Retail Banks?

    D   Discount Houses?

---

6   In a semi-strong form efficient market, which of the following statements is false:

    A   Security prices adjust quickly and accurately to the public release of new information?

    B   Investors can make superior returns by reacting to the advice of newspaper "tipsters"?

    C   Investors cannot make superior returns by studying the pattern of past share price movements?

    D   Security prices only incorporate information which is publicly available?

---

7   Which of the following statements is untrue?

    A   In an efficient capital market, security prices accurately reflect all available information.

    B   In an efficient capital market, the likelihood of anyone consistently beating the market average return is very small.

    C   In an efficient capital market, the chance of beating the market average return in any one year is 50%.

    D   Careful and detailed scrutiny of past share price movements can improve your chances of beating the market average return.

---

8   Which of the following is not likely to be an advantage of setting up a centralised Treasury department?

    A   more efficient cash management.

    B   lower costs of purchasing supplies.

    C   closer relationships with banks.

    D   easier access to financial markets

---

9   Which objective is not appropriate for a Treasury department which is designated as a cost centre?

    A   it aims to minimise the cost of borrowing.

    B   it aims to speculate on foreign exchange transactions.

    C   it aims to manage financial risks.

    D   it aims to optimise liquidity.

10   Which of the following activities are not likely to be part of the Treasury function?

    (i)   control of R&D expenditure.

    (ii)   tax planning.

    (iii)   setting the annual budget for the whole organisation.

    (iv)   arranging finance for new investment projects.

    Choices:

    A   (i)

    B   (iii)

    C   (iv)

    D   (i) and (iii)

11   Which of the following statements is false?

    A   both preference shares and debenture stock can be convertible.

    B   both preference shares and debenture stock can be redeemable.

    C   both preference shares and debenture stock can be secured on fixed assets.

    D   debentures rank ahead of preference shares for payment.

12   Which of the following statements is least likely to constitute a credible reason for selling shares in an IPO?

    A   to repay past borrowings.

    B   to enable the present owners to realise some portion of their equity.

    C   to finance new product development.

    D   to retain key staff via remuneration by share option incentives.

13 Which of the following does not involve raising new finance?

(i) a placing.

(ii) a bonus issue of shares.

(iii) a rights issue.

(iv) a share split.

Choices:

A (ii)

B (ii) and (iii)

C (ii) and (iv)

D (iii)

---

14 Which of the following is not a characteristic of ordinary shares?

A they carry limited liability.

B they will be repaid on a specific date.

C they rank last for payment.

D they cannot be issued at a price below par value.

---

15 Which of the following best describes a share premium account?

A a reserve which records the surplus over the par value of the shares raised in a share issue.

B an account into which the proceeds of a rights are paid.

C the cash generated by a rights issue.

D the balance of monies payable when shares are issued partly paid.

---

16 What is the theoretical ex-rights price (TERP) under the terms of the following rights issue?

Market price = £2; discount to market price of 25%; one new share offered per four existing ones held.

A £2.00

B £1.50

C £1.60

D £1.90

---

17   The main reason for discounting a rights issue is:

    A   to make the shares attractive to shareholders.

    B   to counteract the dilution of owner's equity.

    C   to safeguard against the risk of a fall in market price during the offer period.

    D   to return value to existing shareholders.

---

18   Which of the following statements is correct?

A floating charge debenture is:

    A   loan stock secured on specific company assets.

    B   Loan stock where the security can be transferred from one asset to another with the agreement of the lenders.

    C   Loan stock where the loan is secured on company assets in general.

    D   loan stock where the interest rate is variable.

---

19   Which of the following statements is incorrect?

A loan covenant on a debenture:

    A   may restrict the ability of management to undertake any further borrowing.

    B   is a syndicate of banks formed to jointly offer a loan to a company.

    C   is a limitation on management's freedom of financial decision-making.

    D   may impose a lower limit on a company's stock of tangible fixed assets.

---

20   What is the market value of the warrant in the following example? (Ignore the time value of money).

The warrant gives the right to buy for a price of £4 each two new shares for every three currently held. When the warrant was issued, the ordinary share price was £4, it is now £8.

    A   £4

    B   £24

    C   £8

    D   £12

---

21 Which of the following does not apply to an operating lease?

A   it need not be shown on the balance sheet.

B   it can be easily cancelled.

C   the lessee normally bears the cost of maintenance.

D   lease rentals are tax-deductible.

---

22 XYZ's last dividend payment was 20p per share. It earns 40p per share. It expects to earn a rate of return of at least 12% on retained earnings. Its rate of earnings growth in the future will be:

A   6%

B   12%

C   2.4%

D   4.8%

---

23 The shares of XYZ from the previous example have a market price per share is £4. Assuming an efficient share market, its shareholders appear to require a return of:

A   5%

B   12%

C   11.3%

D   11%

---

24 Which of the following is false?

The dividend valuation model assumes:

(i)   a constant rate of return required by shareholders.

(ii)   a constant rate of dividend growth

(iii)   a constant retention ratio.

(iv)   a constant expected return on investment financed by retained earnings.

Choices:

A   (i)

B   (ii)

C   (i) and (ii)

D   None of the above

---

25 PQR plc has earnings per share of 50p and re-invests half of this on average. The rate of return expected on re-invested earnings is 18%. Shareholders require a minimum rate of return of 12%.

What is today's share price, assuming PQR's shares have just gone ex-dividend?

A   £4.17

B   £9.08

C   £8.33

D   £13.89

---

26 ABC's most recent dividend payments per share have been as follows:

Year 1 – 10p

Year 2 – 16p

Year 3 – 18p

Year 4 – 20p

Which is the relevant growth rate to use in the dividend valuation model?

A   66.7%

B   22.2%

C   26.0%

D   27.9%

---

27 Systematic or market risk is:

A   the degree of variation in the return on the overall market portfolio.

B   the proportion of the total risk of a security that can be diversified away by forming a well-diversified portfolio of shares.

C   the extent to which the return on one particular security varies with variations of that of the market portfolio.

D   the proportion of total risk which cannot be diversified away.

---

28 Which of the following types of risk can be diversified away?

A   variability in return due to general interest rate changes.

B   variability in return due to companies' problems with R&D programmes.

C   variability in return due to exchange rate changes.

D   variability in return due to changes in the government's opinion poll ratings.

---

29   Which of the following statements regarding the Capital Market Line (CML) is false?

   A   the CML is a way of identifying the optimal portfolio of risky assets.

   B   The CML shows how people trade off total risk and return in an efficient capital market.

   C   The CML shows that the definition of the optimal portfolio of risky assets is independent of people's attitudes to risk.

   D   The CML indicates what rate of return firms should achieve to compensate shareholders for risk.

---

30   XYZ plc has a Beta coefficient of 0.75. The rate of return on the market portfolio is 12%, and Treasury Bills offer a return of 7%.

   XYZ's shareholders require a return of:

   A   18%

   B   9%

   C   10.75%

   D   19%

---

31   The Security Market Line (SML) is best described by which of the following statements?

   A   it shows how people trade off risk against return in an efficient capital market.

   B   it predicts returns on all risky securities traded in the market.

   C   it offers guidelines as to how to formulate an efficiently diversified portfolio.

   D   it shows the required premium for different levels of systematic risk.

---

32   Which of the following statements is incorrect?

   A   in an efficient capital market, people are only rewarded for bearing systematic risk.

   B   rational investors will diversify away as much specific risk as possible.

   C   to diversify efficiently, investors should achieve a mix of industrial sectors in their portfolios

   D   to maximise returns, investors should form portfolios comprising securities with the highest Betas.

---

33 Which of the following statements best describe(s) a risk-averting investor?

  A   a risk averter wants to achieve maximum returns for a specified level of risk.

  B   a risk averter wants to maximise returns and to minimise risk.

  C   a risk averter aims for the minimum possible level of risk

  D   a risk averter wants to achieve the minimum risk exposure for a specified expected return.

34 ABC plc's debenture stock (par value £100) sells on the market for £90 ex-interest. It will be redeemed in three years. The coupon rate is 9%. The redemption yield (to the nearest 0.1%) is:

  A   10%

  B   12.4%

  C   11%

  D   13.4%

35 Which of the following statements is false?

  A   the cost of debt for a company is the rate at which it could borrow today, allowing for tax.

  B   the cost of debt for a company is the coupon rate on its existing debt, allowing for tax.

  C   the cost of debt for a company is the yield in the market on its existing debt, allowing for tax.

  D   the cost of debt for a company is the yield on the debt of a company of comparable risk, allowing for tax.

36 XYZ's debentures are redeemable at par of £100 per unit of stock in exactly two year's time. The coupon rate is 8%. They currently yield 10%. What is the market price (ex-interest) today?

  A   £100

  B   £116

  C   £96.5

  D   £80

37   Which of the following statements is incorrect?

    A   undated (or irredeemable) stocks tend to fluctuate less in price than fixed term stocks.

    B   interest rate increases tend to lower stock prices.

    C   tax-deductibility of interest on loan stock lowers the effective cost of borrowing.

    D   a corporation tax reduction, other things being equal, will raise the effective cost of borrowing for companies.

---

38   XYX plc has 3 million 50p shares in issue. The share price is £2.85. The yield on its debt, which has market value of £2m, is 11.6%. Shareholders require a return of 17%.

The WACC for the company is:

    A   14.3%

    B   14.8%

    C   16%

    D   15.3%

---

39   XYZ makes annual sales of £50m. Its operating profit margin is 20%, and its tax charge at the full 30% rate is £2.4m.

Its only debt is a £20m debenture with a 10% coupon rate.

Its interest cover is:

    A   5 times

    B   25 times

    C   4 times

    D   1.2 times

---

40   XZY plc in the previous example incurs fixed operating expenses of £10m. The price charged for its only product is £100 and the variable cost per unit is £40.

Its break-even volume is:

    A   166,667 units

    B   200,000 units

    C   120,000 units

    D   206,667 units

---

41   Which of the following statements is false?

    A   the degree of operating gearing for a company depends on its mix of fixed and variable inputs.

    B   companies with high operating gearing are best advised to restrict their borrowings.

    C   operating gearing has the effect of lowering the company's break-even point.

    D   operating gearing has the effect of magnifying fluctuations in operating profit in relation to sales variations.

---

42   XYZ's most recent P&L shows:

Sales	£100m
Operating Profit	£20m
Interest	£5m
Profit after Tax	£12m
Dividends	£6m

XYZ has 8m shares outstanding with par value of 50p and market price of £20 per share.

Its P:E ratio is:

    A   8:1

    B   10.7:1

    C   26.7:1

    D   13.3:1

---

43   For XYZ above, the dividend cover is:

    A   4 times

    B   2 times

    C   50%

    D   3.3 times

---

44   Also for XYZ, what is the gross dividend yield on its ordinary shares?

    A   3.8%

    B   50%

    C   4.2%

    D   166%

---

45   Also for XYZ, its interest cover is:

      A   4 times

      B   2.4 times

      C   20 times

      D   40%

---

46   Also for XYZ plc, the interest payment relates to a bond issue of £50m par value. Market rates are around 10%. What is XYZ's debt/equity ratio using market values?

      A   125%

      B   150%

      C   31%

      D   320%

---

47   You are now told that XYZ's bonds are convertible into ordinary shares with no further payment required, at the rate of 2 ordinary shares per £100 nominal of stock.

XYZ's fully-diluted EPS is:

      A   £1.50

      B   £1.33

      C   £1.41

      D   21p

---

48   You are planning to invest £1,000 over 5 years. You are offered a choice between simple interest at 8% pa or 6.5%, compounded half-yearly.

What are the respective terminal values that should govern your choice?

      A   £1,400 simple vs £1,650 compound

      B   £1,080 simple vs £1,065 compound

      C   £1,400 simple vs £1,370 compound

      D   £1,400 simple vs £1,325 compound

---

49   People expect inflation to run at 3% pa for the near future. Today's market interest rate is 7%.

What is the precise real rate of interest implied by these rates to one decimal place?

A   4%

B   3.7%

C   3.9%

D   3%

50   I can invest short-term in the bank at 8% pa compounded quarterly. What is the APR on offer?

A   8%

B   2%

C   8.16%

D   8.24%

51   Which of the following would not explain an upward sloping yield curve?

A   people expect inflation to rise in future years.

B   longer-dated stocks are more risky because of liquidity risk.

C   people expect the exchange rate of the pound sterling relative to other currencies to decline.

D   people expect a significant decrease in government funding requirements.

52   Treasury 7% stock is repayable in exactly three years. It currently stands on the market at £109 (ex-interest) per £100 of stock.

The gross yield to redemption is:

A   3.7%

B   minus 2%

C   7%

D   6.4%

53   Which of the following statements is incorrect?

A   Bank overdrafts are an unreliable source of finance as they can be re-called on demand.

B   a bank loan usually confers certainty of cash flow planning regarding interest and capital payments.

C   a bank overdraft is easier to obtain than a loan because no security is required.

D   a bank overdraft is normally cheaper than a a loan as you only pay interest on the outstanding balance.

54   Which of the following statements regarding forfeiting is incorrect?

A   it involves the purchase by a bank of a set of promissory notes signed by an importer due for payment over a period of time.

B   there is right of recourse if the signatory defaults.

C   no credit insurance is required.

D   forfeiting enables exporters to receive advance payment to enable production of goods for export.

55   What is the monthly payment due on the following HP contract?

Equipment cost = £20,000; initial deposit = 30%.

Interest rate = 10%; term of contract = 3 years.

A   £505

B   £469

C   £722

D   £156

56   Which statement is correct?

Net debt is:

A   Total debts to total assets.

B   the sum of long-term and short-term debt less cash holdings, sometimes expressed as a percentage of equity.

C   long-term debts less cash in relation to equity.

D   short-term assets less short-term liabilities as a percentage of short-term assets.

57   Which of the following statements is incorrect?

A Bill of Exchange:

A   is most often used to finance purchase of goods for trading or supplies for production.

B   is payable to the bearer on the maturity date.

C   can be bought and sold several times before it matures.

D   carries a fixed rate of interest.

58   Which of the following types of fixed interest security is the most suitable for investment of short-term cash surpluses?

A   Building Society bonds.

B   Consols.

C   Local Authority bonds.

D   Short-dated government stock.

59   XYZ plc has £1m to invest for one year. It can lock it away at a fixed rate of 7% for the full year, or invest at 6.5% for a three-month term, speculating on an increase in interest rates. Assume the rate available increases to 7.5% after three months and XYZ invests at this rate for the rest of the year.

By how much is XYZ better off from its gamble on interest rates?

A   £2,500

B   £12,836

C   £73,414

D   £3,414

60   Which statement best describes cash balances held for the speculative motive?

A   cash available for investment in government securities in anticipation of a reduction in interest rates.

B   cash available to meet possible liquidity shortages.

C   cash available for taking advantage of short-term opportunities to invest in risky securities.

D   cash available for speculating on foreign exchange movements.

61   Over-trading is best described by which of the following statements?

   A   it occurs when a company tries to grow too rapidly, backed by too small a capital base.

   B   it occurs when a company tries to operate its equipment too far above its designed capacity

   C   it occurs when sales grow rapidly fuelled by extending longer credit periods.

   D   it occurs when a company uses short-term finance in preference to long-term finance.

---

62   A company has sales of £40m, cost of sales of £30m and makes purchases of £15m. Its balance sheet includes among assets and liabilities the following:

   ♦   trade debtors   £4m
   ♦   trade creditors   £3m
   ♦   stocks   £8m

   What is its cash conversion cycle?

   A   206.5 days

   B   60.8 days

   C   36.5 days

   D   97 days.

---

63   XYZ plc has an overall annual stock turnover of 5 times. Its sales are £100m and its gross profit margin is 20%. Raw materials typically make up 30% of its inventory.

   Its raw material turnover figure in days is:

   A   15 days?

   B   73 days?

   C   22 days?

   D   27 days?

---

64   Which of the following will not improve cashflow?

   A   offering an early payment discount to customers.

   B   holding lower stocks.

   C   writing-off capital equipment over ten years instead of eight years.

   D   taking an extra week's credit from suppliers.

---

65   Ignoring interest costs/benefits, which of the above will not, initially at least, improve profits?

    A B C D

---

66   XYZ plc needs to draw down £1 million during the next year from its holdings of marketable securities. Each withdrawal involves a transaction cost of £50. The present yield on its investments is 12% pa.

    What is the optimal encashment quantity?

    A   £83,333

    B   £28,868

    C   £20,000

    D   £120,000

---

67   Which of the following is not a criticism of the Baumol cash management model?

    A   it assumes a constant return on investments in marketable securities.

    B   it assumes a fixed transaction cost.

    C   it ignores the scope for investing temporary cash surpluses.

    D   it assumes a random demand for cash.

---

68   Which of the following is not a cash management facility offered by the banking system?

    A   free same-day cheque-clearing.

    B   provision of tiered-rate interest-bearing deposit facilities.

    C   "sweeping" facilities to automatically move excess amounts in non-interest-bearing deposits into interest-bearing accounts.

    D   itemised statements with entries coded by customer and supplier.

---

69   Which of the following is not an advantage of centralised group cash management?

    A   by aggregating inflows, higher rates on deposits can be secured.

    B   better forecasting of group cash needs can be achieved.

    C   it allows rapid and flexible dealing with local banks.

    D   it avoids the need for individual business units borrowing if there are cash surpluses elsewhere in the group.

70   XYZ plc maintains a minimum cash holding of £10,000. The standard deviation of its daily cash flows is £4,000. The transaction cost per sale or purchase of marketable securities is £40. The daily interest rate is 0.04 per cent per day.

Using the Miller-Orr cash management model, the upper limit to its cash holdings should be:

A   £31,850

B   £41,850

C   £21,850

D   £10,617

---

71   Which of the following is the least suitable way of assessing a new customer's credit-worthiness?

A   bank credit references.

B   references from the firm's other suppliers.

C   examination of the firm's most recent accounts.

D   their readiness to engage in a "cash-only" trial period

---

72   XYZ's sales are £100m of which 95% are made on credit. Start-of-year debtors were £10m and £12m by end-year. 10% of debtors were non-trade related.

What is XYZ's average collection period?

A   36.5 days

B   40 days

C   38 days

D   46 days

---

73   ZXY has start-of-year debtors of £22m and end-of-year debtors of £27m. Sales are £150m, all on credit. The firm can borrow on overdraft at 13% pa.

The interest cost of financing its credit customers is:

A   £3.19m

B   £2.29m

C   £2.81m

D   £2.55m

---

74   ZZZ is planning to appoint an experienced credit manager at an annual salary of £60,000pa. Its sales are £100m pa and average debtors are £13m. The credit manager declares that he can lower bad debts from 3% of sales to 2.75%, the average for the industry, and shorten average debtors from 47 to 40 days.

ZZZ can borrow at 14%.

What is the net value to the firm of the credit manager?

    A   £190,000

    B   £458,492

    C   £268,492

    D   £18,492

75   YZX plc wants to speed up collection of accounts receivable. Its sales are £120m and average debtors are £20m. What are the net savings if it offers a 2% discount for payment within 30 days and half of customers take up the offer?

YZX can borrow on overdraft at 11% pa.

    A   minus £1.2m

    B   minus £0.642m

    C   £1.642m

    D   £1.757m

76   Which of the following ways of dealing with slow payers do you think an experienced credit manager is least likely to adopt?

    A   telephone calls

    B   stopping supplies

    C   personal visits

    D   consider re-scheduling payments.

77   Which of the following is not a disadvantage of factoring schemes?

    A   potential loss of customer goodwill due to intervention of a third party.

    B   inference of liquidity problems if firm employs a factor.

    C   interference with your own marketing and selling decisions.

    D   cost of turnover-based commission.

78   For a fee of 2% of total turnover, a factor undertakes to shorten a firm's debtor days from 60 to 45, to release administrative savings of £50,000 pa, and to reduce bad debts from 2% of turnover to 1.5%.

What is the net benefit of the factor's services, based on a turnover of £20m? The firm can borrow at 11% on overdraft.

A   £90,411

B   £150,000

C   minus £250,000

D   minus £159,589

79   Which of the following statements is incorrect?

A   specific bad debt provisions are written off to the profit and loss account.

B   a general provision for bad debts is written off to the profit and loss account.

C   a bad debt adversely affects cash flow because inputs have been used to produce the goods sold but not paid for.

D   if a bad debtor which has been written off does eventually pay, this affects cash flow but not profits.

80   Shareholders (owners) are last in line in order of priority for payment in a liquidation. But which of the following groups is next to last?

A   holders of floating charges

B   tax authorities

C   the labour force

D   unsecured creditors

81   X plc, with the agreement of its main suppliers, is adopting a new creditor payment system. Instead of settling one month from the date of receiving invoices, X will settle at the end of the month *after* receiving invoices. This will increase the average settlement period from 30 days to 45 days.

X's purchases are £50m pa, and it borrows on overdraft at 14%. There will also be administrative savings of £40,000 pa.

What is the total benefit to X plc of this change?

A   £287,671

B   £327,611

C   £575,342

D   £863,013

82   An aged creditors analysis is:

    A   a listing of trade creditors by date of invoicing.

    B   a listing of trade creditors with whom you are in arrears.

    C   the proportion of purchases by value which are overdue.

    D   a breakdown of trade creditors according to length of time elapsing since the purchase was made.

83   A supplier offers you a 2% discount for payments made within 15 days instead of the normal 30 days. What is the highest rate at which you could afford to borrow on overdraft to take advantage of this offer?   Assume the interest is compounded monthly.

    A   2%

    B   49%

    C   24%

    D   63%

84   Which of the following are likely to tilt the balance of bargaining power over credit terms in favour of the supplier?

    A   the product is a highly specialised component.

    B   the supplier has considerable spare capacity.

    C   the item supplied represents only a small proportion of the costs of the product.

    D   purchasers face little difficulty in switching between alternative suppliers.

85   Cash flow synchronisation is best described by which of the following statements?

    A   suppliers are paid with the same delay taken by customers when settling accounts with you.

    B   suppliers are paid at the same time as customers make payments.

    C   suppliers are paid only when customers cheques clear through the banking system.

    D   cash flows are managed so that inward and reverse floats are equalised.

86   XYZ plc has an average stock-holding period of 45 days. Its cost of sales is £120m, and it borrows on overdraft at 12% pa.

What is its annual interest cost of holding stock?

A   £14.4m

B   £1.78m

C   £14.8m

D   £0.9m

87   XYZ plc buys in components each year for 10p per unit. It pays interest at 12% pa. The ordering cost per order is £20. What is the economic order size given total demand per annum is 100,000 units?

A   6,325 units

B   12,910 units

C   18,257 units

D   5,774 units

88   At the economic order quantity, the relationship between total ordering costs and total holding costs is:

A   holding costs always exceed ordering costs.

B   they are equal.

C   ordering costs always exceed holding costs.

D   could be either.

89   Which of the following would not result from a JIT ordering system?

A   lower holding costs.

B   higher ordering costs.

C   fewer stock outs.

D   shorter lead times.

90 XYZ plc has cost of sales of £300m pa. Its average stocks of raw materials, work-in-progress and finished goods are £15m, £25m and £20m respectively.

Its stock turnover multiple is:

A 27 times

B 72 times

C 5 times

D 15 times

---

91 XYZ has found that the EOQ for a particular component is 300 units of an item whose purchase cost is £2 each. Total usage is 2,000 units pa. It can borrow on overdraft at 10% pa. Its annual interest cost in relation to holding this item of stock is:

A £60
B £150
C £60
D £30

---

92 XYZ plc in the previous example wants to allow for a two-week lead time when replenishing stock. The average safety stock is set at 30 units.

Assuming a 52-week year, the re-order point (to the nearest whole unit) is:

A 227 units
B 107 units
C 42 units
D 36 units

---

93 The ordinary share price of Wobble plc is 180p after the dividend has recently been paid. The dividend paid three years ago was 4p, the most recent dividend was 5p.

Using the dividend growth model what is the cost of equity for Wobble plc?

A 10.7%

B 11.3%

C 11.4%

D 7.6%

94   Yap Ltd is concerned to minimise the costs associated with stock. An investigation has identified the following details for component Z.

Purchases of units per month	300
Cost of processing purchase orders	£10
Annual cost of holding one unit	£5

What is the frequency of orders required per annum for component Z?

A   120 orders

B   60 orders

C   30 orders

D   15 orders

95   Which of the following statements about the efficient market hypothesis is true?

A   The strong form of the hypothesis suggests that investors will always make the correct investment choice.

B   The weak form of the hypothesis suggests that investors base their investment decision on guesses.

C   The semi-strong form of the hypothesis suggests that insider dealing is possible.

D   The semi-strong form of the model suggests that the use of window-dressing of published accounts will not enhance the share price.

96   The G Company has the following information from its own sales ledger together with industry average (benchmark) data for the past year.

Estimated sales	£500,000
Benchmarks	
Asset turnover	4 times
Fixed assets to capital employed	60%
Current ratio	2.5:1
Gross profit margin	40%

What would be an estimated value for the companies current assets?

A   £75,000

B   £50,000

C   £83,333

D   £33,333

97   Which of the following is always true for a finance lease?

A   The lessee is responsible for the servicing and maintenance of the asset.

B   The lessor is responsible for the servicing and maintenance of the asset.

C   The lessor receives the capital allowances from the asset.

D   The asset is purchased by the lessee at the end of the primary rental period.

98   L Ltd has a published equity beta of 1.7. The expected return on the market is at a 9% risk premium. Currently government bonds are trading at 6%.

What is the cost of equity for L Ltd?

A   6%

B   9%

C   11.1%

D   21.3%

99   The S company is looking to float on the stock exchange. It has a market value of £20m and is concerned to issue shares at the lowest possible cost to the company. It is presently unquoted and is considering making 25% of its shares available to the market.

Which method of issuing shares should the company use to minimise the cost of raising equity finance?

A   Rights issue.

B   Bonus issue.

C   Prospectus issue.

D   Placing.

100   B plc has the following information regarding their shares:

Earnings per share	40p
Dividend cover	8 times
Published dividend yield	2%

The price of B plc's ordinary shares are:

A   5p.

B   250p.

C   320p.

D   2000p.

101 If you invest £1,500 at an interest rate of 7% per annum what sum should it generate per annum if invested as a perpetuity?

A £21,429.

B £210.

C £150.

D £105

102 Risk that cannot be diversified away through selecting an appropriate portfolio is:

A Financial risk.

B Market risk.

C Systematic risk.

D Unsystematic risk.

103 The annual interest of a £3m 12% irredeemable bond is about to be paid. Presently holders of similar bonds require a return of 8%. The value of a £100 bond cum int will be?

A £78.67.

B £112.

C £150.

D £162.

104 Which of the following is not a warning of possible over-trading?

A Decreasing current ratio.

B Increase in overdraft.

C Fall in creditor days.

D Sharp increase in sales.

105 A company offers a cash discount of 1.5% for all customers paying within 10 days. Currently the debtors are given 60 days to pay.

What is the annualised cost in percentage terms of offering a cash discount to customers?

A   11.1%

B   11.7%

C   10.95%

D   9.4%

106 The Fake company have just announced a rights issue of 1 new share for 5 existing shares. The current market value of a share is £1.6 per share. Currently there are 2 million shares in circulation. The rights are offered at a deep discount of £1.0 per share.

What is the value of each right to the existing shareholders?

A   £1.5 per share.

B   £0.6 per share.

C   £0.5 per share.

D   £1.0 per share.

107 H and S Ltd has cash outgoings of £4m spread evenly throughout the year. The cash will be generated by selling treasury bills which currently yield 12%. Every treasury bill will cost £6 to sell.

Using the Baumol model what will be the amount sold each time to replenish cash?

A   £20,000.

B   £16,667.

C   £14,142.

D   £10,000.

108 Star plc has the following information from the balance sheet for the previous year:

	£
Debtors	500,000
Sales	3,000,000
Gross profit	600,000

The company is considering the use of a factor who will collect debt over an average of 30 days for the fee of 0.75% of turnover. Debtors are financed by overdraft at 12% pa.

What is the net benefit/(cost) to the company of using the factor?

A £30,411.

B (£253,397)

C £7,910

D £28,397

---

109 Which of the following would not explain the difference between book stock and the stocks physically counted in a stock check?

A Delivery of less units than invoiced by a supplier.

B Theft within the raw material store by employees.

C Oversupply of stock by supplier.

D Theft by customers of finished goods on display.

---

110 Holders of unsecured debentures would have the same claim on a company's assets as:

A Secured debentures.

B Subordinated loan stock.

C Preference shareholders.

D Trade creditors.

---

111 The Smooth company has the following information regarding accounting performance:

	£
Dividend paid	18,000
Profit after tax	30,000
Capital employed	120,000

Using Gordon's growth model calculate the potential growth rate of Smooth?

A   10%

B   15%

C   25%

D   40%

112 BACS (Bankers Automated Clearing Services) is an example of an electronic funds transfer system. Which of the following best described the system?

A   Provides same-day settlement for large sums of money.

B   Is most concerned with processing payrolls and transactions involving standing orders and direct debits.

C   Is a network for repaid transmission of international remittances between participating banks.

D   Requires cheques to be completed to ensure settlement of a transaction.

Questions

Question 1

Corporate Objectives

Required

(a)   'Managers and owners of businesses may not have the same objectives'. Explain this statement, illustrating your answer with examples of possible conflicts of interest.

(7 marks)

(b)   In what respect can it be argued, that companies need to exercise corporate social responsibility? **(7 marks)**

(c)   Explain the meaning of the term 'Value for Money' in relation to the management of publicly owned services/utilities. **(6 marks)**

(Total: 20 marks)

Question 2

Financial Objectives

When determining the financial objectives of a company, it is necessary to take three types of policy decision into account – investment policy, financing policy and dividend policy.

Required

(a)   Discuss the nature of these three types of policy decision, commenting on how they are inter-related and how they might affect the value of the firm (ie the present value of projected cash flows). **(10 marks)**

(b)   Describe the different functions of the treasury and financial control departments of an organisation and comment on the relative contributions of these two departments to policy determination and the achievement of financial objectives. **(10 marks)**

(Total: 20 marks)

Question 3

ABC plc

ABC plc is a UK-based service company with a number of wholly-owned subsidiaries and interests in associated companies throughout the world. In response to the rapid growth of the company, the Managing Director has ordered a review of the company's organisation structure, particularly the finance function. The Managing Director holds the opinion that a separate treasury department should be established. At present, treasury functions are the responsibility of the chief accountant.

Required

(a)   Describe the main responsibilities of treasury department in a company such as ABC plc and explain the benefits which might accrue from the establishment of a separate treasury function.   **(12 marks)**

(b)   Describe the advantages and disadvantages which might arise if the company established a separate treasury department as a profit rather than a cost centre.

(8 marks)

(Total: 20 marks)

Question 4

Inigo

Inigo plc currently has 5 million ordinary shares in issue, which have a market value of £1.60 each. The company wishes to raise finance for a major investment project by means of a rights issue, and is proposing to issue shares on the basis of one for five at a price of £1.30 each.

James Brown currently owns 10,000 shares in Inigo plc and is seeking advice on whether or not to take up the proposed rights.

Required

(a)   Explain the difference between a rights issue and a scrip issue. Your answer should include comment on the reasons why companies make such issues and the effect of the issues on private investors.   **(6 marks)**

(b)   Calculate:

  (i)   the theoretical value of James Brown's shareholding if he takes up his rights; and

  (ii)   the theoretical value of James Brown's rights if he chooses to sell them.

(4 marks)

(c)   Using only the information given below, and applying the dividend growth model formula, calculate the required return on equity for an investor in Inigo plc.

  Inigo plc:

Current share price:	£1.60
Number of shares in issue:	5 million
Current earnings:	£1.5 million

  Dividend paid (pence per share):

20X3:	8
20X4:	9
20X5:	11
20X6:	11
0X7:	12

The formula for the dividend growth model is as follows: $R = (\frac{D_1}{MV} + g) \times 100$.

(4 marks)

Where R = percentage required return on equity.

(d)   If the stock market is believed to operate with a strong level of efficiency, what effect might this have on the behaviour of the finance directors of publicly quoted companies?   **(6 marks)**

(Total: 20 marks)

Question 5

Bardsey plc

Bardsey plc operates a chain of city centre furniture stores, specialising in high quality items. It is 60% owned by the original family founders. Its sales over the past decade have never grown faster than 5% in any one year, even falling during a recent recession. No growth is expected from existing operations in the next few years despite continuing to offer generous credit to customers.

In order to achieve faster growth, the company is considering the development of a number of 'out of town' sites, adjacent to giant supermarkets and DIY stores. During 20X1 this would involve a capital outlay of £50 million plus additional working capital requirements of £20 million in order to finance stock-building. In recent years, Bardsey's capital expenditure, mainly store refurbishments and vehicle replacements, and averaging around £10 million per annum, has been financed entirely from cashflow. This category of investment will continue at about the same level in 20X1. Bardsey's fixed assets were revalued two years ago.

Bardsey's accounting statements for the last financial year are summarised in Exhibit A, and Exhibit B gives information on key financial indicators for the stores sector as a whole (listed companies only).

Bardsey's debentures currently sell on the stock market at £130 per £100 nominal. The current bank base rate is 8%, and economists expect interest rates in general to fall over the next few years. The stock market currently applies a price: earnings ratio of 11: 1 to Bardsey's shares.

Required

As Bardsey's chief accountant, you are instructed to do the following:

(a)   Calculate Bardsey's expected net cashflow in 20X1 without the investment, assuming no changes in the level of net working capital.   **(5 marks)**

Note. A statement in FRS 1 format is not required.

(b)   Prepare a report which compares Bardsey's financial performance and health with the stores sector as a whole.   **(7 marks)**

(c)   Suggest other possible uses of the increasing cash balances if Bardsey rejects the proposed investment.   **(8 marks)**

(Total: 20 marks)

Exhibit A: Bardsey's financial statements

Balance sheet as at 31 December 20X0

	£m	£m
Fixed assets (net)		
Land and premises	200	
Fixtures and fittings	50	
Vehicles	50	
	———	
		300
Current assets		
Stocks	60	
Debtors	100	
Cash	40	
	———	
	200	
	———	
Current liabilities		
Trade creditors	85	
Dividends payable	20	
Tax payable	12	
	———	
	117	
	———	
Net current assets		83
		———
Total assets less current liabilities		383
15% debentures 20X8/X9		(100)
		———
		283
		———
Capital and reserves		
Issued share capital (par value 25p)		100
Revaluation reserve		60
Profit and loss account		123
		———
		283
		———

Profit and loss account for the year ended 31 December 20X0

	£m
Turnover	150.0
Cost of sales (including depreciation of £8m)	(90.0)
	———
Operating profit	60.0
Interest charges	(15.0)
	———
Pre-tax profit	45.0
Corporation tax	(12.0)
	———
Profit after tax	33.0
Dividends proposed	(20.0)
	———
Retained earnings	13.0
	———

Exhibit B: Selected ratios for the store sector

Return on (long-term) capital employed	14.3% (pre-tax)
Return on equity	15.3% (post-tax)
Operating profit margin	26.2%
Fixed asset turnover (sales/fixed assets)	1.2 times
Stock period	180 days
Debtor days	132 days
Gearing (total debt/equity)	42%
Interest cover	3.2 times
Dividend cover	2.1 times
P/E ratio	15:1

Question 6

Nismat and Kemp (ACCA 12/98)

You are an accountant with a practice, which includes a large proportion of individual clients, who often ask for information about traded investments. You have extracted the following data from a leading financial newspaper in 1998.

(i)

Stock	Price	P/E ratio	Dividend yield (% gross)
Nismat plc	160p	20	5
Kemp plc	270p	15	3.33

(ii) Earnings and dividend data for Wild Ideas plc are given below.

	1993	1994	1995	1996	1997
EPS	5p	6p	7p	10p	12p
Dividend per share (gross)	3p	3p	3.5p	5p	5.5p

The estimated before tax return on equity required by investors in Wild Ideas plc is 20%.

(iii) The gross yields to redemption on gilts are as follows.

Treasury 8.5% 2000	7.00%
Exchequer 10.5% 2005	6.70%
Treasury 8% 2015	6.53%

Required

Draft a report for circulation to your private client which explains:

(a) The factors to be taken into account (including risks and returns) when considering the purchase of different types of traded investments. **(6 marks)**

(b) The meanings and the relevance to the investor of each of the following:

    (i) Gross dividend (pence per share);

    (ii) EPS;

    (iii) Dividend cover.

Your answer should include calculation of, and comment upon, the gross dividends, EPS and dividend cover for Nismat plc and Kemp plc, based on the information given above.   **(6 marks)**

(d)   How to estimate the market value of a share. Illustrate your answer by reference to the data in (ii) on Wild Ideas plc, using the information to calculate the market value of 1,000 shares in the company.   **(4 marks)**

(e)   The shape of the yield curve for gilts, based upon the information given in (iii) above, which you should use to construct the curve.   **(4 marks)**

(Total: 20 marks)

Question 7

Newsam (ACCA 12/94)

Newsam plc is a quoted company which produces a range of branded products all of which are well-established in their respective markets, although overall sales have grown by an average of only 2% per annum over the past decade. The board of directors is currently concerned about the company's level of financial gearing, which although not high by industry standards, is near to breaching the covenants attaching to its 15% debenture issue, made twelve years ago at a time of high market interest rates. Issued in order to finance the acquisition of the premises on which it is secured, the debenture is repayable at par value of £100 per unit of stock at any time during the period 20X4–20X7.

There are two covenants attaching to the debenture, which state:

> 'At no time shall the ratio of debt capital to shareholders' funds exceed 50%. The company shall also maintain a prudent level of liquidity, defined as a current ratio at no time outside the range of the industry average (as published by the corporate credit analysts, Creditex), plus or minus 20%.'

Newsam's most recent set of accounts is shown in summarised form below. The buildings have been depreciated since acquisition at 4% per annum, and most of the machinery is only two or three years old, having been purchased mainly via a bank overdraft. The interest rate payable on the bank overdraft is currently 9%. The finance director argues that Newsam should take advantage of historically low interest rates on the European money markets by issuing a medium-term Eurodollar bond at 5%. The dollar is currently selling at a premium of about 1% on the three-month forward market.

Newsam's ordinary shares currently sell at a P/E ratio of 14, and look unattractive compared to comparable companies in the sector which exhibit an average P/E ratio of 18. According to the latest published credit assessment by Creditex, the average current ratio for the industry is 1.35.

The debentures currently sell in the market at £15 above par.

The summarised financial accounts for Newsam plc for the year ending 30 June 20X4 are as follows:

Balance sheet as at 30 June 20X4

	£m	£m
Fixed assets (net)		
Land		5.0
Premises		4.0
Machinery and vehicles		11.0
		20.0
Current assets		
Stocks	2.5	
Debtors	4.0	
Cash	0.5	
	7.0	
Current liabilities		
Bank overdraft	3.0	
Creditors	4.0	
	(7.0)	
Net current assets		0.0
Total assets less current liabilities		20.0
Long-term creditors		
15% debentures 20X4 – 20X7		(5.0)
		15.0
Capital and reserves		
Ordinary shares (25p par value)		5.0
Reserves		10.0
		15.0

Profit and loss account extract for the year ended 30 June 20X4

	£m
Sales	28.00
Operating profit	3.00
Interest payable	(1.00)
Profit before tax	2.00
Taxation	(0.66)
Profit after tax	1.34
Dividend	(0.70)
Retained profit	0.64

Required

(a)   Calculate appropriate gearing ratios for Newsam plc using:

      (i)   book values; and

      (ii)   market values.   **(3 marks)**

(b)   Assess how close Newsam plc is to breaching the debenture covenants.   **(3 marks)**

(c)   Discuss whether Newsam plc's gearing is in any sense 'dangerous'.   **(4 marks)**

(d) Discuss what financial policies Newsam plc might adopt:

    (i)   in order to lower its capital gearing; and

    (ii)   to improve its interest cover. **(10 marks)**

(Total: 20 marks)

Question 8

Cleevemoor (ACCA 12/95)

(a) The Cleevemoor Water Authority was privatised in 20X1, to become Northern Water plc (NW). Apart from political considerations, a major motive for the privatisation was to allow access for NW to private sector supplies of finance. Recent central government controls on capital expenditure had resulted in relatively low levels of investment so that considerable investment was required to enable the company to meet more stringent water quality regulations. When privatised, it was valued by the merchant bankers advising on the issue at £100 million and was floated in the form of 100 million ordinary shares (par value 50p), sold fully-paid for £1 each. The shares reached a premium of 60% on the first day of stock market trading.

(b) Selected *bi-annual* data from NW's accounts are provided below relating to its first six years of operation as a private sector concern. Also shown, for comparison, are the *pro forma* data as included in the privatisation documents. The *pro forma* accounts are notional accounts prepared to show the operating and financial performance of the company in its last year under public ownership as if it had applied private sector accounting conventions. They also incorporate a dividend payment based on the dividend policy declared in the prospectus.

The activities of privatised utilities are scrutinised by a regulatory body which restricts the extent to which prices can be increased. The demand for water in the area served by NW has risen over time at a steady 2% per annum, largely reflecting demographic trends.

Key financial and operating data for year ending 31 December (£m)

	20X1 *(proforma)*	20X3 *(actual)*	20X5 *(actual)*	20X7 *(actual)*
Turnover	450	480	540	620
Operating profit	26	35	55	75
Taxation	5	6	8	10
Profit after tax	21	29	47	65
Dividends	7	10	15	20
Total assets	100	119	151	191
Capital expenditure	20	30	60	75
Wage bill	100	98	90	86
Directors' emoluments	0.8	2.0	2.3	3.0
Employees (number)	12,000	11,800	10,500	10,000
P/E ratio (average)	–	7.0	8.0	7.5
Retail Price Index	100	102	105	109

Required

(a) In what ways might you expect the objectives of an organisation like Cleevemoor/NW to alter following transfer from public to private ownership? **(5 marks)**

(b)   Using the data provided, assess the extent to which NW has met the interests of the following groups of stakeholders in its first six years as a privatised enterprise.

If relevant, suggest what other data would be helpful in forming a more balanced view.

(i)	Shareholders	**(5 marks)**
(ii)	Consumers	**(2 marks)**
(iii)	The workforce	**(4 marks)**
(iv)	The government, through NW's contribution to the achievement of macroeconomic policies of price stability and economic growth.	**(4 marks)**

(Total: 20 marks)

Question 9

Burnsall (ACCA 12/95)

Burnsall plc is a listed company which manufactures and distributes leisurewear under the brand name Paraffin. It made sales of 10 million units worldwide at an average wholesale price of £10 per unit during its last financial year ending at 30 June 20X5. In 20X5/X6, it is planning to introduce a new brand, Meths, which will be sold at a lower unit price to more price-sensitive market segments. Allowing for negative effects on existing sales of Paraffin, the introduction of the new brand is expected to raise total sales value by 20%.

To support greater sales activity, it is expected that additional financing, both capital and working, will be required. Burnsall expects to make capital expenditures of £20 million in 20X5/X6, partly to replace worn-out equipment but largely to support sales expansion. You may assume that, except for taxation, all current assets and current liabilities will vary directly in line with sales.

Burnsall's summarised balance sheet for the financial year ending 30 June 20X5 shows the following.

	£m	£m
Fixed assets (net)		120
Current assets	16	
Stocks	23	
Debtors	6	
Cash		
	45	
Current liabilities		
Corporation tax payable	5	
Trade creditors	18	
	23	
Net current assets		22
Long-term debt at 12%		(20)
		122
Capital and reserves		
Ordinary shares (50p par value)		60
Reserves		62
		122

Burnsall's profit before interest and tax in 20X4/X5 was 16% of sales, after deducting depreciation of £5 million. The depreciation charge for 20X5/X6 is expected to rise to £9 million. Corporation tax is levied at 33%, paid with a one-year delay. Burnsall has an established distribution policy of raising dividends by 10% per annum. In 20X4/X5, it paid dividends of £5 million net.

You have been approached to advise on the extra financing required to support the sales expansion. Company policy is to avoid cash balances failing below 6% of sales.

Required

(a) By projecting its financial statements, calculate how much additional *external* finance Burnsall must raise.

Notes

(1) It is not necessary to present your projection in FRS 1 format.

(2) You may assume that all depreciation provisions qualify for tax relief.

(8 marks)

(b) Evaluate the respective merits of four possible external long-term financing options open to Burnsall. **(12 marks)**

(Total: 20 marks)

Question 10

Phoenix (ACCA 12/97)

Phoenix plc which manufactures building products, experienced a sharp increase in operating profits from the £25 million level in 20X0/X1 to £40 million in 20X1/X2 as the economy emerged from recession, and demand for new houses increased. The increase in profits has been entirely due to volume expansion, with margins remaining static. It still has substantial excess capacity and therefore no pressing need to invest, apart from routine replacements.

In the past, Phoenix has followed a rather conservative financial policy, with restricted dividend payouts and relatively low borrowing levels. It now faces the issue of how to utilise an unexpectedly sizeable cash surplus. Directors have made two main suggestions. One is to redeem the £10 million secured loan stock issued to finance a capacity increase several years previously. The other is to increase the dividend payment by the same amount.

Phoenix's present capital structure is shown below.

	£m
Issued share capital (25p par value)	70
Reserves	130
Creditors: amounts falling due after more than one year	
7% secured loan stock 20X9	10

Further information

♦ Phoenix has not used an overdraft during the two years.

♦ The rate of corporate tax is 33%.

♦ The dividend paid by Phoenix in 20X0/X1 was 1.5 pence per share.

♦ Sector averages currently stand as follows.

Dividend cover	2.6 times
Gearing (long-term debt/equity)	45%
Interest cover	6.5 times

Required

(a)   Calculate the dividend payout ratios and dividend covers for *both* 20X0/X1 *and* for the reporting year 20X1/X2, if the dividend is raised as proposed.   **(6 marks)**

(b)   You have recently been hired to work as a financial strategist for Phoenix, reporting to the finance director. Using the information provided, write a report to your superior, which identifies and discusses the relative merits of the two proposals for utilising the cash surplus.   **(14 marks)**

(Total: 20 marks)

Question 11

Netherby (ACCA 6/94)

Netherby plc manufactures a range of camping and leisure equipment, including tents. It is currently experiencing severe quality control problems at its existing fully-depreciated factory in the south of England. These difficulties threaten to undermine its reputation for producing high quality products. It has recently been approached by the European Bank for Reconstruction and Development, on behalf of a tent manufacturer in Hungary, which is seeking a UK-based trading partner which will import and distribute its tents. Such a switch would involve shutting down the existing manufacturing operating in the UK and converting it into a distribution depot. The estimated exceptional restructuring costs of £5m would be tax-allowable, but would exert serious strains on cashflow.

Importing, rather than manufacturing tents appears inherently profitable as the buying-in price, when converted into sterling, is less than the present production cost. In addition, Netherby considers that the Hungarian product would result in increased sales, as the existing retail distributors seem impressed with the quality of the samples which they have been shown. It is estimated that for a five-year contract, the annual cashflow benefit would be around £2m per annum before tax.

However, the financing of the closure and restructuring costs would involve careful consideration of the financing options. Some directors argue that dividends could be reduced as several competing companies have already done a similar thing, while other directors argue for a rights issue. Alternatively, the project could be financed by an issue of long-term loan stock at a fixed rate of 12%.

The most recent balance sheet shows £5m of issued share capital (par value 50p), while the market price per share is currently £3. A leading security analyst has recently described Netherby's gearing ratio as 'adventurous'. Profit after tax in the year just ended was £15m and dividends of £10m were paid.

The rate of corporation tax is 33%, payable with a one-year delay. Netherby's reporting year coincides with the calendar year and the factory will be closed at the year end. Closure costs would be incurred shortly before deliveries of the imported product began, and sufficient stocks will be on hand to overcome any initial supply problems. Netherby considers that it should earn a return on new investment projects of 15% per annum net of all taxes.

Required

(a)   Is the closure of the existing factory financially worthwhile for Netherby?   **(5 marks)**

(b)   Explain what is meant when the capital market is said to be information-efficient in a semi-strong form.

        If the stock market is semi-strong efficient, and without considering the method of finance, calculate the likely impact of acceptance and announcement of the details of this project to the market on Netherby's share price.   **(4 marks)**

(c)   Explain why a rights issue generally results in a fall in the market price of shares.

        If a rights issue is undertaken, calculate the resulting impact on the existing share price of issue prices of £1 per share and £2 per share respectively. (You may ignore issue costs.)   **(3 marks)**

(d)   Assuming the restructuring proposal meets expectations, assess the impact of the project on earnings per share if it is financed by a rights issue at an offer price of £2 per share, and loan stock, respectively.   **(4 marks)**

        (Again, you may ignore issue costs.)

(e)   Briefly consider the main operating risks connected with the investment project, and how Netherby might attempt to allow for these.   **(4 marks)**

                                                                                        (Total: 20 marks)

Question 12

PAS

Company	Share price (pence)			Dividend Yield (%)	P/E Ratio
	Current	52 week high	52 week low		
Ply	63	112	54	1.8	14.2
Axis	291	317	187	2.1	13.0
Spin	187	201	151	2.3	21.1

Required

(a)   Illustrating your answer by use of data in the table above, define and explain the term P/E ratio, and comment on the way it may be used by an investor to appraise a possible share purchase.   **(6 marks)**

(b)   Using data in the above table, calculate the dividend cover for Spin and Axis, and explain the meaning and significance of the measure from the point of view of equity investors.   **(8 marks)**

(c)   Under what circumstances might a company be tempted to pay dividends which are in excess of earnings, and what are the dangers associated with such an approach?

        You should ignore tax in answering this question.   **(6 marks)**

                                                                                        (Total: 20 marks)

Question 13

AB Ltd

AB Ltd is a new company in the electrical industry. It has been formed by Mr A and Mr B, its joint managing directors, who have been made redundant by a major electrical manufacturer. They intend to employ a number of their former work colleagues who were also made redundant. Mr A and Mr B received a substantial amount of redundancy pay. This money, combined with their savings, will give them £300,000 towards the financing requirements of the company. The rest of their financing will need to be provided by debt and the directors approach their bank with a request for assistance.

The bank has asked for financial information and statements from the company in support of their request. The only information the two directors have available is an estimate of their first year's gross sales together with industry financial ratios/averages for the current year, obtained from the Inter Company Comparisons' (ICC) *Industrial Performance Analysis*. This information is as follows:

Estimated sales for 19X4	£1.4 million
Industry financial ratios/averages for 19X3	
Current ratio	1.83 times
Net operating profit	10%
Sales to capital employed	2.8 times
Average collect period	50 days
* Average payment period (trade creditors)	60 days
Sales to stock	5.6 times
Fixed assets to capital employed	60%
Cost of sales to sales	60%
Operating expenses to sales	30%

*You should assume that all cost of sales is on credit and all operating expenses are for cash.

Ignore taxation.

Required

(a)   Draft a report for the bank based on the above information for inclusion in a formal request for financing;   **(9 marks)**

(b)   State the assumptions necessary in your calculations and comment on other information which would be useful to support your request for finance;   **(5 marks)**

(c)   Advise the company on alternative sources of short- and medium-term financing which could be considered if the bank refuses finance.   **(6 marks)**

(Total: 20 marks)

Question 14

X and Y plc

The directors of X plc are comparing some of the company's year-end statistics with those of Y plc, the company's main competitor. X plc has had a fairly normal year in terms of profit but Y plc's latest profits have been severely reduced by an exceptional loss arising from the closure of an unsuccessful division. Y plc has a considerably higher level of financial gearing than X plc.

The board is focusing on the figures given below:

	X plc	*Y plc*
Share price	450p	525p
Nominal value of shares	50p	100p
Earnings yield	6.67%	4%
Dividend yield	4%	3.2%
Price/earnings ratio	15	25
Proportion of profits earned overseas	60%	0

In the course of the discussion a number of comments are made, including those given below.

Required

Respond critically to comments (a) to (e), making use of the above data where appropriate.

(a)   "There is something odd about the p/e ratios. Y plc has had a particularly bad year. Its p/e should surely be lower than ours."   **(4 marks)**

(b)   "Y plc's earnings yield is lower than ours. This gives them the benefit of a lower cost of capital."   **(4 marks)**

(c)   "One of the factors which may explain Y plc's high p/e is its high financial gearing."   **(4 marks)**

(d)   "The comparison of our own p/e ratio, dividend yield and earnings yield with those of Y plc is not really valid. The shares of the two companies have different nominal values."   **(3 marks)**

(e)   "These figures will not please our shareholders. The dividend yield is below the return an investor could currently obtain on risk-free government bonds."   **(5 marks)**

(Total: 20 marks)

Question 15

S plc

S plc issues a debenture at par carrying a 9% coupon. The debenture is redeemable in five years and each unit of £100 is convertible into 20 ordinary shares at any time prior to redemption. At the date of issue the yield on comparable debentures is 12% and the company's shares are quoted at 400p.

Required

(a) Calculate the conversion premium on the debenture at the date of issue and explain in general terms the relationship between the conversion premium and the coupon rate on convertible debentures; **(5 marks)** (b)	Assuming a 10% annual growth rate in share price, calculate the conversion value of the debenture three years after issue and explain why the debenture's market value is likely to exceed this figure;	**(5 marks)**

(c)	Explain why the market value of a convertible debenture is likely to be affected by the dividend policy of the issuing company;	**(5 marks)**

(d)	Explain what strategy a company might be pursuing when raising capital in the form of a convertible as distinct from raising straight debt or straight equity.	**(5 marks)**

(Total: 20 marks)

Question 16

CP plc

CP plc is a company operating primarily in the distribution industry. It has been trading for 15 years and has shown steady growth in turnover and profits for most of those years, although a failed attempt at diversification into retailing four years ago caused profits to fall by 30% for one year. The figures for the latest year for which audited accounts are available are:

Turnover	£35.2 million
Profit before tax	£13.7 million

The company has been financed to date by ten individual shareholders, three of whom are senior managers in the company, and by bank loans. Shares have changed hands occasionally over the past 15 years but the present shareholders are predominantly those who invested in the company when it was formed.

Some of the shareholders are now keen to realise some of the profits their shareholdings have earned over the years. At the last Annual General Meeting, it was proposed that the company should consider a full listing on the Stock Exchange.

Required

(i)	Discuss the advantages and disadvantages of a flotation on the stock exchange in the circumstances described above;	**(6 marks)**

(ii)	Explain and compare the following methods by which the company's shares could be brought to the market:

- private placing;
- offer for sale at fixed price;
- offer for sale by tender.	**(6 marks)**

(b)	Describe the services which are likely to be provided by the following institutions in connection with a public offering of shares:

(i)	merchant banks;

(ii)	stockbrokers;

(iii)	institutional investors.	**(8 marks)**

(Total: 20 marks)

Question 17

4D plc

(a)   Briefly explain the factors which a company's treasurer should consider before investing in marketable securities.   **(6 marks)**

(b)   4D plc is a manufacturing company whose shares are listed on the London International Stock Exchange. It is expecting to have surplus cash resources available for at least 12 months. The board has decided to develop an investment portfolio of marketable securities. The company's financial advisers have recommended four securities for the board to consider. These are as follows:

Security 1:   regularly traded shares in a medium-sized UK retailing company. The equity beta is quoted as 1.2.

Security 2:   shares in a relatively small but rapidly growing UK company in a high-technology industry. The shares have an equity beta of 1.6.

Security 3:   shares in an American bank which are listed on US stock exchanges but not in the UK. They are currently quoted at US$ 25.50. An equity beta is unavailable but 4D plc's stockbroker estimates that the required rate of return on the shares is 12% per annum.

Security 4:   short-dated government bonds.

The expected return on Treasury Bills is 5% per year, and that of the market is 12%.

4D plc's own equity beta is 0.8 and this is not expected to change in the foreseeable future.

The board can invest in one or more of these securities in any proportion.

Required

(i)   Calculate the risk and expected return of the investment portfolio assuming 30% of available funds is invested in each of securities 1 and 2 and 20% in each of securities 3 and 4.   **(4 marks)**

(ii)   Write a report for the board advising which, if any, of the four securities listed above should be considered as suitable investments for a company such as 4D plc. Also comment on the types of marketable securities, other than those listed above, which could be considered by 4D plc.   **(10 marks)**

(Total: 20 marks)

Question 18

Howgill (ACCA 6/96)

(a)   Briefly explain the main features of the following.

♦   Sale and leaseback
♦   Hire purchase
♦   Financial leasing   **(6 marks)**

(b)   Howgill Limited is the leasing subsidiary of a major commercial bank. It is approached by Clint plc, a company entirely financed by equity, which operates in the pharmaceutical industry, with a request to arrange a lease contract to acquire new computer-controlled manufacturing equipment to further automate its production line. The outlay involved is £20 million. The equipment will have only a four-year operating life owing to the fast rate of technical change in this industry, and no residual worth. The basic project has a positive net present value when operating cashflows are discounted at the shareholders' required rate of return.

Howgill would finance the purchase of the machinery by borrowing at a pre-tax annual interest rate of 15%. The purchase would be completed on the final day of its accounting year, when it would also require the first of the annual rental payments. Howgill currently pays tax at 33%, 12 months after its financial year end. A writing-down allowance is available based on a 25% reducing balance.

Under the terms of the lease contract, Howgill would also provide maintenance services, valued by Clint at £750,000 per annum. These would be supplied by Howgill's computer maintenance sub-division at no incremental cost as it currently has spare capacity which is expected to persist for the foreseeable future.

Clint has the same financial year as Howgill, also pays tax at 33% and its own bank will lend at 18% before tax.

Required

(Calculate the minimum rental which Howgill would have to charge in order to just break even on the lease contract.

Note. You may assume that the rental is wholly tax-allowable as a business expense.

(7 marks)

(c)   Assume that Howgill does proceed with the contract and charges an annual rental of £7 million.

Calculate whether, on purely financial criteria, Clint should lease the asset or borrow in order to purchase it outright:

(i)   ignoring the benefit to Clint of the maintenance savings   **(6 marks)**

(ii)   allowing for the maintenance savings.   **(7 marks)**

(Total: 20 marks)

Question 19

Acme

(a)   Explain the cashflow characteristics of a finance lease, and compare it with the use of a bank loan or cash held on short-term deposit. Your answer should include some comment on the significance of a company's anticipated tax position on lease versus buy decisions.   **(8 marks)**

(b)   Acme Printing plc has the opportunity to replace one of its pieces of printing equipment. The new machine, costing £120,000, is expected to lead to operating savings of £50,000 per annum and have an economic life of five years. The company's after-tax cost of capital for the investment is estimated at 15%, and operating cashflows are taxed at a rate of 30%, one year in arrears.

The company is trying to decide whether to fund the acquisition of the machine via a five-year bank loan, at an annual interest rate of 13%, with the principal repayable at the end of the five-year period. As an alternative, the machine could be acquired using a finance lease, at a cost of £28,000 per annum for five years, payable in advance. The machine would have zero scrap value at the end of five years.

Note: Because of its current tax position, the company is unable to utilise any capital allowances on the purchase until year one.

Required

Assuming that writing down allowances of 25% per annum are available on a reducing balance basis, recommend, with reasons, whether Acme Printing should replace the machine, and if so whether it should buy or lease. **(12 marks)**

(Total: 20 marks)

Question 20

MRF

MRF is a charitable organisation and exempt from all taxes. It is about to acquire some new capital equipment for a special project. The President of the charity has been advised that it might be advantageous to acquire the equipment with a finance lease. The cost to the charity of the equipment, if it were purchased outright, would be £22.5 million. However, the leasing company would be able to negotiate a 20% discount on this price because of its long-term commercial relationship with suppliers of the type of equipment being purchased. This discount would not be available to the charity if it purchased the equipment with a bank loan.

The leasing company is nearing its year end and is keen to obtain the tax advantages denied to MRF because of its charitable status. It has therefore offered what it considers to be very favourable terms. Payments by MRF would be £7.5 million per annum for 6 years, payable at the end of each year of the lease contract.

Writing down allowances are available to the leasing company at 25% on a reducing balance basis. At the end of year 6, it is estimated that the second-hand value of the equipment would be £4 million. Insurance and maintenance would be the responsibility of the charity, whether it leases or purchases the equipment.

The cost of a bank loan to the charity would be 12%. The opportunity cost of capital for the leasing company would be 14%.

Assume no time lag in tax payments or refunds.

You should work to two decimal places throughout.

Required

(a)   Assume you are MRF's treasurer. Evaluate the financial aspects of the lease and recommend to the President whether the charity should purchase with a bank loan or use a finance lease. You should state the reasons for your recommendation and any assumptions you make in arriving at your decision. **(8 marks)**

(b)   Now assume that you are an account negotiator for the leasing company. You have been informed that MRF has decided to buy the equipment with a bank loan at 12% interest. Your boss, Helen, has asked you to advise her whether the lease terms could be reduced so as to be competitive with the bank loan. The leasing company pays tax at the marginal rate of 33%. Assume that the lease receipts from MRF are full taxable

Write a short report advising Helen:

♦   of the annual lease payments required for the charity to be indifferent between the bank and the leasing company;

♦ the effect on the leasing company's evaluation if the lease payments were reduced to the amount calculated above (if you are unable to calculate a figure, assume £5 million per annum);

♦ of other actions which the company could take to rescue the deal.

Supporting calculations should be provided were appropriate. **(12 marks)**

(Total: 20 marks)

Question 21

Investment and Risk

(a) You are the company accountant with a medium-sized, privately-owned company. The company has surplus funds which it does not believe it will be able to invest in company operations for at least five years. The majority shareholders are also the directors of the company and they do not wish the surplus funds to be distributed as dividends. A board meeting has therefore been called to discuss the proposal that the funds be invested in a portfolio of medium to long-term securities.

Three of the directors have recently attended a short course at the local university on '*Investment and the Management of Risk*'. They make the following comments at the meeting, based on their interpretations of what they have learnt on the course:

"If we hold a portfolio of stocks, we need only consider the systematic risk of the securities."

"As a cautious investor we must always consider total risk."

"We should not buy anything if the expected return is less than that on the market as a whole, and certainly not if it is below the return on the risk-free asset."

Required

(i) Explain to the members of the board the meaning of systematic, unsystematic and total risk and advise them, briefly, how all three types of risk can be measured.

(ii) Discuss the directors' comments. **(12 marks)**

(b) The following two comments were drawn from separate articles in a highly-respected financial newspaper:

"Market efficiency does not mean that share prices can be forecast with accuracy."

"The research department of a large firm of stockbrokers has developed a multiple regression model, based on data collected between 1964 and 1994, which is claimed to give statistically significant results for predicting share prices."

Required

Discuss these comments and explain why they are not contradictory. **(8 marks)**

(Total: 20 marks)

Question 22

Leisure International

The following is an extract from the balance sheet of Leisure International plc at 30 June 19X2:

	£000
Ordinary shares of 50p each	5,200
Reserves	4,850
9% preference shares of £1 each	4,500
14% debentures	5,000
Total long-term funds	19,550

The ordinary shares are quoted at 80p. Assume that the market estimate of the next ordinary dividend is 4p, growing thereafter at 12% per annum indefinitely. The preference shares, which are irredeemable, are quoted at 72p and the debentures are quoted at par. Corporation tax is 35%.

Required

(a)   Use the relevant data above to estimate the company's weighted average cost of capital (WACC) ie, the return required by the providers of the three types of capital, using the respective market values as weighting factors.   **(6 marks)**

(b)   Explain how the capital asset pricing model would be used as an alternative method of estimating the cost of equity, indicating what information would be required and how it would be obtained.   **(7 marks)**

(c)   Assume that the debentures have recently been issued specifically to fund the company's expansion programme under which a number of projects are being considered. It has been suggested at a project appraisal meeting that because these projects are to be financed by the debentures, the cut-off rate for project acceptance should be the after-tax interest rate on the debentures rather than the WACC. Comment on this suggestion.   **(7 marks)**

(Total: 20 marks)

Question 23

GLC Ltd

GLC is a medium sized business in a mature but highly cyclical industry. It is intending to expand considerably requiring substantial investment in fixed assets. The board has provided the following sales data for the past two years together with estimates for the next five years (2002-2006).

Year	2000	2001	2002	2003	2004	2005	2006
	£000's	£000's	£000's	£000's	£000's	£000's	£000's
Sales	500	300	400	550	750	900	700

10% of receipts are received one year in advance due to the specialist nature of the products. 30% are received in the year in which they are incurred, and the remaining sales are paid in staged payments equally over three years commencing in the year of sales.

Variable costs of sale are 60% of the sales, one third being labour cost, the remainder being materials. Labour is paid in the year incurred, the material is purchased two years in advance (a key part of the process).

Fixed costs (all cash) of £200,000 per annum are incurred each year. The company intends to invest £200,000 in fixed assets in both 2002 and 2004. Interest of £20,000 is to be paid each year to cover outstanding debts. The current cash balance at 31/12/01 is £50,000.

Required

(a)   Prepare a cash budget for four years from 2002 to 2005.   **(8 marks)**

(b)   What short and medium sources of finance should GLC Ltd consider to ensure that cash is in balance for the years in question.   **(12 marks)**

(Total: 20 marks)

Question 24

Long-Term and Short-Term

(a)   Identify the advantages and disadvantages of financing a company with short-term funds as opposed to long-term funds.   **(8 marks)**

(b)   Illustrate and describe the yield curve and state the situations where the curve may be downward sloping.   **(12 marks)**

(Total: 20 marks)

Question 25

Interest Rates

(a)   Describe the principal of time value for money in layman terms, illustrating the description with an example using marketable securities.   **(7 marks)**

(b)   Explain the relationship of real to money interest rates and identify the link between a real rate of 6% and a money rate of 2%. Why may the answer be considered strange?   **(5 marks)**

(c)   Estimate the flat and the gross redemption yields on the following securities and determine which debt instrument should be held by a rational investor. The yields are to be calculated as at the end of 2001.

   Potential investments

   (i)   8% 2005 Market value £108 (redeemable at par).

   (ii)   4% 2007 Market value £90 (Redeemable at a discount of £4 to par).   **(8 marks)**

(Total: 20 marks)

Question 26

Cash Discount: TLC Company

The TLC company products, two products love and kindness. It is particularly concerned with the management of its working capital.

The managing director is of the opinion that extended credit has lead to excess funding requirements and wants the financial manager to encourage early payment by offering a cash discount.

The sales manager is unhappy with this suggestion and counters that extended credit is the key to their current sales success. She suggests that present debtor balances could be financed through debtor factoring. A result of a recent CIMA sponsored masterclass on 'financial management for non accountants'.

The production director is keen to reduce inventories as part of a just-in-time exercise but is still concerned with the level of debtors and suggests 'cash on delivery' should be the terms used.

The proposed terms for the cash discount are either a 1% discount for payment after 20 days or a 1.25% discount for payment after 10 days. Existing sales are £5m and trade debtors in the previous balance sheet stood at £0.833m. Assume 360 days per annum.

Required

(a)   Calculate the annualised percentage cost of the cash discounts. From the perspective of a prospective supplier whose current cost of capital is 10%, decide whether either or both discounts would be accepted. Suggest reasons other than the cost of capital why a supplier may accept the cash discount.   **(8 marks)**

(b)   Discuss the alternative debtor financing and collection policies. Decide which policy you would undertake stating reasons for your choice.   **(7 marks)**

(c)   List four additional short-term sources of finance and describe each of them briefly.
                                                                                        (5 marks)

                                                                            (Total: 20 marks)

Question 27

BYO plc

The treasurer of BYO plc has successfully managed cash to such an extent that a surplus is growing in the current account. During the current year the funds have grown £500,000 from a starting point of a £200,000 overdraft.

An investigation by the management accounting team has identified the following information regarding the company's cash requirements next year.

Transaction cost	£300 per transaction
Overdraft rate	0.04% per day
Variance of cashflows	£9,000,000
Buffer cash balance	£15,000

Required

(a)   Suggest four possible short-term uses of funds for BYO plc during the current year.
                                                                                        (6 marks)

(b)   Using the Miller-Orr model calculate the return point and spread and describe how they may be used for next year's data.   **(8 marks)**

(c) Discuss three ways in which cash shortages may be eased over the short-term without recourse to external funding. **(6 marks)**

(Total: 20 marks)

Question 28

Ewden (ACCA 6/94)

Ewden plc is a medium-sized company producing a range of engineering products which it sells to wholesale distributors. Recently, its sales have begun to rise rapidly following a general recovery in the economy as a whole. However, it is concerned about its liquidity position and is contemplating ways of improving its cashflow. Ewden's accounts for the past two years are summarised below.

Profit and loss account for the year ended 31 December

	20X2	20X3
	£000	£000
Sales	12,000	16,000
Cost of sales	7,000	9,150
Operating profit	5,000	6,850
Interest	200	250
Profit before tax	4,800	6,600
Taxation (after capital allowances)	1,000	1,600
Profit after tax	3,800	5,000
Dividends	1,500	2,000
Retained profit	2,300	3,000

Balance sheet as at 31 December

	20X2		20X3	
	£000	£000	£000	£000
Fixed assets (net)		9,000		12,000
Current assets				
Stock	1,400		2,200	
Debtors	1,600		2,600	
Cash	1,500		100	
		4,500		4,900
Current liabilities				
Overdraft	–		200	
Trade creditors	1,500		2,000	
Other creditors	500		200	
		(2,000)		(2,400)
10% loan stock		(2,000)		(2,000)
Net assets		9,500		12,500
Capital and reserves				
Ordinary shares (50p)		3,000		3,000
Profit and loss account		6,500		9,500
		9,500		12,500

In order to speed up collection from debtors, Ewden is considering two alternative policies. One option is to offer a 2% discount to customers who settle within 10 days of despatch of invoices rather than the normal 30 days offered. It is estimated that 50% of customers would take advantage of this offer. Alternatively Ewden can utilise the services of a factor. The factor will operate on a service-only basis, administering and collecting payment from Ewden's customers. This is expected to generate administrative savings of £100,000 per annum and, it is hoped, will also shorten the debtor days to an average of 45. The factor will make a service charge of 1.5% of Ewden's turnover. Ewden can borrow from its bankers at an interest rate of 18% per annum.

Required

(a)   Identify the reasons for the sharp decline in Ewden's liquidity and assess the extent to which the company can be said to be exhibiting the problem of 'overtrading'.

Illustrate your answer by reference to key performance and liquidity ratios computed from Ewden's accounts.   **(13 marks)**

(*Note:* It is not necessary to compile an FRS 1 statement.)

(b)   Determine the relative costs and benefits of the two methods of reducing debtors, and recommend an appropriate policy.   **(7 marks)**

(Total: 20 marks)

Question 29

Keswick (ACCA 6/96)

(a)   (i)   Discuss the significance of trade creditors in a firm's working capital cycle.
(4 marks)

(ii)   Discuss the dangers of over-reliance on trade credit as a source of finance.
(4 marks)

(b)   Keswick plc traditionally follows a highly aggressive working capital policy, with no long-term borrowing. Key details from its recently compiled accounts appear below.

	£m
Sales (all on credit)	10.00
Earnings before interest and tax (EBIT)	2.00
Interest payments for the year	0.50
Shareholders' funds (comprising £1m issued share capital, par value 25p, and £1m revenue reserves)	2.00
Debtors	0.40
Stocks	0.70
Trade creditors	1.50
Bank overdraft	3.00

A major supplier which accounts for 50% of Keswick's cost of sales is highly concerned about Keswick's policy of taking extended trade credit. The supplier offers Keswick the opportunity to pay for supplies within 15 days in return for a discount of 5% on the invoiced value.

Keswick holds no cash balances but is able to borrow on overdraft from its bank at 12%. Tax on corporate profit is paid at 33%.

Required

Determine the costs and benefits to Keswick of making this arrangement with its supplier, and recommend whether Keswick should accept the offer.

Your answer should include the effects on each of the following.

- The working capital cycle

- Interest cover

- Profits after tax

- Earnings per share

- Return on equity

- Capital gearing.   **(12 marks)**

(Total: 20 marks)

Question 30

Ripley (ACCA 12/96)

(a)   The Treasurer of Ripley plc is contemplating a change in financial policy. At present, Ripley's balance sheet shows that fixed assets are of equal magnitude to the amount of long-term debt and equity financing. It is proposed to take advantage of a recent fall in interest rates by replacing the long-term debt capital with an overdraft. In addition, the Treasurer wants to speed up debtor collection by offering early payment discounts to customers and to slow down the rate of payment to creditors.

As his assistant, you are required to write a brief memorandum to other Board members explaining the rationales of the old and new policies and pin-pointing the factors to be considered in making such a switch of policy.   **(6 marks)**

(b)   Bramham plc, which currently has negligible cash holdings, expects to have to make a series of cash payments (P) of £1.5m over the forthcoming year. These will become due at a steady rate. It has two alternative ways of meeting this liability.

Firstly, it can make periodic sales from existing holdings of short-term securities. According to Bramham's financial advisers, the most likely average percentage rate of return (i) on these securities is 12% over the forthcoming year, although this estimate is highly uncertain. Whenever Bramham sells securities, it incurs a transaction fee (T) of £25, and places the proceeds on short-term deposit at 5% per annum interest until needed. The following formula specifies the optimal amount of cash raised (Q) for each sale of securities.

$$Q = \sqrt{\frac{2 \times P \times T}{i}}$$

The second policy involves taking a secured loan for the full £1.5 million over one year at an interest rate of 14% based on the initial balance of the loan. The lender also imposes a flat arrangement fee of £5,000, which could be met out of existing balances. The sum borrowed would be placed in a notice deposit at 9% and drawn down at no cost as and when required.

Bramham's Treasurer believes that cash balances will be run down at an even rate throughout the year.

Required

Advise Bramham as to the most beneficial cash management policy.

Note. Ignore tax and the time value of money in your answer.   **(9 marks)**

(c)   Discuss the limitations of the model of cash management used in part (b).   **(5 marks)**

(Total: 20 marks)

Question 31

Marton (ACCA 12/97)

Marton Limited produces a range of specialised components, supplying a wide range of UK and overseas customers, all on credit terms. Twenty% of UK turnover is sold to one firm. Having used generous credit policies to encourage past growth, Marton now has to finance a substantial overdraft and is concerned about its liquidity. Marton borrows from its bank at 13% per annum interest. No further sales growth in volume or value terms is planned for the next year.

In order to speed up collection from UK customers, Marton is considering two alternative policies.

Option one

Factoring on a with-recourse, service only basis, the factor administering and collecting payment from Marton's UK customers. This is expected to generate administrative savings of £200,000 per annum and to lower the average debtor collection period by 15 days. The factor will make a service charge of 1% of Marton's UK turnover and also provide credit insurance facilities for an annual premium of £80,000.

Option two

Offering discounts to UK customers who settle their accounts early. The amount of the discount will depend on speed of payment as follows.

◆   Payment within 10 days of despatch of invoices: 3%

◆   Payment within 20 days of despatch of invoices: 1.5%

It is estimated that UK customers representing 20% and 30% of Marton's sales respectively will take up these offers, the remainder continuing to take their present credit period.

Another opportunity arises to engage in a just-in-time stock delivery arrangement with the main UK customer, which normally takes 90 days to settle accounts with Marton. This involves borrowing £0.5 million on overdraft to invest in dedicated handling and transport equipment. This would be depreciated over five years on a straight-line basis. The customer is uninterested in the early payment discount but would be prepared to settle after 60 days and to pay a premium of 5% over the present price in exchange for guarantees regarding product quality and delivery. Marton judges the probability of failing to meet these guarantees in any one year at 5%. Failure would trigger a penalty payment of 10% of the value of total sales to this customer (including the premium).

In addition, Marton is concerned about the risk of its overseas earnings. All overseas customers pay in US dollars and Marton does not hedge currency risk, invoicing at the prevailing spot rate, which is currently US$1.45 : £1. It is considering the use of an overseas factor and also hedging its US dollar income on the forward market. Its bank has offered to buy all of its dollar earnings at a fixed rate of US$1.55: £1. Marton's advisers estimate the following chances of various dollar/sterling rates of exchange.

US dollars per £	Probability
1.60	0.1
1.50	0.2
1.45	0.4
1.40	0.2
1.30	0.1

Extracts from Marton's most recent accounts are given below

	£000	£000
Sales (all on credit)		
Home	20,000	
Export	5,000	
		25,000
Cost of sales		(17,000)
Operating profit		8,000
Current assets		
Stock	2,500	
Debtors*	4,500	
Cash	–	

*There are no overseas debtors at the year end.

Note. Taxes and inflation can be ignored in this question.

Required

(a) Calculate the relative costs and benefits *in terms of annual profit before tax* of each of the two proposed methods of reducing domestic debtors, and recommend the most financially advantageous policy. Comment on your results. **(14 marks)**

(b) Calculate the improvement *in profits before tax* to be expected in the first trading year after entering into the JIT arrangement. Comment on your results. **(8 marks)**

(c) Suggest the benefits Marton might expect to derive from a JIT agreement in addition to the benefits specified in the question. **(6 marks)**

(d) Briefly outline the services provided by an overseas factor. **(4 marks)**

(e) (i) Calculate the maximum loss which Marton can sustain through movements in the dollar/sterling exchange rate if it does not hedge overseas sales. **(2 marks)**

(ii) Calculate the maximum opportunity cost of selling dollar earnings forward at US$1.55 : £1. **(2 marks)**

(iii) Briefly discuss whether Marton should hedge its foreign currency risk. **(4 marks)**

(Total: 40 marks)

Question 32

Wastell (ACCA 6/99)

Wastell Security plc are manufacturers and wholesalers of locks and household security fittings. Over the last twelve months the company has encountered increasing problems with late payment by debtors.

The last twelve months of credit sales of £67.5 million show an increase of 10% over the previous year, but the company's overdraft, on which it is charged 12% per annum has also increased (by £1.8 million) over the last year. The company is concerned to reduce its working capital requirements by reducing the debtor collection period.

Wastell's management accountant has extracted an aged debtors profile which is shown below.

% of total debtor payments (by value)	Average collection period
5	30
28	45
10	60
30	75
16	90
11	120

Bad debts currently stand at £2 million per annum.

Wastell is considering the introduction of early settlement discounts. The current invoicing terms require payment to be made within 30 days of the date of issue of the invoice. The management accountant has suggested that a 1% discount be offered to all customers who comply with these payment terms, and he estimates that 50% of total payments (by value) would be on these terms (an average settlement period of 30 days for these payments can be assumed). The discount scheme would be expected to be taken up by customers who already pay in 75 days or less.

As an alternative way of reducing the debtors figure, Wastell could use a with recourse debt collection service, which has quoted a price of 1% of sales receipts. It is estimated that using the service will have the effect of reducing debtor days by 20 and eliminating 50% of bad debts.

Required

(a)   Calculate the change in working capital requirements and bad debts which would result from:

   (i)   the introduction of the early settlement discounts
   (ii)   the use of the debt collection service

   and recommend which (if either) policy should be adopted by Wastell. Your answer should clearly show all workings.   **(10 marks)**

(b)   There are a number of methods that can be adopted to assess the credit-worthiness of a potential credit customer. Describe and comment upon two such methods that Wastell could adopt to help reduce the current level of bad debts.   **(5 marks)**

(c)   Explain the term 'invoice discounting' and the pros and cons of its use as a way of improving cashflow.   **(5 marks)**

(Total: 20 marks)

Question 33

Fleming plc

Fleming plc established a new subsidiary company on 1 November specifically for the manufacture and selling of a new product. The holding company will inject, for working capital purposes, £30,000 cash on 1 December. Fixed capital assets are being transferred from another company in the group.

Required

Using the data given you are required to prepare a cash budget for each of the months of December, January, February and March. Calculations are to be made to the nearest £1.

Data

The variable production cost per unit is expected to be:

	£
Direct materials	4.0
Direct wages	3.0
Variable production overhead	1.5
Variable production cost	8.5

Fixed overhead estimated at £48,000 per annum is expected to be incurred in equal amounts each month from 1 December.

Production will commence in December and sales on 1 January. The estimated sales for the first four months are:

19X1	Units	Sales Value £
January	6,200	65,100
February	6,800	70,720
March	5,400	59,400
April	6,000	63,000

The following information is to be taken into consideration:

1   Stocks, finished goods: 75% of each month's invoiced sales units to be produced in the month of sale and 25% of each month's invoiced sales units to be produced in the previous month.

2   Stocks, direct materials: 50% of direct materials required for each month's production to be purchased in the previous month. Direct materials to be paid for in the month following purchase.

3   Direct wages to be paid 75% in the month used and 25% in the following month.

4   Variable production overhead: 40% to be paid in the month of usage and the balance in the following month.

5 ˙   Fixed overhead: 30% to be paid in the month in which it is incurred and 40% in the following month, the balance represents depreciation of fixed assets.

6   Payments to be received from customers as follows:

January   £12,369
February   £45,987
March   £59,666   **(20 marks)**

Question 34

Credit Management

(a)   Recent research has shown that a large percentage of small company failures were due to poor financial management skills and poor credit management.

Required

Explain the problems faced by small companies in respect of credit management, and discuss internal actions which they could take to minimise the effects of these problems.   **(8 marks)**

(b)   A medium sized manufacturing company is suffering a fall in sales of many of its product lines. It is reviewing its business strategy and the heads of all departments have been asked to review their activities. The accounting department has been asked to review specifically the company's credit control policy. At present the company offers its goods to customers on 30 days' credit (from date of invoice), subject to satisfactory trade references. It does not offer a discount for prompt payment.

Required

Assume you are a management accountant working in the company's credit control department. Write a report to the Credit Manager which

(i)   discusses the contribution that credit control policy can make to overall business strategy,

(ii)   assesses the advantages and disadvantages of introducing discounts for prompt payment. Include in your assessment a calculation and comment on the true cost of discounts. For the sake of your discussion you should assume a 1% discount for payment within 10 days if the normal credit period allowed continues at 30 days.   **(12 marks)**

(Total: 20 marks)

Question 35

EFT Miller

(a)   Explain the advantages and disadvantages to a company of paying suppliers by using an electronic funds transfer system instead of cheques by post.   **(5 marks)**

(b)   The treasurer of a local government department is reviewing her cash management procedures. She plans to introduce the use of cash management models and has asked you to investigate their applicability to the department. The following information is available.

◆ The department has agreed with its bank that it will maintain a minimum daily cash balance of £15,000. Severe financial penalties will apply if this balance is not maintained.

◆ A forecast of daily cash movements for the next twelve months shows a standard deviation of daily cashflows of £3,000.

◆ The daily interest rate is at present 0.0236% and this is not expected to change for the foreseeable future.

◆ The transaction cost for each sale or purchase is £25.

Assume you are a newly recruited accountant in the department.

Required

Write a report to the treasurer which discusses:

(i)   the advantages and disadvantages of cash management models over more traditional methods of cash forecasting, making specific reference to their applicability to a public sector organisation such as a local authority;   **(6 marks)**

(ii)   how one such model, the Miller-Orr, would operate in practice, using the information given above. Your report should include calculations of the upper and lower limits for cash balances and the return point. Assume a spread of £26,820.   **(9 marks)**

Note: The Miller-Orr formula is given in the *Mathematical Tables*. You do not need it to calculate the spread as this is given above, but you should explain the terms used in the Miller-Orr model.   **(Total: 20 marks)**

Question 36

XYZ plc

XYZ plc is an unlisted company which has been trading for almost 10 years. The board of directors is concerned about the cost and level of the company's overdraft which have been increasing over the past two years. The company's financial manager estimates the deterioration will continue into 19X5 and beyond unless action is taken. The directors agree that the company should take action to improve its liquidity and debt collection procedures, and as a consequence, reduce the overdraft. The options available are:

(1)   Offer a cash discount to all credit customers of 1.5% for payment within 10 days. The normal terms of trade allow for 60 days although many customers regularly exceed this limit. Approximately 70% of sales are on credit and all credit customers trade regularly up to their maximum credit limit. If this scheme is introduced, approximately half of all credit customers are expected to take advantage. Bad debts are expected to fall by 50%.

(2)   Employ a debt factoring company. The factor has agreed to accept 90% of XYZ plc's credit customers and will charge a commission of 2% of acceptable debtors' value. Finance charges will be 11%, which is 5% over base rate. XYZ plc will take the maximum finance available and use it to turn the overdraft into a cash balance. The use of a debt factor is expected to result in a saving of £65,000 on XYZ plc's in-company credit management costs.

(3)   Raise £500,000 by taking out a 10 year mortgage secured on the company's premises and use the proceeds to reduce the overdraft. The interest rate on this debt will be 9%.

XYZ plc pays overdraft interest at 4% over base rate. Its opportunity cost of capital is 12%. Summary financial information is as follows:

	19X5 *Forecast* *£000*
Turnover	4,850
Cost of sales	2,862
Bad debts	48
Profit after tax	325
Stock	455
Trade debtors	850
Total current assets	1,305
Trade creditors	550
Overdraft	565
Total current liabilities	1,115
Net current assets	190
Shareholders' funds	1,575
Director's loan (13% unsecured 2000)	450

Required

Evaluate for **each** of the **three** options

(i)   the net financial benefit to the company

(ii)   the effect on current ratio and debtors' days

and to recommend, with reasons, which should be chosen to meet the directors' objectives.

(20 marks)

Question 37

V plc

V plc manufactures engineering equipment. The company has received an order from a new customer for five machines at £5,000 each. V plc's terms of sale are 10% of the sales value payable with order. This deposit has been received from the new customer. The balance is payable 12 months after acceptance of the order by V plc.

V plc's past experience has been that only 60% of similar customers pay within 12 months. Customers who do not pay within 12 months are referred to a debt collection agency to pursue the debt. The agency has in the past had a 50% success rate of obtaining immediate payment once they became involved. When they are unsuccessful the debt is written off by V plc. The agency's fee is £500 per order, payable by V plc with the request for service. This fee is not refundable if the debt is not recovered.

You are an accountant in V plc's credit control department and, based on the company's past experience and on discussions with the sales and credit managers, you do not expect the pattern of payment and collection to change.

Incremental costs associated with the new customer's order are expected to be £3,600 per machine. 70% of these costs are for materials and are incurred shortly after the order has been accepted. The remaining 30% is for all other costs which you can assume are paid shortly before delivery, that is in 12 month's time. The company is not at present operating at full production capacity.

V plc's opportunity cost of capital is 16%. Ignore taxation.

Required

Write a report to the credit control manager which:

(a)   evaluates, from a purely financial point of view, whether V plc should accept the order from the new customer on the basis of the above information;   **(9 marks)**

(b)   comments on what other factors should be considered before a decision to grant credit is taken;   **(6 marks)**

(c)   discusses, briefly, methods which might be used to evaluate the creditworthiness of this particular customer.   **(5 marks)**

(Total: 20 marks)

Question 38

Sprinter plc

Sprinter plc is a UK based company which produces 'designer' watches targeted at the youth market. The company also exports its watches to Canada, the USA and Japan, invoicing foreign customers in their local currency. (Assume Sprinter's policy is to hold sterling prices constant.) The company has traditionally hedged its foreign currency exposure by the use of forward contracts, but is now considering abandoning their use.

Exhibit A shows the geographic breakdown of Sprinter's sales for 1998. Exhibit B contains information extracted from the annual report and accounts of Sprinter plc for the year ended 31 December 1998.

Exhibit A: **Geographic Sales Breakdown: based on Sterling Value**

Country 1998	
UK	70%
USA	15%
Japan	10%
Canada	5%
Total	100%

Exhibit B: **Information extracted from the accounts of Sprinter plc for the year ended 31 December 1998**

Stocks:	Total	UK only
Raw materials	£1,404,000	£812,500
WIP	£980,000	£568,750
Finished Goods	£1,120,000	£650,000
Purchases	£6,720,000	£3,900,000
Cost of Goods Sold	£8,130,000	£5,525,000
Sales	£9,290,000	£6,500,000
Debtors	£3221,000	£1,300,000
Trade Creditors	£773,300	£448,000

Assume 365 days per working year.

The average cost of capital for Sprinter is 12%.

Required

(a)   Briefly explain how forward contracts may be used to hedge foreign exchange exposure.   **(2 marks)**

(b)   Calculate the length of the working capital cycle in respect of:

      (i)   UK sales, and

      (ii)   total sales (worldwide).   **(6 marks)**

(c)   Why is the working capital cycle longer for total sales than for UK sales?   **(6 marks)**

(d)   Calculate and comment upon the profit impact of the longer working capital cycle associated with foreign sales.   **(6 marks)**

(Total: 20 marks)

Question 39

Delcars

Delcars plc own a total of ten franchises, in a variety of United Kingdom locations, for the sale and servicing of new and used cars. Six of the franchises sell just second hand vehicles, with the remaining four operating a car service centre in addition to retailing both new and used vehicles. Delcars operate different systems for banking of sales receipts, depending on the type of sale. All monies from new car sales must be banked by the garage on the day of the sale; receipts from second hand car sales are banked once a week on Mondays, and receipts from car servicing work are banked twice a week on Wednesdays and Fridays. No banking facilities are available at the weekend ie Saturdays and Sundays. The sales mix of the three elements (as a percentage of Delcars' total revenue) is as follows: 60% new vehicles; 25% second hand vehicles; 15% servicing. Total sales for all three business areas amounted to £25 million in 1999. Delcars pays interest at a rate of 8.5% per annum on an average overdraft of £65,000, and the company's finance director has suggested that the company could significantly reduce the interest charge if all sales receipts were banked on the day of sale. All the garages are open every day except Sunday. Assume that the daily sales value (for all three areas of business) is spread evenly across the week.

Required

(a)   Calculate the value of the annual interest which could be saved if all ten franchises adopted the finance director's suggestion of daily banking.   **(12 marks)**

(b)   Using the example of a car dealership such as Delcars, as given in (a) above, outline the advantages and disadvantages of centralisation of the treasury function.   **(8 marks)**

(Total: 20 marks)

PILOT PAPER

INTERMEDIATE LEVEL

Finance

Instructions to candidates

Section A contains **20** multiple choice questions: candidates should answer **all** of these. Section B contains **five** questions: candidates should answer **three** of these.

Time allowed: **3 hours**.

This is a **Pilot Paper** and is intended to be indicative of the style of questions that will appear in the future. It does not purport to cover the range of the syllabus learning outcomes.

The mark allocations for particular topics within the paper are subject to change in the future, as is the range of topics covered. The layout of the printed paper may be subject to slight variation in the future.

PILOT PAPER QUESTIONS

Section A: 40 marks

Answer all 20 questions in this section: 2 marks each

Each of the questions below has only one correct answer

Question 40 (Question 1 of Pilot Paper)

40.1   A yield curve shows the relationship between the yield and term to maturity for a number of financial assets, eg government stocks. In theory, the yield curve will normally be upward sloping so that long-term financial assets offer a higher yield than short-term financial assets.

Which of the following best explains the reason for this?

   A   Interest rates are expected to fall in the future.

   B   Interest rates have been increased on a number of occasions in the past year in an attempt to combat high inflation.

   C   The investor must be compensated for the additional risk of tying up money in the asset for a longer period of time.

   D   The market prices of long-term financial assets will tend to be lower than for short-term financial assets.

40.2   The ordinary share price of NS plc is currently 150p. Dividends are paid once a year, and the dividend for the previous year has very recently been paid. The net dividend for the year was 3p and a 15% annual growth rate is expected for dividend payments for the foreseeable future.

Using the dividend growth model, what is the cost of equity for NS plc?

   A   2.4%

   B   15.0%

   C   17.0%

   D   17.3%

40.3 The following data relates to shares of RB plc at the end of the day on 20 July 1999.

	Share price			Closing prices, 20 July	
High for year		Low for year	Selling price	Mid-market price	Buying price
330p		205p	280p	290p	300p

The earnings per share for the year to 31 January 1999 were 20p.

What is the P/E for the company that would be reported in the financial press on 21 July 1999?

A   14.0

B   14.5

C   15.0

D   16.5

40.4 In certain circumstances the Stock Exchange may grant a quotation for a company, even though the company is not making any new shares or existing shares available to the market.

This method of obtaining a quotation is known as:

A   placing.

B   prospectus issue.

C   tender issue.

D   introduction.

40.5 Which of the following is *not* true for a finance lease?

A   The lessee receives capital allowances from the asset.

B   The lease has a primary period which covers all or most of the useful economic life of the asset.

C   The lessee is responsible for servicing and maintenance of the asset.

D   The lessee records the leased asset as a fixed asset in its balance sheet.

40.6 SB plc has a published equity beta of 1.4. The expected return on three-month Treasury bills is 6%. The expected return on the market is 11%.

The cost of equity for SB plc may be estimated as:

A   11%

B   12.4%

C   13%

D   15.4%

40.7 Which one of the following statements about certificates of deposits is *not* true?

A   Certificates of deposit are negotiable deposits issued by banks.

B   Certificates of deposit will typically have maturity periods of between one month and five years.

C   Certificates of deposit are non-negotiable.

D   Certificates of deposit are issued in bearer form.

40.8 AC Ltd is a new company, whose directors have approached its bank for financial assistance. The bank has asked for draft profit and loss and balance sheet information to support the request for finance. The only information the directors have available is an estimate of sales for the first year, together with some industry averages for the current year.

Industry averages

Cost of sales to sales	50%
Sales to capital employed	2.5 times
Fixed assets to capital employed	70%
Current ratio	1.5:1
Estimated sales for the year	£760,000

In the draft balance sheet for AC Ltd, what would be the total of current assets?

A   £91,200

B   £182,400

C   £273,600

D   £570,000

40.9 PB Ltd uses 2,500 units of component X per year. The company has calculated that the cost of placing and processing a purchase order for component X is £185, and the cost of holding one unit of component X for a year is £25.

What is the economic order quantity (EOQ) for component X, and assuming a 52 week year, what is the average frequency at which purchase orders should be placed?

	EOQ	*Frequency of orders*
A	136 units	3 weeks
B	136 units	6 weeks
C	192 units	4 weeks
D	192 units	5 weeks

40.10 BACS (Bankers Automated Clearing Services) is an example of an electronic funds transfer system. Which of the following best describes the system?

    A   Provides same-day settlement for large sums of money.

    B   Is most concerned with processing payrolls and transactions involving standing orders and direct debits.

    C   Is a network for rapid transmission of international remittances between participating banks.

    D   Requires cheques to be completed to ensure settlement of a transaction.

40.11 Which one of the following statements about the efficient markets hypothesis is *false?*

    A   The strong form of the hypothesis implies that it is possible to predict changes in share prices.

    B   The strong form of the hypothesis implies that share prices will reflect all available information that could possibly affect the share price.

    C   The semi-strong form of the hypothesis implies that share prices will reflect information such as earnings forecasts and announcements of acquisitions.

    D   The semi-strong form of the hypothesis implies that it is not worthwhile for an investor to study company reports and accounts to try to achieve superior returns.

40.12 ABC plc and DEF plc are listed companies in the same country. Their P/E ratios and share prices are shown below.

	P/E ratio	*Current share price ex div.*
ABC plc	8	£5.00
DEF plc	12	£3.90

Which of the following statements will best explain the higher P/E ratio of DEF plc?

    A   DEF plc is a much larger company than ABC plc.

    B   DEF plc is regarded as a higher-risk investment than ABC plc.

    C   DEF plc has higher earnings per share growth prospects than ABC plc.

    D   DEF plc retains a higher proportion of its annual post-tax profits than ABC plc.

40.13 A company maintains a minimum cash holding of £1,000. The variance of its daily cashflows has been measured as £250,000. The transaction cost for each sale or purchase of treasury bills is £20. The daily interest rate is 0.025% per day and is not expected to change in the foreseeable future. Using the Miller-Orr cash-management model, the maximum cash holding level would be:

A   £1,594

B   £2,594

C   £7,400

D   £8,400

40.14 The following information relates to the ordinary shares of BC plc:

Earnings per share	50p
Dividend cover	2.5
Published dividend yield	3.2%

The price of BC plc's ordinary shares implied by the above data is:

A   78p

B   153p

C   625p

D   3,906p

40.15 The projected profit and loss account of SD plc for the year to 30 June 2000 shows the following figures:

	£000
Operating profit	100
Interest payable	40
Profit before tax	60
Corporation tax (30%)	18
Profit after tax	42

The directors of SD plc estimate that the additional purchase of new equipment on 1 July 1999 for £140,000 would increase the projected operating profit for the year by £18,000. The machine would be financed by a loan raised on 1 July 1999 with a coupon rate of 5%.

What would the projected interest cover for the company become if the directors purchased the new machine?

A   0.66

B   0.94

C   2.13

D   2.51

40.16   If £1,700 is invested at an interest rate of 9% per annum, compounded monthly, the sum it will give in three years' time is:

A   £1,738

B   £2,159

C   £2,202

D   £2,225

40.17   Which of the following is *not* a method used for raising finance to fund export sales?

A   Bills of exchange.

B   Credit insurance.

C   Documentary credits.

D   Countertrade.

40.18   Which of the following statements about warrants is incorrect?

A   Warrants are a device sometimes offered by a company to its ordinary shareholders, or attached to a loan issue as part of a package.

B   Warrants are sometimes issued by investment trusts in a bid to compensate investors for the discount to net asset backing at which the shares often trade.

C   Warrants have a fixed life, and once this has expired, the warrant may be sold back to the issuing company at the nominal value of the ordinary shares.

D   Warrants offer no income, but give the holder the right to apply for the ordinary shares of that company at a fixed price.

40.19 A company has cash outgoings of £1,260,000 per annum, spread evenly throughout the year. The interest rate on a Treasury bill is 8% per annum, and every sale of treasury bills costs £20. According to the Baumol cash-management model, the optimum amount of Treasury bills to be sold each time cash is replenished is:

A   £7,937

B   £17,748

C   £25,100

D   £88,741

40.20 Which of the following statements about venture capital is correct?

A   Venture capital would not be appropriate to finance a management buyout.

B   Venture capital organisations may provide loan finance as well as equity finance to a company.

C   Secured medium-term bank loans are a form of venture capital.

D   Companies with a stock market quotation would have no difficulty raising finance from a venture capital organisation.

(Total marks = 40)

Section B: 60 marks

Answer three questions only

Question 41 (Question 2 of Pilot Paper)

KM plc

The finance director of KM plc has recently reorganised the finance department following a number of years of growth within the business, which now includes a number of overseas operations. The company now has separate treasury and financial control departments.

Required

(a)   Describe the main responsibilities of a treasury department, and comment on the advantages to KM plc of having separate treasury and financial control departments.

(14 marks)

(b)   Identify the advantages and disadvantages of operating the treasury department as a profit centre rather than a cost centre.   **(6 marks)**

(Total marks = 20)

Question 42 (Question 3 of Pilot Paper)

SF Ltd

SF Ltd is a family-owned private company with five main shareholders.

SF Ltd has just prepared its cash budget for the year ahead, details of which are shown below. The current overdraft facility is £50,000 and the bank has stated that it would not be willing to increase the facility at present, without a substantial increase in the interest rate charged, due to the lack of assets to offer as security.

The shareholders are concerned by the cash projections, and have sought advice from external consultants.

All figures, £000

	J	F	M	A	M	J	J	A	S	O	N	D
						MONTH						
Collections from customers	55	60	30	10	15	20	20	25	30	40	55	80
Dividend on investment						10						
Total inflows	55	60	30	10	15	30	20	25	30	40	55	80
Payments to suppliers		20		20		25		28		27		25
Wages and salaries	15	15	15	15	15	20	20	15	15	15	15	15
Payments for fixed assets			2		5	10		15				
Dividend payable				25								
Corporation tax									30			
Other operating expenses	5	5	5	5	7	7	7	7	7	7	8	8
Total outflows	20	40	22	65	27	62	27	65	52	49	23	48
Net in or (out)	35	20	8	(55)	(12)	(32)	(7)	(40)	(22)	(9)	32	32
Bank balance (overdraft):												
Opening	20	55	75	83	28	16	(16)	(23)	(63)	(85)	(94)	(62)
Closing	55	75	83	28	16	(16)	(23)	(63)	(85)	(94)	(62)	(30)

The following additional information relating to the cash budget has been provided by SF Ltd:

♦ all sales are on credit. Two months' credit on average is granted to customers;

♦ production is scheduled evenly throughout the year. Year-end stocks of finished goods are forecast to be £30,000 higher than at the beginning of the year;

♦ purchases of raw materials are made at two-monthly intervals. SF Ltd typically takes up to 90 days to pay for goods supplied. Other expenses are paid in the month in which they arise;

♦ the capital expenditure budget comprises:

Office furniture	March	£2,000
Progress payment on building extensions	May	£5,000
Car	June	£10,000
New equipment	August	£15,000

Required

Assume you are an external consultant employed by SF Ltd. Prepare a report for the board advising on the possible actions it might take to improve its budgeted cashflow for the year, and consider the possible impact of these actions on the company's business. Your report should also identify possible short-term investment opportunities for the cash surpluses identified in the first part of the budget year. **(20 marks)**

Question 43 (Question 4 of Pilot Paper)

D plc

The summarised balance sheet of D plc at 30 June 1999 was as follows:

	£000	£000
Fixed assets		15,350
Current assets	5,900	
Creditors falling due within one year	(2,600)	
Net current assets		3,300
9% debentures		(8,000)
		10,650
Ordinary share capital (25p shares)		2,000
7% preference shares (£1 shares)		1,000
Share premium account		1,100
Profit and loss account		6,550
		10,650

The current price of the ordinary shares is 135p ex dividend. The dividend of 10p is payable during the next few days. The expected rate of growth of the dividend is 9% per annum. The current price of the preference shares is 77p and the dividend has recently been paid. The debenture interest has also been paid recently and the debentures are currently trading at £80 per £100 nominal. Corporation tax is at the rate of 30%.

Required

(a)   Calculate the gearing ratio for D plc using:

    (i)   book values

    (ii)   market values   **(4 marks)**

(b)   Calculate the company's weighted average cost of capital (WACC), using the respective market values as weighting factors.   **(6 marks)**

Assume that D plc issued the debentures one year ago to finance a new investment.

(c)   Discuss the reasons why D plc may have issued debentures rather than preference shares to raise the required finance.   **(4 marks)**

(d)   Explain what services a merchant bank may have provided to D plc in connection with the raising of this finance.   **(6 marks)**

(Total marks = 20)

Question 44 (Question 5 of Pilot Paper)

ABC Ltd

ABC Ltd is a small manufacturing company which is suffering cashflow difficulties. The company already utilises its maximum overdraft facility. ABC Ltd sells an average of £400,000 of goods per month at invoice value and customers are allowed 40 days to pay from the date of invoice. Two possible solutions to the company's cashflow problems have been suggested.

♦ **Option 1.** The company could factor its trade debts. A factor has been found who would advance ABC Ltd 75% of the value of its invoices immediately on receipt of the invoices, at an interest rate of 10% per annum. The factor would also charge a service fee amounting to 2% of the total invoices. As a result of using the factor, ABC Ltd would save administration costs estimated at £5,000 per month.

♦ **Option 2.** The company could offer a cash discount to customers for prompt payment. It has been suggested that customers could be offered a 2% discount for payments made within 10 days of invoicing.

Required

(a)   Identify the services that may be provided by factoring organisations.   **(4 marks)**

(b)   Calculate the annual net cost (in £) of the proposed factoring agreement.   **(6 marks)**

(c)   Calculate the annualised cost (in percentage terms) of offering a cash discount to customers.   **(3 marks)**

(d)   Discuss the relative merits of the two proposals.   **(7 marks)**

(Total marks = 20)

Question 45 (Question 6 of Pilot Paper)

KB plc

(a)   KB plc has a paid-up ordinary share capital of £1,500,000 represented by 6 million shares of 25p each. It has no loan capital. Earnings after tax in the most recent year were £1,200,000. The P/E ratio of the company is 12.

The company is planning to make a large new investment which will cost £5,040,000 and is considering raising the necessary finance through a rights issue at 192p.

Required

(i)   Calculate the current market price of KB plc's ordinary shares.   **(2 marks)**

(ii)   Calculate the theoretical ex-rights price, and state what factors in practice might invalidate your calculation.   **(6 marks)**

(iii)   Briefly explain what is meant by a deep-discounted rights issue, identifying the main reasons why a company might raise finance by this method. **(3 marks)**

(b)   As an alternative to a rights issue KB plc might raise the £5,040,000 required by means of an issue of convertible loan stock at par, with a coupon rate of 6%. The loan stock would be redeemable in seven years' time. Prior to redemption, the loan stock may be converted at a rate of 35 ordinary shares per £100 nominal loan stock.

Required

(i)   Explain the term *conversion premium* and calculate the conversion premium at the date of issue implicit in the data given.   **(4 marks)**

(ii)   Identify the advantages to KB plc of issuing convertible loan stock   instead of the rights issue to raise the necessary finance.   **(5 marks)**

(Total marks = 20)

RATIONALE

General

This pilot paper attempts to address the main aims of the syllabus which, in summary, are:

♦ to build on the material covered at the previous level, particularly Economics for Business, Business Mathematics, and Financial Accounting Fundamentals;

♦ to test the candidate's ability to:

- explain the role and purpose of financial management;

- identify and evaluate sources of finance;

- calculate cost of capital;

- analyse the overall management of working capital;

- evaluate debtor and creditor management policies.

The method of assessment is by a three-hour, unseen examination. The paper contains six questions. Question 1 is a compulsory 40-mark question containing 20 multiple choice sub-questions. Questions 2 – 6 are 20-mark questions and candidates are required to answer three of these.

Section A

Question 1

The 20 multiple choice questions are designed to test techniques and understanding from across the range of the syllabus. There is a mix of numerical and non-numerical questions.

Section B

Question 2

This question deals with the role and management of the treasury function which forms one of the key elements of section (i) of the syllabus: *The finance function*. Candidates are required to comment on the advantages of establishing a separate treasury function, and the advantages and disadvantages of operating this function as a profit centre.

Question 3

This question deals with analysis of cashflow forecasts. The question tests for an ability to evaluate working capital control and cash-management techniques, and asks candidates to consider the possible impact of their suggested actions on the business. The question is drawn mainly from section (iv) of the syllabus: *Working capital management*, but also draws from topic areas in section (iii) of the syllabus: *Sources of short-term finance*, as the question also asks candidates to consider opportunities for investing short-term cash surpluses.

Question 4

This question is aimed at testing gearing ratios, the cost of capital and the role of merchant banks in connection with an issue of new finance. It asks candidates to discuss why a particular form of financing might be preferred. The topics covered here are from section (ii) of the syllabus: *Sources of long-term finance* and section (i): *The finance function*.

Question 5

This question requires candidates to summarise the services provided by factoring organisations, and to calculate the net cost of a particular factoring agreement. The question also tests knowledge of alternative methods of managing debtors, requiring the calculation of cash discounts and an evaluation of cash discounts as against factoring. This question is drawn from topics within section (iv) of the syllabus: *Working capital management*.

Question 6

This question tests knowledge of two potential long-term sources of finance. The question asks candidates to carry out relevant calculations for both sources, to discuss the advantages of issuing convertible loan stock rather than making a rights issue, and to briefly explain what is meant by a deep-discounted rights issue. The question is drawn from topic areas in section (ii) of the syllabus: *Sources of long-term finance*.

May 2001 Exam Questions

Question 46 (Question 1 of Exam Paper)

46.1   A company has a current ratio of 1.75. It has decided in future to pay its trade creditors after 40 days, rather than after 30 days as it has in the past.

What will be the effect of this change on the company's current ratio and its cash operating cycle?

	Current ratio	Cash operating cycle
A	Increase	Increase
B	Increase	Decrease
C	Decrease	Increase
D	Decrease	Decrease

46.2   A perpetuity series of cash flows of £10,000 each year commences in two years. The relevant rate of interest is 10% each year.

What is the present value, to the nearest £1, of the cash flows?

A   £100,000

B   £90,909

C   £82,645

D   £110,000

46.3   A company uses additional debt to finance a new investment. Equity capital and the level of operating risk are unchanged.

What is the most likely effect upon the company's cost of equity capital?

A   It remains constant.

B   It increases.

C   It decreases.

D   It either increases or decreases.

46.4   The traditional theory of gearing states that, as gearing increases, a company's weighted average cost of capital:

A   rises initially then falls.

B   remains constant.

C   falls consistently.

D   falls initially then rises.

46.5 Company X and Company Y operate in the same industry but have different price earnings (P/E) ratios as follows:

	P/E ratio
Company X	7
Company Y	13

Which of the following is the most probable explanation of the difference in the P/E ratios between the two companies?

A   Company Y has a greater profit this year than Company X.

B   Company Y is higher risk than Company X.

C   Company Y has higher expected growth than Company X.

D   Company Y has higher gearing than Company X.

46.6 Which of the following best describes an equity warrant?

A   A security issued independently of the company concerned, by financial institutions, entitling the holder to subscribe for a different security at a pre-determined price at the option of the holder.

B   A security issued by the company concerned, containing a standardised expiry date and exercise price, requiring the holder to purchase the number of shares in the company specified in the warrant.

C   A security issued by a company giving a holder the right to be allotted ordinary shares in that company on terms specified in the warrant.

D   A security issued by the manufacturer of a product to the customer guaranteeing the minimum quality of its product.

46.7 FGH plc requires a rate of return of 12.85% each year.

Two of FGH plc's suppliers, P Ltd and Q Ltd, are offering the following terms for immediate cash settlement:

Company	*Discount*	*Normal settlement period*
P Ltd	1%	1 month
Q Ltd	2%	2 months

Which of the discounts should be accepted to achieve the required rate of return?

A   Both P Ltd and Q Ltd.

B   P Ltd only.

C   Q Ltd only.

D   Neither of them.

46.8   Which of the following is most likely to reduce a firm's working capital?

A   Paying creditors early.

B   Lengthening the period of credit given to debtors.

C   Repaying an overdraft out of cash.

D   Giving a discount to a debtor for immediate cash settlement.

46.9   Assume that a stock market is semi-strong form efficient. An ordinary dividend is proposed and paid, the amount being as the stock market expected.

Assuming there are no other events occurring at the same time, what is the most probable response of the company's share price at each of the following times:

(i)   dividend payment date?

(ii)   ex-dividend date?

	Dividend payment date	*Ex-dividend date*
A	Unchanged	Decrease
B	Decrease	Decrease
C	Unchanged	Unchanged
D	Decrease	Unchanged

46.10   Examine the validity of the following statements:

Statement 1

A portfolio of about 25 shares will normally diversify away over 95% of systematic (that is, market) risk.

Statement 2

Risk averse investors always aim to minimise their investment risk.

	Statement 1	*Statement 2*
A	True	True
B	True	False
C	False	True
D	False	False

46.11   The following money and real rates of interest are expected over the next two years:

	Year 1	*Year 2*
Money rate	9%	10%
Real rate	4%	5%

Calculate the average rate of inflation expected over the 2 years as implied by the stated money and real rates (to 2 decimal places).

A   4.76%

B   4.78%

C   4.81%

D   5.00%

46.12   A retailing company had cost of sales of £60,000 in April. In the same month, trade creditors increased by £8,000 and stock decreased by £2,000.

What payment was made to suppliers in April?

A   £50,000

B   £54,000

C   £66,000

D   £70,000

46.13   A listed company makes a rights issue. Which of the following rankings of prices is most valid? (Note: the symbol '<' below means 'is less than'.)

A   Ex-rights < Cum rights < Issue price

B   Ex-rights < Issue price < Cum rights

C   Cum rights < Ex-rights < Issue price

D   Issue price < Ex-rights < Cum rights

46.14   A company is considering whether to purchase or lease two different machines. It has a cost of capital of 10% each year.

Machine 1   can be purchased for £100,000, payable immediately, with a residual value of £10,000 after 5 years. It can be leased for six annual rentals of £20,000, the first one being payable immediately.

Machine 2   can be purchased for £48,000, payable immediately, with a zero residual value. It can be leased for five annual rentals of £14,500, the first being payable in two years time.

What is the appropriate action for purchasing or leasing the machines in order to minimise the cost in present value terms?

	Machine 1	*Machine 2*
A	Purchase	Purchase
B	Purchase	Lease
C	Lease	Purchase
D	Lease	Lease

46.15   Which of the following statements about venture capital is most valid?

    A   Venture capital is a low risk and low return form of finance.

    B   Companies listed on major stock exchanges normally use venture capital to raise new finance.

    C   Venture capital can be appropriate for a management buyout.

    D   Venture capital normally takes the form of debt finance.

46.16   A company commenced trading on 1 January and total sales for January were £150,000. Sales are made up to 60% on credit and 40% for cash. Sales grow at a monthly rate of 10%.

Bad debts were 3% of credit sales. Half of the remaining debtors paid in the month following the sale and the remainder in the month after that.

The cash received during February was:

    A   £107,670

    B   £153,300

    C   £103,650

    D   £109,650

46.17   The yield curve for bonds shows the relationship between the redemption yield and the term to maturity.

If the yield curve for a series of government bonds is upward sloping, this is most likely to indicate that:

    A   the coupon interest rate declines over time.

    B   market interest rates are expected to fall in future.

    C   short-term bonds offer a higher redemption yield than long-term bonds.

    D   long-term bonds offer a higher redemption yield than short-term bonds.

46.18   The cum div price of a company's shares is currently £10, its annual cost of equity capital is 10%. The market expects that the dividend, which is due immediately, and next year's dividend will both be zero, but a dividend will be paid in two years' time. Thereafter it is expected that there will be a constant growth in dividends of 5% each year.

What level of dividend, to one decimal place, does the market expect of the company when it recommences paying a dividend in two years' time?

    A   50.0 pence

    B   55.0 pence

    C   57.7 pence

    D   52.5 pence

46.19 A participating preference share is one which:

A accumulates unpaid preference dividends to a subsequent year, at which time the holder will participate in profits.

B entitles the holder to participate in profits above a pre-determined level at a fixed rate of interest per share.

C carries the right for holders to participate in share price gains by giving them the option to convert preference shares into ordinary shares at a pre-determined ratio, over a specified period of time.

D carries the right to an additional preference dividend when equity shareholders are paid an ordinary dividend exceeding a pre-determined level.

46.20 A company's shares have gone ex-div having just declared a dividend of 20p per share, but the market expects this dividend to decline by 2% each year in perpetuity. The annual cost of equity capital is 8%.

What is the ex-dividend price per share (to the nearest 1p)?

A £1.96

B £2.00

C £2.24

D £3.27   **(Total = 20 marks)**

Question 47 (Question 2 of Exam Paper)

James Williams

James Williams intends to set up a new company, Williams Ltd, on 1 January 2002. The company will sell hand-made leather shoes to a number of specialist retail outlets.

Production during January and February 2002 is to be used entirely to build up finished goods stocks and will be equal in each of these two months. By the end of February, it is intended to accumulate finished goods stock with a sales value of £300,000, and thereafter it will be maintained at this level. The company holds no raw material stocks or work-in-progress.

From March 2002 onwards sales are expected to be:

	£
March	100,000
April	125,000
May	125,000
Thereafter	150,000 each month

20% of the total sales value is expected to be for cash, the remaining 80% being sold on credit terms of one month.

Bad debts are estimated to be 2% of credit sales. The remaining trade debtors are equally divided between those who are expected to comply with the credit terms and pay after one month, and those who take a further month to pay.

Gross profit (that is, the excess of sales value over wages and material costs) is estimated at 25% of sales. Wage costs are expected to be equal to material costs. Wages will be paid in the month they are incurred, but materials will be purchased on one month's credit.

Overheads, which are payable in the month in which they are incurred, are estimated at £5,000 each month.

Fixed assets of £150,000 will be purchased and paid for on 1 January 2002. They are estimated to have, on average, a 5-year useful economic life with a zero residual value.

The majority of sales are expected to arise from a small number of customers and can be predicted with a high degree of certainty.

Mr Williams intends to subscribe £250,000 of his own money as the entire initial share capital of Williams Ltd on 1 January 2002. To the extend that this amount is insufficient, he is intending to approach his bank for finance in the form of a fixed term loan and/or an overdraft. In order to do so, he needs to quantify his precise financial requirements.

Required

(a)   Prepare a monthly cash budget for Williams Ltd for the 6-month period ending 30 June 2002. It should show the net cash flow for each month and the cumulative budgeted cash surplus or overdraft at the end of each month, assuming that no loan is given by the bank.

         Ignore interest and taxation payments.   **(12 marks)**

(b)   Write a brief memorandum to James Williams which identifies the financing needs of the company. It should include the following issues:

         (i)   the factors that should be considered in determining the most appropriate mix of short-term financing (such as an overdraft) and long-term financing (such as a fixed term bank loan).

         (ii)   the extent to which improved working capital management might contribute towards the company's financing, and a description of how this might be achieved.   **(8 marks)**

         Where appropriate, show supporting calculations.   **(Total = 20 marks)**

Question 48 (Question 3 of Exam Paper)

Deaton plc

Deaton plc is a listed company which manufactures quality cut-glass products. The company's sole manufacturing site and 95% of its sales are in the United Kingdom. The company is, however, currently considering entering into a contract to sell a specialist range of glassware to a Japanese retailer. The revenues from the Japanese contract are expected to amount to 25% of all future sales and 15% of future profit. It will require a significant initial investment, but it is expected that the money could be borrowed from the company's bank.

The Deaton family and other directors own the majority of the equity share capital, the remainder being held by employees and small shareholders. The total share capital amounts to 12 million £1 ordinary shares and has been unchanged for many years. Dividends per share paid on 31 May each year have been:

1997	1998	1999	2000
35.64 pence	37.78 pence	40.05 pence	42.45 pence

The dividend on 31 May 2001 will be 45.00 pence per share.

The company also has £12.5 million of 8% loan stock to be redeemed on 31 May 2002. Interest is payable annually in arrears on 31 May.

At 31 May 2001, the company's ordinary shares were quoted at £5.50 (cum div) and the loan stock at £98 per £100 nominal (ex-interest).

The corporation tax rate can be assumed to be 30% for the foreseeable future.

Interest is allowable for tax purposes.

Ignore any taxation of dividends.

The directors' meeting

The directors of Deaton plc were uncertain whether to proceed with the Japanese contract and in particular they were concerned about the discount rate that should be used for assessing the project.

The *marketing director* argued: 'We should use the weighted average cost of capital. This is the rate we have used in the past and it reflects the average cost of acquiring funds.'

The *production director* disagreed: 'If we are going to borrow to finance this project, then we have to pay interest. So long as the cash flows from the project cover the interest payments, we will make a profit on the contract. Commonsense dictates that we should therefore simply use the interest rate charged to us by the bank as the discount rate.'

The *finance director* argued: 'The real issue in deciding the relevant discount rate is the finance that we use. I suggest that instead of paying more and more dividends each year, largely to ourselves as individual shareholders, we should reduce dividends and use the cash saved to decrease the company's debt. If the company can earn a better rate of return than individual shareholders, then the cash should be retained in the company. As it is, the company is in effect borrowing to pay a dividend. Also, this project is high risk and therefore demands a high-risk premium in the discount rate.'

Required

(a)   Calculate Deaton plc's weighted average cost of capital at 31 May 2001.   **(8 marks)**

(b)   As a member of the treasury team, write a memorandum to the directors of Deaton plc which considers the views expressed by the directors. In so doing, and so far as the information permits, describe the factors to be considered in determining a discount rate for the Japanese project.   **(12 marks)**

(Total = 20 marks)

Question 49 (Question 4 of Exam Paper)

Stokko Ltd

Stokko Ltd imports bicycles from Eastern Europe for sale to the public by mail order. The company sells only two types of bicycle – the LXX and the GYY. The expected annual sales are 14,400 LXX bicycles imported from a Russian manufacturer and 3,600 GYY bicycles imported from a Polish manufacturer.

The *purchasing director* is concerned by the company's stockholding policy and wishes to introduce the use of the economic order quantity model (EOQ model). He has established that both suppliers make a transport charge of £500 per delivery. The purchase price of each type of bicycle is £40 and annual holding costs are 25% of the purchase price per unit. He has also established that supplies can be delivered reliably and regularly. Demand is constant throughout the year.

The new *company accountant* would prefer to control stock by using accounting ratios. He would wish to maintain a *stock/cost of sales* ratio of 0.25 for each type of bicycle. (Thus cost of sales for the year would be four times larger than the stock at the end of the year.)

The *finance director* believes that he can negotiate a quantity discount with the Polish manufacturer which would establish the following prices per bicycle for an entire order:

Order quantity	Cost per unit £
up to 499	40.10
500 – 719	40.00
720 and over	39.90

Required

(a) For each of Stokko Ltd's two products, calculate the economic order quantity, assuming that no discounts are available. Compare and comment upon these calculations. **(7 marks)**

(b) Calculate the level of stocks for each product that would be necessary to maintain a *stock/cost of sales* ratio of 0.25. In so doing ignore any discounts.

   Compare and contrast this method of controlling stocks for Stokko Ltd with the EOQ model used in (a) above. **(6 marks)**

(c) Calculate the optimal order quantity of GYY bicycles from the Polish manufacturer using the EOQ model, assuming that the discounts specified by the finance director are available. **(7 marks)**

(Total = 20 marks)

Question 50 (Question 5 of Exam Paper)

Rump plc

Rump plc is an all equity financed, listed company which operates in the food processing industry. The Rump family owns 40% of the ordinary shares; the remainder are held by large financial institutions. There are 10 million £1 ordinary shares currently in issue.

The company has just finalised a long-term contract to supply a large chain of restaurants with a variety of food products. The contract requires investment in new machinery costing £24 million. This machinery would become operational on 1 January 2002, and payment would be made on the same date. Sales would commence immediately thereafter.

Company policy is to pay out all profits as dividends and, if Rump plc continues to be all equity financed, there will be an annual dividend of £9 million in perpetuity commencing 31 December 2002.

There are two alternatives being considered to finance the required investment of £24 million:

(1) A 2-for-5 rights issue, in which case the annual dividend would be £9 million. The cum rights price per share would be £6.60.

(2)   Issuing 7.5% irredeemable debentures at par with interest payable annually in arrears. For this alternative, interest would be paid out of the £9 million otherwise available to pay dividends.

For either alternative, the directors expect the cost of equity to remain at its present annual level of 10%.

Required

(a)   Calculate the issue and ex-rights share prices of Rump plc assuming a 2-for-5 rights issue is used to finance the new project at 1 January 2002. Ignore taxation.   **(4 marks)**

(b)   Calculate the value per ordinary share in Rump plc at 1 January 2002 if 7.5% irredeemable debentures are issued to finance the new project. Assume that the cost of equity remains at 10% each year. Ignore taxation.   **(3 marks)**

(c)   Write a report to the directors of Rump plc which:

(i)   compares and contrasts the rights issue and the debenture issue methods of raising finance – you may refer to the calculations in your answer to requirements (a) and (b) and to any assumptions made; and

(ii)   explains and evaluates the appropriateness of the following alternative methods of issuing equity finance *in the specific circumstances* of Rump plc:

a placing,

an offer for sale,

a public offer for subscription.   **(13 marks)**

(Total = 20 marks)

Question 51 (Question 6 of Exam Paper)

Imlico plc

Imlico plc is an all equity financed listed company. It develops customised software for clients which are mainly large civil engineering companies. Nearly all its shares are held by financial institutions.

Imlico plc's chairman has been dissatisfied with the company's performance for some time. Some directors were also concerned about the way in which the company is perceived by financial markets. In response, the company recently appointed a new finance director who advocated using the capital asset pricing model as a means of evaluating risk and interpreting the stock market's reaction to the company.

The following initial information was put forward by the finance director for two rival companies operating in the same industry:

Company	Beta
Aztaz plc	0.7
Borran plc	1.4

The *finance director* suggests that the betas of the two companies are used by the stock market to calculate their required rates of return. He also notes, however, that the risk-free rate is 5% each year and the expected return on the market portfolio is 15% each year.

The *chairman* set out his concerns at a meeting of the board of directors: 'I fail to understand these calculations. Aztaz plc operates largely in overseas markets with all the risk which that involves, yet you seem to be arguing that it is a lower risk company than Borran plc, whose income is mainly derived from long-term contracts in our domestic UK building industry. I am very concerned that we can take too much notice of the stock market. Take last year for instance, we had to announce a loss and the share price went up.'

Required

(a)   Calculate, using the capital asset pricing model, the required rate of return on equity of:

        Aztaz plc

        Borran plc   **(4 marks)**

(b)   Calculate the beta of Imlico plc assuming its required annual rate of return on equity is 17% and the stock market uses the capital asset pricing model to calculate this return.

        (3 marks)

(c)   As the new finance director, write a memorandum to the chairman which explains, in language understandable to a non-financial manager, the following:

    (i)   the assumptions and limitations of the capital asset pricing model; and

    (ii)   an explanation of why Imlico plc's share price could rise following the announcement of a loss.

In so doing, comment upon the observations and concerns expressed by the chairman. You may refer, where appropriate, to your calculations in (a) and (b) above. **(13 marks)**

(Total = 20 marks)

November 2001 Exam Questions

Question 52 (Question 1 of Exam Paper)

52.1 Which ONE of the following is *least* likely to act as a financial (that is, investment) intermediary?

A   Bank.

B   Pension fund.

C   Credit rating agency.

D   Unit trust.

52.2 Which ONE of the following lists of securities is ranked in order of increasing risk to the investor (commencing with the lowest risk)?

A   Warrant; Unsecured loan; Preference share.

B   Unsecured loan; Preference share; Warrant.

C   Preference share; Unsecured loan; Warrant.

D   Warrant; Preference share; Unsecured loan.

52.3 Examine the validity of the following statements.

Statement 1   If share prices move randomly, then technical analysis (that is, Chartism) will normally fail to predict future share price movements.

Statement 2   If a stock market is semi-strong form efficient, then share prices will not respond to new information.

	Statement 1	*Statement 2*
A	True	False
B	True	True
C	False	False
D	False	True

52.4 A company currently has 10 million $1 shares in issue with a market value of $3 per share. The company wishes to raise new funds using a 1-for-4 rights issue. If the theoretical ex rights price per share turns out to be $2.80, how much new finance was raised?

A $2,500,000.

B $4,000,000.

C $5,000,000.

D $7,000,000.

52.5   A debenture has a fixed annual coupon rate of 7% and it will be repaid at its face value of $100 in one year's time. Similar debentures have a redemption yield (that is, yield to maturity) of 8% each year.

Ignoring tax, what is the current ex interest value of the debenture?

A $99.07.

B   £100.00.

C $100.93.

D $106.07.

52.6   If the financial gearing of a company increases, then

A   the required return on equity increases.

B   the required return on debt decreases.

C   the level of dividend decreases.

D   market interest rates increase.

52.7   The current annual risk-free rate of return is 6% and the required annual rate of return on a security with a beta of 1.2 is 15.6%. Using the capital asset pricing model, what is the required annual rate of return on the market portfolio?

A   11.52%.

B   13.00%.

C   14.00%.

D   17.52%.

52.8   Examine the validity of the following statements with respect to the yield curve showing the term structure of interest rates.

Statement 1   When interest rates are expected to fall consistently, short-term interest rates are likely to be higher than long-term interest rates.

Statement 2   When interest rates are expected to fall consistently, a yield curve would normally be downward sloping.

	Statement 1	*Statement 2*
A	True	False
B	True	True
C	False	False
D	False	True

52.9 What is the present value of an amount of $100, receivable in 10 years from now, at an interest rate of 10% each year (to the nearest $1)?

A $39.

B $42.

C $259.

D $614.

52.10 Which ONE of the following would most appropriately describe *commercial paper*?

A   Secured long-term loan notes issued by companies.

B   Secured short-term loan notes issued by companies.

C   Unsecured long-term loan notes issued by companies.

D   Unsecured short-term loan notes issued by companies.

52.11 In 2 years from now, $100,000 will be invested for a further 5 years at an annual compound rate of 8%. What will be the terminal value of the investment at the end of this period (that is, 7 years from now)?

A $85,734.

B $146,933.

C $171,382.

D $586,703.

52.12 Which ONE of the following most appropriate describes *forfaiting*?

A   It is a method of providing medium-term export finance.

B   It provides long-term finance to importers.

C   It provides equity finance for the redemption of shares.

D   It is the surrender of a share because of the failure to make a payment on a partly-paid share.

52.13 A company has a current ratio of 1.5 : 1. It decides to use surplus cash balances to settle 30% of its total current liabilities.

The current ratio will:

A   decrease by more than 30%.

B   decrease by less than 30%.

C   increase by more than 30%.

D   increase by less than 30%.

52.14 A company buys goods on credit and then, before payment is made, it is forced to sell all of these goods on credit for less than the purchase price. What is the consequence of these two transactions immediately after the sale has taken place?

A Stock decreases and cash decreases.

B Cash decreases and creditors increase.

C Stock decreases and debtors increase.

D Debtors increase and creditors increase.

52.15 Which ONE of the following would not normally be considered a cost of holding stock?

A Stock obsolescence.

B Insurance cost of stocks.

C Lost interest on cash invested in stocks.

D Loss of sales from a stock-out.

52.16 The following items were extracted from a company's budget for next month:

	$
Purchase on credit	360,000
Expected decrease in stock over the month	12,000
Expected increase in trade creditors over the month?	15,000

What is the budgeted payment to trade creditors for the month?

A $333,000.

B $345,000.

C $357,000.

D $375,000.

52.17 Examine the validity of the following statements with respect to the Miller-Orr cash management model.

Statement 1 The greater the variability in cash flows, the greater is the spread between the upper and lower cash balance limits.

Statement 2 The return point is the lower limit plus one third of the spread.

	Statement 1	*Statement 2*
A	True	False
B	True	True
C	False	False
D	False	True

52.18 A retailing company has an annual turnover of $36 million. The company earns a constant margin of 20% on sales. All sales and purchases are on credit and are evenly distributed over the year. The following amounts are maintained at a constant level throughout the year:

Stock $6 million

Debtors $8 million

Creditors $3 million

What is the company's cash cycle to the nearest day (that is, the average time from the payment of a supplier to the receipt from a customer)?

A   81 days.

B   111 days.

C   119 days.

D   195 days.

52.19 A company uses the economic order quantity model (EOQ model). Demand for the company's product is 36,000 units each year and is evenly distributed each day. The cost of placing an order is $10 and the cost of holding a unit of stock for a year is $2.

How many orders should the company make in a year?

A   60.

B   120.

C   300.

D   600.

52.20 Working capital is most likely to increase when

A   payments to creditors are delayed.

B   the period of credit extended to customers is reduced.

C   fixed assets are sold.

D   stock levels are increased.

Question 53 (Question 2 of Exam Paper)

XYZ plc

XYZ plc is a large company whose shares are listed on a major international stock exchange. It manufactures a variety of concrete and clay building materials. It has decided to replace 100 of its grinding machines with 100 of a new type of machine that has just been launched. The company is unable to issue any further equity and is therefore considering alternative methods of financing the new machines.

The company's accounting year end is 31 December.

Option 1 – Issue debt to purchase the machines

The machines are expected to cost $720,000 each on 31 December 2001 and on average are expected to have a useful economic life of 10 years. After this time, the company expects to scrap the machines, but it has no idea what proceeds would be generated from the sale.

If XYZ plc issues debt, it would do so on 31 December 2001 for the full purchase price in order to finance the investment. The debt would be issued at a discount of 10% on par value (that is, at $90 per $100 nominal) being redeemable at par on 31 December 2011 and carrying a coupon annual interest rate of 6%. Debt interest is tax allowable and the corporation tax rate can be assumed to be 30% (ignore any tax on the redemption).

The debt would be secured by fixed and floating charges.

Option 2 – Long-term lease

The machines can be leased with equal annual rentals payable in arrears. The lease term would be eight years, but this can be extended indefinitely at the option of the company at a nominal rent. The lease cannot be cancelled within the minimum lease term of eight years. The company would need to pay its own maintenance costs.

Option 3 – Short-term leases

The machines can be leased using a series of separate annual contracts. Maintenance costs would be paid by the lessor under these contracts but, even so, the average lease rentals would be much higher than under *Option 2*. There is no obligation on either party to sign a new annual contract on the termination of the previous lease contract.

Required

(a)   Calculate the after tax cost of debt at 31 December 2001 to be used in *Option 1*.**(8 marks)**

(b)   Explain whether the after tax cost of debt would be an appropriate discount rate for evaluating XYZ plc's investment in grinding machines.

        Calculations are not required.   **(4 marks)**

(c)   Write a memorandum to the directors of XYZ plc which discusses the factors that should be considered when deciding which of the three methods of financing the grinding machines is the most appropriate.   **(8 marks)**

(Total = 20 marks)

Question 54 (Question 3 of Exam Paper)

OVR Ltd

OVR Ltd manufactures and sells specialist aluminium scooters. The company has been very successful, with sales growing rapidly over recent years. A number of new retail outlets have been opened to extend the company's geographical coverage and cope with the rapid expansion in demand. Each retail outlet holds a wide range of available stock.

Despite profits increasing over the past few years, the company's overdraft has risen significantly to the point where it is approaching the limit of its overdraft facility, which is currently $5.5 million.

Extracts from OVR Ltd's accounts for the last two years show the following:

Balance sheets at 30 September

	2001 $000	2001 $000	2001 $000	2000 $000	2000 $000	2000 $000
Fixed assets			10,600			6,000
Current assets:						
Stock		2,400			1,600	
Trade debtors		3,300			2,200	
		5,700			3,800	
Current liabilities:						
Overdraft	5,200			2,700		
Trade creditors	1,000			500		
		(6,200)			(3,200)	
Net current (liabilities)/ assets			(500)			600
Bank loan			(5,000)			(3,000)
Net assets			5,100			3,600
Share capital			1,000			1,000
Profit and loss account			4,100			2,600
			5,100			3,600

Profit and loss account extracts for the years to 30 September

	2001 $000	2000 $000
Sales	12,000	8,000
Cost of sales	6,000	4,000
Gross profit	6,000	4,000
Other costs	4,500	3,000
Profit for the financial year	1,500	1,000

Additional information

(1)   The company's policy is to maintain a high level of stock in order to provide a significant choice to customers. The level of stock has increased in proportion to sales. At 30 September 1999, closing stock was $1,200,000. Stocks are valued at full cost.

(2)   Credit is taken by all customers. The terms of credit vary depending on the value of the sale, but normally take the form of paying in a number of equal instalments. OVR Ltd is considering doubling the credit period available to customers in order to compete more effectively with rival companies.

(3)   Sales tend to vary significantly from month to month with the peak months being July, August and September.

(4)   The cost of sales comprises approximately 50% labour costs and 50% material and other production costs.

Required

(a)   Calculate the following ratios for OVR Ltd for the years ended 30 September 2000 and 30 September 2001:

(i)   stock turnover period (in days);

(ii)   debtors' turnover period (that is, the number of days credit taken by customers);

(iii)   creditors' turnover period (that is, the number of days credit given by suppliers).

In calculating the above ratios, use the year-end figures for stock, debtors and creditors.

In each case, state any relevant assumptions and critically appraise the usefulness of the ratios in assessing working capital policy in OVR Ltd's particular circumstances.

Ignore taxation.   **(12 marks)**

(b)   Write a memorandum to the directors of OVR Ltd which explains alternative methods (other than ratio analysis) that OVR Ltd could use to manage the company's working capital position more efficiently.

No further calculations are necessary.   **(8 marks)**

(Total = 20 marks)

Question 55 (Question 4 of Exam Paper)

AEF plc

AEF plc is listed on an international stock exchange. It has an issued share capital of 2 million ordinary shares. Most of the shares are held by large financial institutions.

The company currently has an overdraft of $70 million which is carrying an annual interest rate of 10%. The company has no other borrowings.

The company's summary profit and loss account for the year ended 30 September 2001 was as follows:

	$000
Operating profit	22,000
Interest paid	7,000
Profit before taxation	15,000
Taxation	3,000
Profit after taxation	12,000
Ordinary dividend paid	3,000
Retained profit for the year	9,000

Earnings and dividends are expected to grow at a constant rate of 4% each year in perpetuity. Assume, for simplicity, that the dividend is paid on 30 September each year.

The company is now considering accepting a major new project which would commence on 30 September 2002. The project is a high-risk investment but the directors expect it to increase the company's annual growth rate of total earnings and total dividends from 4% to 7%. The project would be financed by a 1-for-4 rights issue at an issue price of $10 on 30 September 2002.

The required return by equity shareholders is currently 10% each year, but the directors believe it would rise to 12% each year if the new project is accepted.

One of the directors is concerned about the impact of the project on the overall risk of the company. She is also concerned about the impact of the project on earnings per share. In particular, she is concerned that if earnings per share falls, the share price might be adversely affected.

Required

(a)   Ignoring the impact of the new project, calculate the following at 30 September 2001:

     (i)   the price per share (using the dividend growth model);

     (ii)   earnings per share;

     (iii)   dividend cover;

     (iv)   price earnings ratio;

     (v)   gearing (using market value for equity).   **(7 marks)**

(b)   Write a memorandum to the directors of AEF plc which, as far as the information permits, evaluates the potential impact of the new project at 30 September 2002 (including financing) on:

     (i)   the value of the company;
     (ii)   the risk profile of the company;
     (iii)   the earnings per share of the company.

     Show any relevant calculations to support your arguments.   **(13 marks)**

Note

In all relevant calculations, assume that financial markets believe the directors' estimates of future dividends and cost of equity.   **(Total = 20 marks)**

Question 56 (Question 5 of Exam Paper)

CF Ltd

CF Ltd is about to commence trading as a wholesaler of hats. CF Ltd's only shareholders, Mr and Mrs Topper, worked as employees of a hat retailer for many years, but have recently been made redundant. They intend to subscribe $200,000 as the initial share capital.

Sales in 2002 are expected to be as follows:

	Units
January	2,400
February	3,600
March	4,800
Thereafter	9,600 each month

The average selling price of each hat is to be $10. All sales will be made on credit terms, requiring settlement two months after the date of sale. However, if settlement is made by customers within one month, a 2.5% cash discount will be given. Of the total sales, 60% are expected to be settled two months after the date of sale and 40% (before any discount is deducted) are expected to be settled one month after the date of sale.

The average purchase price for each hat will be $7. CF Ltd intends to make purchases at the end of each month in order to maintain stocks at a sufficient level to cover the following month's sales. Initially, therefore, purchases of 2,400 hats will be made in December 2001. Payment for purchases will be made one month in arrears.

Fixed assets are expected to cost $250,000, payable in January 2002. Depreciation on these assets will be $5,000 each month, commencing January 2002. These fixed assets are likely to have a low net realisable value.

Annual rent is expected to be $24,000 and will be payable quarterly in advance, commencing January 2002.

Monthly wages are expected to be $4,000 and are payable in the month they are incurred. Other overheads are expected to be $6,000 each month, half of which are payable in the month they are incurred and half are payable one month later.

Mr and Mrs Topper are considering approaching the bank for an overdraft or loan finance, or a mixture of both. They are also unsure of the conditions that might attach to any finance that the bank may offer.

Required

(a)   Prepare a monthly cash budget for CF Ltd for the period January 2002 to May 2002 inclusive. It should show the expected net cash flow for each month and the cumulative budgeted cash surplus or deficit at the end of each month. Assume for the purposes of this cash budget that the bank has not provided any loan finance. Ignore interest charges and taxation payments. **(10 marks)**

(b)   Write a memorandum to Mr and Mrs Topper explaining the factors that the bank would be likely to consider:

(i)   in deciding whether to provide finance to CF Ltd; and

(ii)   in determining the amount and nature of the finance to be provided.

Where appropriate, show supporting calculations. **(10 marks)**

(Total = 20 marks)

Question 57 (Question 6 of Exam Paper)

DF Ltd

DF Ltd is a manufacturer of sports equipment. All of the share of DF Ltd are held by the Wong family.

The company has recently won a major three year contract to supply FF plc with a range of sports equipment. FF plc is a large company with over 100 sports shops The contract may be renewed after three years.

The new contract is expected to double DF Ltd's existing total annual sales, but demand from FF plc will vary considerably from month to month.

The contract will, however, mean a significant additional investment in both fixed and current assets. A loan from the bank is to be used to finance the additional fixed assets, as the Wong family is currently unable to supply any further share capital. Also, the Wong family does not wish to raise new capital by issuing shares to non-family members.

The financing of the additional current assets is yet to be decided. In particular, the contract with FF plc will require orders to be delivered within two days. This delivery period gives DF Ltd insufficient time to manufacture items, thus significant stocks need to be held at all times. Also, FF plc requires 90 days' credit from its suppliers. This will result in a significant additional investment in debtors by DF Ltd.

If the company borrows from the bank to finance current assets, either using a loan or an overdraft, it expects to be charged annual interest at 12%. Consequently, DF Ltd is considering alternative methods of financing current assets. These include debt factoring, invoice discounting and offering a 3% cash discount to FF plc for settlement within 10 days rather than the normal 90 days.

Required

(a)   Calculate the annual equivalent rate of interest implicit in offering a 3% cash discount to FF plc for settlement of debts within 10 days rather than 90 days.

Briefly explain the factors, other than the rate of interest, that DF Ltd would need to consider before deciding on whether to offer a cash discount.   **(6 marks)**

(b)   Write a report to the Wong family shareholders explaining the various methods of financing available to DF Ltd to finance the additional current assets arising from the new FF plc contract. The report should include the following headings:

bank loan;

overdraft;

debt factoring;

invoice discounting.   **(14 marks)**

(Total = 20 marks)

May 2002 Exam Questions

ANSWER *ALL* TWENTY SUB-QUESTIONS – 2 MARKS EACH

Each of the sub-questions numbered from 1.1 to 1.20 inclusive, given below, has only ONE correct answer.

Question 58 (Question 1 of Exam Paper)

1.1   Which ONE of the following is one of the *3Es* "value for money" concept?

    A   Earnings.

    B   Equity.

    C   Evaluation.

    D   Effectiveness.

1.2   Which ONE of the following may be regarded as an advantage to shareholders of obtaining a quotation on a major stock market?

    A   Reduced disclosure requirements.

    B   Larger dividends can be paid.

    C   Shares become more readily marketable.

    D   It entitles a company to put "plc" (that is, public limited company) after its name.

1.3   Examine the validity of the following statements:

Statement 1

In a strongly efficient market, the price/earnings ratios (that is, P/E ratios) of all companies would be the same.

Statement 2

In a semi-strong efficient market, the share price for a particular company should not change when its financial statements are made public.

	Statement 1	*Statement 2*
A	True	True
B	False	True
C	True	False
D	False	False

1.4 $1,000 is invested for a period of 10 years. The interest rate for the first 8 years is 10% a year, and for the final 2 years it is 5% a year. To what value (to the nearest $1) will the $1,000 accumulate after 10 years?

    A $1,900

    B $2,363

    C $9,918

    D $17,194

1.5 Dividend cover may be defined as

    A   dividend per share divided by earnings per share.

    B   earnings per share divided by dividend per share.

    C   dividend per share divided by retained profit per share.

    D   retained profit per share divided by dividend per share.

1.6 A company makes a 2-for-3 rights issue at an issue price of $2. The cum rights price is $4. The theoretical ex rights price is

    A $2·50

    B $2·80

    C $3·00

    D $3·20

1.7 A company is to use a lease agreement to acquire machinery on 31 May 2002. The lease term is 5 years and lease rentals of $10,000 each year are payable annually in advance. The present value of the lease rental payments at 31 May 2002 using an annual discount rate of 10% is

    A $4,170

    B $6,209

    C $37,910

    D $41,700

1.8   A cashier misappropriates cash takings in week 1. The cashier then uses the cash takings in week 2 to make up exactly the shortfall from week 1. The cash takings from week 3 are then used to make up the shortfall in cash takings from week 2. This type of fraudulent behaviour is known as

   A   teeming and lading.

   B   advanced fee fraud.

   C   removal and substitution.

   D   fraudulent payments.

1.9   A company retains 70% of its earnings and distributes the remaining 30%. Capital investment projects generate an annual post-tax return on investment of 15% and a pre-tax return of 20%. Using the Gordon Growth Model, what is the annual rate of growth?

   A   4·5%

   B   6·0%

   C   10·5%

   D   14·0%

1.10 Examine the validity of the following statements:

   Statement 1

   In order to reduce the risk of a portfolio, the returns on its securities must be negatively correlated.

   Statement 2

   A risk-averse investor will always seek to minimise risk.

	Statement 1	*Statement 2*
A	False	False
B	False	True
C	True	False
D	True	True

1.11 With respect to the term structure of interest rates, the inverse yield curve is

   A   upward sloping.

   B   downward sloping.

   C   U-shaped.

   D   horizontal.

1.12 Which ONE of the following services is NOT normally undertaken by a debt factor?

A Taking customer orders and invoicing.

B Attempting to recover doubtful debts.

C Making payments to companies before the cash is received from debtors.

D Administering a company's sales ledger.

1.13 Examine the validity of the following statements:

Statement 1

In a period of high inflation, one would normally expect interest rates to be higher than in a period of low inflation.

Statement 2

Overdraft interest rates will normally increase in direct proportion to the balance outstanding.

	Statement 1	*Statement 2*
A	False	False
B	False	True
C	True	False
D	True	True

1.14 A company's current assets exceed its current liabilities (which include an overdraft). The company pays a trade creditor, taking advantage of a cash discount. What will be the effect of this transaction upon the company's working capital and on its current ratio?

	Working capital	*Current ratio*
A	Constant	Decrease
B	Constant	Increase
C	Decrease	Decrease
D	Increase	Increase

1.15 A company uses the economic order quantity model (that is, the EOQ model) to manage stocks.

Situation 1 – interest rates rise.

Situation 2 – sales volumes increase.

What would happen to the economic order quantity in each of these two situations?

	Situation 1	*Situation 2*
A	Increase	Increase
B	Increase	Decrease
C	Decrease	Increase
D	Decrease	Decrease

1.16 A company uses the Baumol cash management model. Cash disbursements are constant at $20,000 each month. Money on deposit earns 5% a year, while money in the current account earns a zero return. Switching costs (that is, for each purchase or sale of securities) are $30 for each transaction.

What is the optimal amount (to the nearest $100) to be transferred in each transaction?

A $500

B $1,700

C $4,900

D $17,000

1.17 Which ONE of the following transactions is most likely to affect the overall amount of working capital?

A   Receipt of full amount of cash from a debtor.

B   Sale of a fixed asset on credit at its net book value.

C   Payment of a creditor.

D   Purchase of stock on credit.

1.18 Which ONE of the following transactions would NOT affect the amount of a bank overdraft?

A   A payment by direct debit.

B   A bad debt write off.

C   An investment in treasury bills.

D   Bank charges.

1.19 A company commenced business on 1 April 2002. Sales in April 2002 were $20,000, but this is expected to increase at 2% a month. Credit sales amount to 60% of total sales. The credit period allowed is one month. Bad debts are 3% of credit sales, but other debtors pay on time. Cash sales represent the other 40% of sales.

The cash expected to be received in May 2002 is

A $19,560

B $19,640

C $19,800

D $20,160

1.20   If the current ratio for a company is equal to its acid test (that is, the quick ratio), then

A   the current ratio must be greater than one.

B   the company does not carry any stock.

C   debtors plus cash is greater than creditors minus stock.

D   working capital is positive.   **(Total = 40 marks)**

SECTION B – 60 MARKS

ANSWER THREE QUESTIONS ONLY

Question 59 (Question 2 of Exam Paper)

DEB plc

DEB plc is a listed company that sells fashion clothes over the Internet. Financial markets have criticised the company recently because of the high levels of debt that it has maintained in its balance sheet.

The company's debt consists of $150 million of 8% debentures that are due for repayment by 31 March 2005. Financial markets indicate it would not be possible to issue a new loan under the same conditions. The market value of the debentures is $90 per $100 nominal.

DEB plc's draft balance sheet at 31 March 2002 was as follows:

	$ million
Ordinary shares of $1	100
Reserves	20
	120
8% debentures (at nominal value)	150
	270
Fixed assets	200
Net current assets	70
	270

Fixed assets consist of $150 million of capitalised development costs and $50 million of land and buildings.

The company's share price has fallen consistently over the past two years as follows:

	Price per share
31 March 2000	$20
31 March 2001	$8
31 March 2002	$4

The company intends to make a 1-for-2 rights issue at an issue price of $2·50 on 30 June 2002. It is assuming that the cum rights price at the issue date will be $4. Immediately thereafter, all the proceeds will be used to redeem debt at its nominal value and thereby reduce its gearing.

Required

(a)   Calculate the gearing (that is, debt/equity) of DEB plc at 31 March 2002 using both

     (i)   book values; and

     (ii)   market values.   **(3 marks)**

(b)   Evaluate

     (i)   the weaknesses; and

     (ii)   the benefits

     of the two methods used to calculate gearing in requirement (a) above.   **(6 marks)**

(c)   Calculate the gearing of DEB plc in market value terms, immediately after the rights issue and redemption of debt.   **(6 marks)**

(d)   Briefly explain the advantages and disadvantages for DEB plc of redeeming part of its debt using an issue of equity shares.   **(5 marks)**

(Total = 20 marks)

Question 60 (Question 3 of Exam Paper)

STF plc

STF plc is a listed company operating in the building industry. The company recently sold its motorway maintenance division to concentrate on its core activity of house building.

The directors are unsure what to do about the surplus funds generated by the sale of the motorway maintenance division. They wish to invest in the company's core activity of house building by buying a smaller house-building company – possibly overseas – in order to expand geographically. This is unlikely to happen next year, and may take much longer. Nevertheless, the company wishes to maintain sufficient cash resources to make a take-over bid at any time.

At a meeting of the board, the *finance director* has suggested investing the surplus funds in a portfolio of three equity shares as follows:

	Equity Beta	*Investment* *$ million*	*Industry*
Loecost plc	0·9	20	Supermarket
Inter IT plc	1·5	10	Information technology
BankGlobal plc	1·2	30	Bank

The finance director argued: "This portfolio would give a spread across non-building industries and represent diversification for the company, thereby lowering risk. The investments could also be sold quickly when the need arose."

The chairman was unsure about the wisdom of investing in equities: "I am particularly concerned about risk and we must remember that we might need the cash to be available at short notice. I would therefore favour low-risk, short-term investments in marketable securities."

The marketing director argued: "If we have surplus funds that we do not know what to do with, we should return them to the shareholders in the form of a dividend and let them decide how to invest them. If we need funds in the future then we should raise new capital appropriate for the purpose."

Treasury bills yield 5% a year while the expected return on the market is 10% a year.

Required

(a)   Using the capital asset pricing model, calculate the required rate of return on the portfolio of three securities suggested by the finance director.   **(5 marks)**

(b)   For STF plc, briefly describe FIVE types of marketable security that may be suitable for short-term investment.   **(5 marks)**

(c)   As STF plc's management accountant, write a memorandum to the board that discusses the arguments of each of the three directors with respect to the use of surplus short-term funds.   **(10 marks)**

(Total = 20 marks)

Question 61 (Question 4 of Exam Paper)

WCM Ltd

WCM Ltd is a private company that sells a wide range of specialist electrical and manual tools to professional builders through a trade catalogue.

The company is considering the improvement of its working capital management in order to reduce its current overdraft. Most customers are required to pay cash when they place an order and thus there is little that can be done to reduce debtors. The focus of the board's attention is therefore on creditors and stock.

The working capital position at 30 April 2002 was as follows:

	$	$
Stock	300,000	
Trade debtors	50,000	
	———	
		350,000
Trade creditors	150,000	
Overdraft	550,000	
	———	
		(700,000)
		———
Net current liabilities		(350,000)
		———

Creditors

WCM Ltd has two major suppliers, INT plc and GRN Ltd.

INT plc supplies electrical tools and is one of the largest companies in the industry, with international operations. GRN Ltd is a small, local manufacturer of manual tools of good quality. WCM Ltd is one of its major customers.

Deliveries from both suppliers are currently made monthly, and are constant throughout the year. Delivery and invoicing both occur in the last week of each month. Details of the credit terms offered by suppliers are as follows:

Supplier	Normal credit period	Cash discount	Average monthly purchases
INT plc	40 days	2% for settlement in 10 days	$100,000
GRN Ltd	30 days	none	$50,000

WCM Ltd always takes advantage of the cash discount from INT plc and pays GRN Ltd after 30 days.

Stock

The company aims to have the equivalent of 2 months' cost of sales (equal to 2 months' purchases) in stock immediately after a delivery has been received.

New working capital policy

At a meeting of the board of directors, it was decided that from 1 May 2002 all payments would be based upon taking the full credit period of 40 days from INT plc, and similarly taking 40 days before paying GRN Ltd.

A review of stocks is also to be commissioned to assess the level of safety (that is buffer) stocks held. In particular, it would examine the feasibility of a just-in-time stock management system. Meanwhile, it was decided to make no purchases in May in order to reduce stock levels.

While most of the board supported these changes, the *purchasing manager* disagreed, arguing that working capital would be even worse after the changes.

Required

(a) Calculate the annual rate of interest implied in the cash discount offered by INT plc. Assume a 365-day year. **(3 marks)**

(b) Calculate the anticipated current ratio of WCM Ltd at 31 May 2002, assuming that the changes in creditor payment policy take place, and that there are no stock purchases during May 2002.

Assume for this purpose that, in the absence of any change to creditor policy, the overdraft would have remained at its 30 April 2002 level.

Clearly state any assumptions made. **(5 marks)**

(c)   As a management accountant of WCM Ltd, write a memorandum to the directors that evaluates:

(i)   the proposed changes to the creditor payment policy; and

(ii)   the proposed policy to introduce a just-in-time system for stock management.

(12 marks)

(Total = 20 marks)

Question 62 (Question 5 of Exam Paper)

WEB plc

WEB plc operates a low-cost airline and is a listed company. By comparison to its major competitors it is relatively small, but it has expanded significantly in recent years. The shares are held mainly by large financial institutions.

The following are extracts from WEB plc's budgeted balance sheet at 31 May 2002:

	$ million
Ordinary shares of $1	100
Reserves	50
9% debentures 2005 (at nominal value)	200
	350

Dividends have grown in the past at 3% a year, resulting in an expected dividend of $1 per share to be declared on 31 May 2002. (Assume for simplicity that the dividend will also be paid on this date.) Due to expansion, dividends are expected to grow at 4% a year from 1 June 2002 for the foreseeable future. The price per share is currently $10·40 ex div. and this is not expected to change before 31 May 2002.

The existing debentures are due to be redeemed at par on 31 May 2005. The market value of these debentures at 1 June 2002 is expected to be $100·84 (ex interest) per $100 nominal. Interest is payable annually in arrears on 31 May and is allowable for tax purposes. The corporation tax rate for the foreseeable future is 30%. Assume taxation is payable at the end of the year in which the taxable profits arise.

New finance

The company has now decided to purchase three additional aircraft at a cost of $10 million each. The board has decided that the new aircraft will be financed in full by an 8% bank loan on 1 June 2002.

Required

(a)   Calculate the expected weighted average cost of capital of WEB plc at 31 May 2002.

(8 marks)

(b)   Without further calculations, explain the impact of the new bank loan on WEB plc's

(i)   cost of equity;

(ii)   cost of debt;

(iii) weighted average cost of capital (using the traditional model).   **(8 marks)**

(c)   Explain and distinguish

   (i)   debentures; and

   (ii)   a bank loan.

   In so doing, explain why, in the circumstances of WEB plc, the cost of debt may be different for the two types of security.   **(4 marks)**

(Total = 20 marks)

Question 63 (Question 6 of Exam Paper)

PRT Ltd

PRT Ltd is a rapidly growing printing company that uses the latest technology to operate a quick and efficient service to other businesses and to private individuals. Some printing is undertaken to order, while other work, such as posters, is held in stock until sold. Sales to business customers are on credit, while sales to individuals are for cash.

Expansion has been rapid, as indicated by the number of print shops owned at each financial year ended 31 March:

Year	1998	1999	2000	2001	2002
Number of print shops	8	12	18	27	40

While expansion has been very rapid, concerns have arisen regarding the increasing overdraft, which is now approaching the limit of $1 million set by the bank. The company has used equity and debt finance to expand in recent years, but is unlikely to be able to raise further finance from these sources in the immediate future.

Extracts from the financial statements for the years ended 31 March are as follows:

	2001 $000	2002 $000
Raw material stocks	55	80
Finished goods stocks	185	185
Purchases of raw materials	600	850
Cost of sales	1,570	1,830
Administrative expenses	45	65
Sales	1,684	1,996
Trade debtors	114	200
Trade creditors	50	70
Overdraft	400	950
Additions to fixed assets	700	900

Cost of sales includes all relevant production costs including manufacturing overheads and labour.

Required

(a)   Calculate the length in days of PRT Ltd's operating cycle, for the year ended 31 March 2002.   **(5 marks)**

(b)   So far as the information permits, calculate the cash generated from operating activities for PRT Ltd for the year ended 31 March 2002. State any relevant assumptions. **(4 marks)**

(c)   As PRT Ltd's management accountant, write a memorandum to the board that analyses the company's cash and working capital position, recommending appropriate actions. Indicate any additional information that would be needed to make a fuller assessment.

(11 marks)

(Total = 20 marks)

November 2002 Exam Questions

Question 64 (Question 1 of Exam Paper)

Objective test questions

64.1 A company wishes to raise capital by issuing new ordinary shares to the public using an offer for sale. Which ONE of the following institutions would be most likely to assist the company in making the issue?

A   Capital house

B   Clearing house

C   Issuing house

D   Discount house

64.2 The Stock Exchange may grant a quotation for a company without that company making any new shares available to the market.

This method of obtaining a quotation is known as:

A   an offer for sale

B   an introduction

C   a placing

D   a scrip issue

64.3 Which ONE of the following would be least likely to be a function of a treasury department?

A   Managing relationships with banks

B   Liquidity management including investment of surplus funds

C   Currency management

D   Investment appraisal

64.4 A company makes a rights issue and the following prices apply:

Cum rights price	£10
Issue price	£6
Theoretical ex rights price	£9

What were the terms of the rights issue?

A   1 for 3

B   3 for 1

C   1 for 4

D   4 for 1

64.5 A company has a cost of debt of 5%, a weighted average cost of capital of 8% and a *debt : equity* ratio of 1 : 2. What is its cost of equity?

A 3%

B 7%

C 9.5%

D 14%

64.6 Examine the validity of the following statements:

Statement 1

Following a rights issue, a company's share price is likely to fall.

Statement 2

Following a rights issue, the total value of the company's ordinary shares is likely to fall.

	Statement 1	*Statement 2*
A	True	True
B	True	False
C	False	True
D	False	False

64.7 A company is considering whether to buy or lease two assets.

Asset 1 has a 10 year economic life with a zero residual value. It can be purchased for £80,000 payable immediately. Alternatively, it can be leased for 10 lease rentals of £12,000 per annum payable annually in advance.

Asset 2 has a 5 year economic life. It can be purchased for £81,000 payable immediately and will have a residual value of £40,000 after 5 years. Alternatively, it can be leased for 5 lease rentals of £14,000 per annum payable annually in arrears and the asset will be handed back to the lessor at the end of this 5 year contract.

The required rate of return is 10% per annum. Ignore taxation.

How should the company finance each asset?

	Asset 1	*Asset 2*
A	Lease	Lease
B	Lease	Buy
C	Buy	Lease
D	Buy	Buy

64.8   Examine the validity of the following statements:

Statement 1

All other things being equal, the higher the price earnings ratio (P/E ratio) the greater the *growth* expected by financial markets.

Statement 2

All other things being equal, the higher the price earnings ratio (P/E ratio) the greater the *risk* expected by financial markets.

	Statement 1	*Statement 2*
A	True	True
B	True	False
C	False	True
D	False	False

64.9   Extracts from company Y's accounts are as follows:

Turnover	£200 million
Operating profit	£50 million
Interest payable	£10 million
Profit before tax	£40 million
Profit after tax	£20 million

What is company Y's interest cover?

A   20 times

B   5 times

C   4 times

D   2 times

64.10   Four investments are available:

Investment A pays interest of	1.6%	every	3 months
Investment B pays interest of	3.5%	every	6 months
Investment C pays interest of	5.2%	every	9 months
Investment D pays interest of	7%	every	12 months

Which investment gives the best annual rate of return?

A   Investment A

B   Investment B

C   Investment C

D   Investment D

64.11 In respect of the *term structure of interest rates*, which of the following would best explain a downward sloping yield curve?

    A   Short-term interest rates are higher than long-term rates

    B   Inflation is expected to rise in future

    C   There is increasing uncertainty over future long-term interest rates

    D   The central bank has lowered short-term interest rates on a temporary basis to stimulate the economy

64.12 In October, a company made credit purchases of £18,000 and credit sales of £24,000. All sales are made on the basis of cost plus 25%. By how much will working capital increase in October as a result of these transactions?

    A   £2,000

    B   £4,000

    C   £4,800

    D   £6,000

64.13 The following items have been extracted from a company's budget for next month:

	£
Sales on credit	240,000
Expected increase in stock next month	20,000
Expected decrease in trade debtors next month	12,000

What is the budgeted receipt from trade debtors next month?

    A   £228,000

    B   £232,000

    C   £252,000

    D   £272,000

64.14 A company has a positive level of working capital but has an overdraft. What will be the impact of the following transactions on the current ratio?

Transaction 1

Cash is received from debtors and is then used to reduce the overdraft.

Transaction 2

A fixed asset is sold for cash and this is used to reduce the overdraft.

	Transaction 1	*Transaction 2*
A	Increase	Increase
B	Increase	Decrease
C	Decrease	Increase
D	Decrease	Decrease

64.15 If payments to creditors are delayed, what is the impact on the total level of working capital (ignore cash discounts)?

A   Increase

B   Decrease

C   No effect

D   Depends on whether working capital is positive or negative

64.16 Which of the following is not normally associated with overtrading?

A   Falling sales

B   Increasing overdraft

C   Falling current ratio

D   Rising profit

64.17 The Clearing House Automated Payment System (CHAPS) provides:

A   a system to clear cheques for customers within 3 working days

B   same day settlements between banks which are members of the clearing system

C   a system of payment for the purchase of shares within the settlement period

D   a financial transfer system, normally for the payment of payrolls by companies

64.18 A company has decided to issue new share capital using an offer for sale by tender. The company estimates that the following tenders would be received:

Price £	Number of shares applied for at each price
5.00	500,000
4.50	800,000
4.00	200,000
3.50	100,000

What strike price would maximise the proceeds from the issue?

A   £5.00

B   £4.50

C   £4.00

D   £3.50

64.19 What is the operating cycle of company Z given the following?

Stock cycle	30 days
Trade debtors' cycle	38 days
Trade creditors' cycle	44 days

A   112 days

B   68 days

C   36 days

D   24 days

64.20 Invoice discounting normally involves:

A   offering a cash discount for early settlement of invoices

B   selling an invoice to a discount house at a profit

C   selling an individual invoice for cash to a factory organisation at a discount

D   writing off an invoice, partly or in total, as a bad debt

(Total : 40 marks)

Question 65 (Question 2 of Exam Paper)

AAD Ltd

AAD Ltd is a newly-created subsidiary of a large listed company. It commenced business on 1 October 2002, to provide specialist contract cleaning services to industrial customers. All sales are on credit.

More favourable credit terms are offered to larger customers (class A) than to smaller customers (class B). All sales are invoiced at the end of the month in which the sale occurs. Class A customers will be given credit terms requiring payment within 60 days of invoicing, while class B customers will be required to pay within 30 days of invoicing.

Since it is recognised, however, that not all customers comply with the credit terms they are allowed, receipts from debtors have prudently been estimated as follows:

Customer type	Within 30 days	31 to 60 days	61 to 90 days	91 to 120 days	Bad debts
Class A		50%	30%	15%	5%
Class B	60%	25%	10%		5%

The above table shows that debtors are expected either to pay within 60 days of the end of the credit period, or not at all. Bad debts will therefore be written off 60 days after the end of the credit period.

Budgeted credit sales for each class of customer in the first 4 months of trading are as follows:

Customer	October £000	November £000	December £000	January £000
Class A	100	150	200	300
Class B	60	80	40	50

Assume all months are of 30 days.

Required

(a)   Prepare a statement showing the budgeted cash to be received by AAD Ltd from debtors in each of the three months of November 2002, December 2002 and January 2003, based upon the prudently estimated receipts from debtors.   **(7 marks)**

(b)   Prepare a budgeted age analysis of debtors for AAD Ltd at 30 January 2003 for each of the two classes of customer. It should show the total budgeted debtors outstanding at that date analysed into each of the following periods:

      (i)   within credit period.
      (ii)   up to 30 days overdue.
      (iii)   30 to 60 days overdue.   **(8 marks)**

(c)   Explain the purposes of companies preparing an age analysis of debtors analysed by individual debtors.   **(5 marks)**

(Total : 20 marks)

Question 66 (Question 3 of Exam Paper)

STK Ltd

STK Ltd sells bathroom fittings throughout England. In order to obtain the best price, it has decided to purchase all its annual demand of 10,000 shower units from a single supplier. After investigation, it has identified two possible manufacturers – SSS plc and RRR Ltd. Each has offered to provide the required number of showers each year under an exclusive long-term contract.

Demand for shower units is at a constant rate all year. The cost to STK Ltd of holding one shower unit in stock for one year is £4 plus 3% of the purchase price.

SSS plc is located only a few miles from the STK Ltd main showroom. It has offered to supply each shower unit at £400 with a transport charge of £200 per delivery. It has guaranteed such a regular and prompt delivery service that STK Ltd believes it will not be necessary to hold any safety stock (that is buffer stock) if it uses SSS plc as its supplier.

RRR Ltd is located in the Far East. It has offered to supply each shower unit at £398 but transport charges will be £500 per delivery. There is also a minimum order size of 1,000 shower units. Deliveries will be by ship and will therefore take some time to arrive. There is also significant uncertainty about the lead time which means that STK Ltd will need to hold a safety stock of 600 shower units.

Required

(a)   Using the economic order quantity model (EOQ model), calculate the optimal order size, assuming that SSS plc is chosen as the sole supplier of shower units for STK Ltd.

                                                         (4 marks)

(b)   (i)   Prepare calculations to determine whether SSS plc or RRR Ltd should be chosen as the sole supplier of shower units for STK Ltd.   **(7 marks)**

      (ii)   Describe any further factors that STK Ltd should consider before making a final choice of supplier.   **(4 marks)**

(c)   Assume you are a consultant advising the Far East based company RRR Ltd. Write a brief memorandum explaining how RRR Ltd could finance the necessary working capital for its proposed contract to supply STK Ltd.   **(5 marks)**

(Total : 20 marks)

Question 67 (Question 4 of Exam Paper)

CAP plc

CAP plc is a listed company that owns and operates a large number of farms throughout the world. A variety of crops are grown.

Financing structure

The following is an extract from the balance sheet of CAP plc at 30 September 2002.

	£ million
Ordinary shares of £1 each	200
Reserves	100
9% irredeemable £1 preference shares	50
8% loan stock 2003	250
	600

The ordinary shares were quoted at £3 per share ex div on 30 September 2002. The beta of CAP plc's equity shares is 0.8, the annual yield on treasury bills is 5% and financial markets expect an average annual return of 15% on the market index.

The market price per preference share was £0.90 ex div on 30 September 2002.

Loan stock interest is paid annually in arrears and is allowable for tax at a corporation tax rate of 30%. The loan stock was priced at £100.57 ex interest per £100 nominal on 30 September 2002. Loan stock is redeemable on 30 September 2003.

Assume that taxation is payable at the end of the year in which taxable profits arise.

A new project

Difficult trading conditions in European farming have caused CAP plc to decide to convert a number of its farms in Southern Europe into camping sites with effect from the 2003 holiday season. Providing the necessary facilities for campers will require major investment, and this will be financed by a new issue of loan stock. The returns on the new campsite business are likely to have a very low correlation with those of the existing farming business.

Required

(a)   Using the capital asset pricing model, calculate the required rate of return on equity of CAP plc at 30 September 2002. Ignore any impact from the new campsite project.

Briefly explain the implications of a beta of less than 1, such as that for CAP plc.

(5 marks)

(b)   Calculate the weighted average cost of capital of CAP plc at 30 September 2002 (use your calculation in answer to requirement (a) above for the cost of equity). Ignore any impact from the new campsite project.   **(10 marks)**

(c)   **Without further calculations**, identify and explain the factors that may change CAP plc's equity beta during the year ending 30 September 2003.   **(5 marks)**

(Total : 20 marks)

Question 68 (Question 5 of Exam Paper)

HRD Ltd

HRD Ltd owns a number of small hotels. The room occupancy rate varies significantly from month to month. There are also high fixed costs. As a result, the cash generated each month has been very difficult to estimate.

Christmas is normally a busy period and large cash surpluses are expected in December. There is, however, a possibility that a rival group of hotels will offer large discounts in December and this could damage December trade for HRD Ltd to a significant extent.

January is a poor period for the industry and therefore all the company's hotels will close for the month, resulting in a negative cash flow. The Finance Director has identified the following possible outcomes and their associated probabilities:

	£000s	Probability
Expected cash balance at 30 November 2002	+175	1.0
Net operating cash flow in December 2002	+700 -300	0.7 0.3
Net operating cash flow in January 2003	-900	1.0

Assume cash flows arise at month ends.

Money can be put on deposit at the following rates:

Maturity period	*Compounded annualised yield*
1 month	5% (ie 0.4074% per month)
2 months	6% (ie 0.9759% for two months)

The company's overdraft carries a compounded annualised interest rate of 10% (ie 0.7974% per month).

After January 2003, trade is expected to improve but there is still a high degree of uncertainty in relation to the cash surpluses or deficits that will be generated in each month.

Required

(a)   Calculate the expected cash balance or overdraft of HRD Ltd at 31 January 2003.

   Briefly comment, with reasons, on whether this figure should be used for short-term cash planning.   **(5 marks)**

(b)   As a member of the treasury team of HRD Ltd, write a memorandum to the Directors, with supporting calculations, advising them regarding the investment of short-term cash balances in December 2002 and January 2003.

   Ignore transaction costs and make all calculations to the nearest £1.   **(10 marks)**

(c)   Consider whether the use of the Miller-Orr model would be useful for determining HRD Ltd's policy for investment of short-term cash balances *beyond* January 2003. Calculations are **not** required.   **(5 marks)**

(Total : 20 marks)

Question 69 (Question 6 of Exam Paper)

COE plc

COE plc is an all-equity financed, listed company in the pharmaceutical industry which produces a small, specialist range of drugs that treat heart disorders. The drugs are protected by international patent as soon as new research and development has progressed sufficiently.

On 1 March 2002, following many years of testing, a new drug, kryothin, was given government approval in the United Kingdom. It was approved for use in most other countries during April and May 2002. Sales of kryothin will commence on 1 January 2003. The company's accounting year end is 31 December.

Including the earnings generated by sales of kryothin, the company could pay a *total* annual dividend of £32.2 million in each of the years ending 31 December 2003 to 31 December 2007. Thereafter, it is expected that competitors will develop similar drugs and most of the excess profits will disappear, in which case the company could pay a total annual dividend of £19 million from 31 December 2008 onwards. (Assume for simplicity that dividends are declared and paid on 31 December each year.)

In order to manufacture kryothin, it will be necessary to raise £80 million of new capital on 1 January 2003 to finance the purchase of equipment.

The financing options being considered are:

Option 1 An offer for sale at the market price per share on 1 January 2003.

Option 2 An issue at par of 7% irredeemable corporate bonds. In this case, the interest would reduce the amount otherwise available to pay dividends.

The directors of COE plc assume that the annual cost of equity will remain at its current level of 10%. The company currently has in issue a share capital of 20 million £1 ordinary shares.

Required

(a) Assuming a semi-strong efficient market, explain the nature and timing of the share price reaction to the new drug kryothin at each stage of its development. Calculations are **not** required. **(7 marks)**

(b) Calculate COE plc's price per share at 2 January 2003 under each of the following options for raising the £80 million of new finance:

  Option 1 An offer for sale.
  Option 2 An issue at par of 7% irredeemable corporate bonds.

  Assume that the directors are correct in assuming that the annual cost of equity will remain at 10%, and that financial markets believe the directors' forecasts of future dividends.

  Ignore taxation. **(13 marks)**

(Total : 20 marks)

Objective test answers

1	D
2	D
3	C
4	D
5	B
6	B
7	D
8	B
9	B
10	D
11	C
12	A
13	C
14	B
15	A
16	D

$$\text{Theoretical ex rights price} = \frac{\text{MV of shares pre rights issue} + \text{Proceeds of rights issue}}{\text{Number of shares post rights issue}}$$

$$= \frac{\pounds 2/\text{share} \times 4\,\text{shares} + \pounds 1.5/\text{share} \times 1\,\text{share}}{5\,\text{shares}}$$

$$= \pounds 1.9/\text{share}$$

17   C

---

18   C

---

19   B

---

20   C

MV of warrant	= MV of shares/warrant - purchase price of shares/warrant
	= £8 × 2 - £4 × 2
	= £16 - £8 = £8/warrant

---

21   C

---

22   A

Gordon's growth model = rb

where r = ROCE   b = retention rate

r = 12% $b = \dfrac{20p}{40p} = 50\%$

rb = 12% × 50% = $\underline{6}$%

---

23   C

$K_e = \dfrac{d_1}{P_0} + g$

$d_1 = 20p \times 1.06 = 21.2p$

$P_0 = 400p$

$g = 6\%$

$K_e = \dfrac{21.2}{400} + 0.06$

$= 11.3\%$

---

24   D

---

25   B

g = rb   r = 18%   b = 50%   g = 18% × 50% = $\underline{9}$%

$P_0 = \dfrac{D_0(1+g)}{K_e - g}$ $=$ $\dfrac{25p \times 1.09}{0.12 - 0.09}$ $=$ $\underline{908}$

26 C

Use $1 + g = \sqrt[3]{d_o / d_n} = \left(\dfrac{d_o}{d_n}\right)^{\frac{1}{3}}$

$d_o = 20p$ $d_n = 10p$

                      $g = 26\%$

---

27 D

---

28 B

---

29 D

---

30 C

$K_e = R_f + \left(R_m - R_f\right)\beta$

    $= 7\% + \left(12\% - 7\%\right)0.75$

    $= 10.75\%$

---

31 D

---

32 D

---

33 D

---

34 D

			D.F.		P.V.	
Year	Cashflow	@ 10%	@ 15%	@ 10%	@ 15%
0	(90)	1.000	1.000	(90)	(90)
1-3	9	2.487	2.283	22.38	20.547
3	100	0.751	0.658	75.1	65.8
				+7.48	-3.65

IRR $= 10\% + 5\% \times \dfrac{7.48}{11.13}$

       $= 13.36\%$

---

35 B

---

36   C

Current market value

Coupon = $\dfrac{£8}{0.1}$ = £80

Additional return to redemption = £100 - £80 = £20

PV of addition return = £20 × 0.826 = £16.5

Total value of debt

= £80 + £16.5 = £96.5

---

37   A

---

38   C

WACC

$$K_o = K_e \left[\frac{V_E}{V_E + V_D} \right] + K_d \left[\frac{V_D}{V_E + V_D} \right]$$

K_e =   17%

K_d =   11.6%

V_E =   3m × 2.85   =   £8.55m

V_D =   £2m

K_o = $17\% \times \dfrac{8.55}{10.55} + 11.6\% \times \dfrac{2}{10.55}$

          =   <u>16%</u>

---

39   A

Interest cover	=	$\dfrac{\text{PBIT}}{\text{Interest}}$
PBIT	=	£50m × 20% = £10m
Interest	=	£20m × 10% = £2m
Interest cover	=	$\dfrac{£10m}{£2m}$ = 5 times

---

40   A

Contribution/unit	=	£100 - £40
	=	£60/unit
Fixed cost	=	£10m
Breakeven point (units)	=	$\dfrac{£10,000,000}{£60 / \text{unit}}$
	=	166,667 units

---

41   C

---

42   D

	£m
Operating profit	20
Less interest	(5)
Profit before tax	15
Less tax	(3)
Profit after tax	12
No. of shares	8
Earning per share	£1.5/share
P/E ratio	20 ÷ 1.5 = 13.33:1

---

43   B

Dividend cover

$$= \frac{\text{Earnings per share}}{\text{Dividend per share}}$$

$$= \frac{£12m}{£6m} = 2 \text{ times}$$

---

44   A

Gross dividend yield

$$= \frac{\text{Dividend per share}}{\text{Market price}}$$

$$= \frac{£6m \div 8m}{£20} = \frac{£0.75}{£20}$$

$$= 0.0375 = 3.75\%$$

---

45   A

Interest cover

$$= \frac{\text{Operating profit}}{\text{Interest}}$$

$$= \frac{£20m}{£5m} = 4 \text{ times}$$

---

46   C

Debt to equity ratio

$$= \frac{\text{Debt}}{\text{Equity}} \times 100$$

$$= \frac{£50m}{£160m} \times 100 = 31\%$$

47   B

Total number of shares post conversion

$$= \quad \frac{£50m}{£100} \times 2 + 8m$$

$$= \quad 1m + 8m = 9m \text{ shares}$$

Fully diluted EPS $= \dfrac{£12m}{9m \text{ shares}} = £1.33/\text{share}$

48   C

Simple $£1,000 \times (1 + 5r) = 1000 \times 1.40 = £1,400$

Compound $£1,000\,(1+r)^5 = 1000 \; 1.065^5 = £1,370$

49   C

$$1 + i \quad = \quad \frac{1+m}{1+r}$$

$$= \quad \frac{1.07}{1.03} \quad = \quad 1.039$$

$$i \quad = \quad \underline{3.9\%}$$

50   D

Interest per compounding period   = 2%
Number of periods per annum   = 4

$$\text{APR} = 1.02^4 \quad = \quad 1.0824$$
$$= \quad 8.24\%$$

51   D

52   A

Gross redemption yield =

$$\text{Flat yield} + \left[\frac{(\text{Redemption Value} - \text{Market Value}) \div \text{Number of Years}}{\text{Market Value}} \right] \times 100$$

$$\text{Flat yield} = \left[\frac{\text{Coupon Rate} \times \text{Nominal Value}}{\text{Market Value}} \right] \times 100$$

$$\text{Flat yield} = \left(\frac{7\% \times £100}{£109} \right) \times 100 = 6.42\%$$

$$\text{Gross redemption yield} = 6.42\% + \left[\frac{(100 - 109) \div 3}{109} \right] \times 100$$

$$= 6.42\% - 2.75\% = 3.67\%$$

53   C

---

54   B

---

55   A

Interest is charged at a flat rate of 10% per annum on the full balance outstanding.

Total interest	= £14,000 × 10% × 3 years = £4,200
Total balance	= borrowing + interest = £14,000 + £4,200 = £18,200
Payment per annum	= £18,200 ÷ 36 months = £505/month

---

56   B

---

57   D

---

58   D

---

59   D

Total interest @ 7% per annum	= £1m × 7% = £70,000
Total interest @ 6.50% for 3 months	= £1m × 6.5% × $\frac{1}{4}$ = 16,250
Interest for remaining 9 months	£1,016,250 × 7.5% × $\frac{3}{4}$ = £57,164
Total interest	= 16,250 + 57,164 = £73,414
Difference	= 73,414 – 70,000 = £3,414

---

60   C

---

61   A

---

62   B

		Days
Stock days	$\frac{8}{30}$ × 365	97.3
Debtor days	$\frac{4}{40}$ × 365	36.5
Creditor days	$\frac{3}{15}$ × 365	(73)
Working capital cycle		60.8 days

63 C

---

64 C

---

65 A

---

66 B

Baumol Model $\qquad = \sqrt{\dfrac{2\,Cod}{Ch}}$

Co   -   £50
d   -   £1,000,000
Ch   -   12%

Encashment quantity $\qquad = \sqrt{\dfrac{2 \times 50 \times 1{,}000{,}000}{0.12}}$

= £28,868

---

67 D

---

68 A

---

69 C

---

70 B

Spread $\qquad = 3\left[\dfrac{\tfrac{3}{4} \times \text{Transaction Cost} \times \text{Variance of Cashflow}}{\text{Interest Rate}}\right]^{\tfrac{1}{3}}$

$\qquad\qquad = 3\left[\dfrac{\tfrac{3}{4} \times 40 \times 4{,}000^2}{0.0004}\right]^{\tfrac{1}{3}}$

$\qquad\qquad = 31{,}879$

Upper limit $\qquad = 31{,}879 + 10{,}000$

$\qquad\qquad = £41{,}879$

---

71 A

---

72   C

Total debtors		£
On sales = £100m × 95%	=	95.00
Other £95m × $\dfrac{10}{90}$		10.55
		_____
		105.55
		_____

Average debtor balance	=	$\dfrac{10m + 12m}{2}$
	=	£11m
Debtor period = $\dfrac{11m}{105.55m} \times 365$	=	38 days

---

73   A

Average debtors = $\dfrac{£22m + £27m}{2}$	=	£24.5m

Interest cost of credit customer

£24.5m × 13%	=	£3.185m

---

74   **B**

Savings	£
Bad debts £100m × 0.25%	250,000
Reduction in credit cost	
£100m × $\dfrac{7}{365}$ × 14%	268,493
Cost of salary	(60,000)
	_____
	458,493
	_____

---

75   **B**

Existing debtor days = $\dfrac{20}{120} \times 365$ = 60.8 days

	£
Saved interest costs	
£120m × $\dfrac{30.83}{365}$ × 11% × 50%	0.557
Foregone revenue	
£120m × 50% × 2%	(1.2)
	_____
	(0.643)
	_____

---

76   B

---

77   C

---

78   D

	£
Cost/benefits	
Fee £20m × 2%	(400)
Saved interest	
£200 × $\dfrac{15}{365}$ × 11%	90.4
Admin savings	50
Reduction in bad debts	
£20m × 0.5%	100
	159.6

---

79   D

---

80   D

---

81   B

	£000's
Savings/(Costs)	
Additional credit period	
£50m × $\dfrac{15}{365}$ × 14%	287.7
Admin savings	40.0
	327.70

---

82   D

---

83   D

Annual interest cost:

$$\left(1 + \frac{2}{98}\right)^{\frac{365}{15}} \quad = \quad 1.635$$

$$= \quad 63.5\%$$

---

84   A

---

85   B

---

86   B

$$\text{Interest cost} \quad = \quad £120m \times \frac{45}{365} \times 12\% \quad = \quad £1.78m.$$

87   C

$$\text{EOQ} \quad = \quad \sqrt{\frac{2\,\text{Cod}}{\text{Ch}}}$$

$$= \quad \sqrt{\frac{2 \times 20 \times 100{,}000}{0.1 \times 0.12}}$$

$$= \quad 18{,}257 \text{ units}$$

88   B

89   B

90   C

91   D

$$\text{Interest cost} \quad = \quad \frac{1}{2} \times \text{EOQ} \times \text{Purchase Cost} \times \text{Interest Rate}$$

$$= \quad \frac{1}{2} \times 300 \text{ units} \times £2/\text{unit} \times 10\%$$

$$= \quad £30 \text{ per annum}$$

92   B

| Reorder point | = | Buffer Stock | = | Two Weeks Leadtime Usage |

$$\frac{2000 \text{ units}}{52 \text{ weeks}} \quad = \quad 38.5 \text{ units/week}$$

Reorder Point   =   30 units + 2 × 38.5 units
                 =   107 units

93   A

$$1 + g \quad = \quad \left(\frac{d_o}{d_n}\right)^{1/n} \quad = \quad \left(\frac{5}{4}\right)^{1/3} \quad = \quad 1.077$$

$$K_e \quad = \quad \frac{D_o(1+g)}{P_o} \quad + \quad g \quad = \quad \frac{5p \times 1.077}{180p} \quad + \quad 0.077$$

$$= \quad \underline{10.7\%}$$

94 A

$$\text{EOQ} = \sqrt{\frac{2\,\text{Cod}}{\text{Ch}}} = \sqrt{\frac{2 \times 10 \times 3600}{5}}$$

$$= \quad 120 \text{ orders}$$

---

95 C

---

96 C

Workings

Total assets	=	$\dfrac{£500,000}{4}$	=	£125,000
Working capital	=	$£125,000 \times \dfrac{40\%}{100\%}$	=	£50,000

Current ratio (2.5:1)

$$\therefore 1.5 = \text{Difference} = £50,000$$

$$\therefore \text{Current assets} = \frac{2.5}{1.5} \times £50,000$$

$$= \underline{£83,333}$$

---

97 C

---

98 D

$$
\begin{aligned}
K_e &= R_f + \left(R_m - R_f\right)\beta \\
&= 6\% + \left(15\% - 6\%\right)1.7 \\
&= 21.3\%
\end{aligned}
$$

---

99 D

---

100 B

Dividend per share   =   40p   ÷   8   = 5p
Share price   =   5p   ÷   2%   = 250p

---

101 D

$$\text{PV of perpetuity} = \frac{\text{Annual Payment}}{r}$$

$$
\begin{aligned}
\therefore \text{Perpetuity per annum} &= PV \times r \\
&= 1500 \times 0.07 \\
&= £105
\end{aligned}
$$

---

102   C

---

103   D

Value of bond cum int

$$= \frac{\text{Coupon Rate}}{\text{Rate of Return}} + \text{Coupon Rate}$$

$$= \frac{12}{8\%} + £12$$

$$= £162$$

---

104   C

---

105   B

$$\left(\frac{\text{Discount}}{100\% - \text{Discount}}\right)^{\text{No of periods per annum}}$$

$$= \left(1 + \frac{1.5}{98.5}\right)^{\frac{365}{50}} = 1.01523^{7.3}$$

$$= 11.7\%$$

---

106   C

Theoretical ex rights price $= \dfrac{\text{MV of Shares Pre Rights Issue} + \text{Proceeds of Rights Issue}}{\text{No. of Shares Post Rights Issue}}$

$$= \frac{2m \times £1.6 + 0.4m \times £1.0}{2.4m}$$

$$= £1.5/\text{share}$$

Value of a right
$$= \text{Theoretical ex rights price - Cost of right}$$
$$= £1.5 - £1.0$$
$$= \underline{£0.5/\text{share}}$$

---

107   A

$$Q = \sqrt{\frac{2\,\text{Cod}}{\text{Ch}}}$$

C_o -   £6

d -   £4m

C_h -   12%

$$Q = \sqrt{\frac{2 \times 6 \times 4,000,000}{0.12}} = £20,000$$

108 C

Existing debtor days $= \dfrac{500,000}{3,000,000} \times 365 = 60.83$ days

Benefit/(Cost)

	£
Fee 0.75% × £3,000,000	(22,500)
Interest saving	
$\dfrac{60.83-30}{365} \times £3,000,000 \times 12\%$	30,410
	7,910

109 C

110 D

111 B

Gordon's Growth Model

$\quad = \quad$ Rb

R $\quad = \quad$ ROCE $\quad = \dfrac{£30,000}{£120,000} \times 100 \quad = \quad 25\%$

b $\quad = \quad$ Retention Rate $\quad = \dfrac{£18,000}{£30,000} \times 100 = \quad 60\%$

Growth $= 25\% \times 60\% \quad = \quad 15\%$

112 B

Answers

Answer 1

Corporate Objectives

(a) The underlying success of the business must be beneficial to both managers and owners. As the company increases its size and profitability this should ensure that both parties are adequately compensated. There are conflicts between the needs of managers and owners.

Remuneration

The management will be concerned to maximise their pay and bonuses, the higher the cost base of the company the lower the return to shareholders.

More specifically share options at a beneficial price are often provided to managers to encourage better performance. The shareholder must balance the additional performance gain by such incentives against the dilution of their own shareholding.

Time horizons

It is often argued that managers are concerned with short-term performance to achieve bonus targets at the expenses of long-term growth in the value of the company.

Conversely the shareholder may be argued to be fickle, willing to divest unless short-term performance is strong enough. Managers can be expected to demand longer term stability to ensure a period of stable employment.

Mergers/takeovers

Managers often view being taken over as failure and taking over another company as success. They are more likely to enhance their earnings and avoid redundancy.

Shareholders tend to receive a better return on being taken over and may lose share value as the result of paying too much of a premium when taking over another company.

(b) Companies are required to exercise corporate social responsibility for the following reasons:

Statutory requirements

The government encourages social responsibility by requiring companies to adhere to for example a minimum wage, health and safety legislation, wider employment legislation and environmental legislation. Failure to do so will make the company liable to prosecution.

Investors

If a company is considered to be failing to adhere to the social norms, maybe because it is a major pollutant or has poor worldwide employment practice this will have an adverse impact on the share price. Not practising good corporate responsibility may lead to greater investor risk.

Customers

The customer may decide that the company is not in step with their own ethical stance. This would lead the customer to punish the company by switching to another company.

(c) A value for money audit is a means of assessing the provision of services for a non profit making organisation. It is a measure used by government to assess the efficiency with which services are provided. It is separated in the 3 E's.

Economy	-	The inputs to the service provider must be purchased at the lowest cost.
Efficiency	-	The services output must be maximised for a given level of input.
Effectiveness	-	The outputs must match the need and be the most appropriate service.

Answer 2

Financial Objectives

(a)   There are 3 basic decisions for the financial manager, whether to invest, how to finance and the level of dividend to be paid.

Investment

The decision to invest considers the purchase of capital assets or a company containing capital assets. The importance of this decision is in the long-term nature of the assets, meaning a poor decision will have long-term implications.

The appraisal normally uses discounted cash flow techniques which allow the present values of future inflows to be compared to the initial investment (NPV).

Financing

The company must make a number of funding decisions including gearing (debt to equity), short -term to long-term funds and whether to lease or buy assets.

The key to most funding decisions is to minimise the cost of funding, typically debt is cheaper than equity and short-term funds may be cheaper than long-term funds. In the lease or buy decision taxation may have the effect of making leasing more advantageous.

The other consideration is the level of risk associated with the finance. Debt is more risky than equity to the company due to the fixed nature of the interest payment. Short-term funds may be considered to be more risky because of their less permanent nature requiring more frequent replenishment.

Dividends

The dividend policy of a company is a key consideration of investors in deciding whether to invest in a share. It represents the only cash return associated with holding a share.

The dividend is used as a means of valuing the share using the dividend valuation model.

Inter-relationship

The decision to invest in new assets will directly affect the amount of finance required. Likewise the level of dividends will determine the amount of internally generated funds and hence the need to finance externally.

(b)   **Treasury department**

Function - A treasurer is responsible for the financing of the business in particular the flow of funds as and when required and regulating the cost of capital of the business. The treasurer must act as the interface between the company and the sources of funds (eg, banks, institutions and shareholders). The treasurer will also operate on a day to day basis to manage cash flows and deal with foreign exchange possibly hedging to avoid exchange exposure.

The treasurer is concerned with achieving financial objectives by enabling the availability of funds as and when required. They must be fully conversant with and included within policy determination to ensure that any funding requirements are determined at the earliest opportunity, ensuring that they are accepted as feasible.

Financial control department

Function - A financial controller has the role of enabling the functions of the business in financial terms. They operate from a prosaic level of collecting debt and paying suppliers to identifying and appraising investment opportunities. Their role is to ensure that all management decisions are underpinned by an analysis of the financial implications.

The financial controller will have a role at policy determination in appraising the competing aims of a business. The financial objectives of a business may be both set and achieved by the financial controller.

Interface

The financial controller and treasurer work in unison but at very different roles. Their roles will however meet because the funding raised by the treasurer is used by the financial controller.

It may be said that the treasurer determines the cost of capital of the business which is then used by the financial controller for appraisal purposes.

Answer 3

ABC plc

A treasury department in such a company would have the following functions:

1   Funding the company using a range of sources of finance. The treasurer must decide on the level of gearing and achieving a level of gearing that minimises the weighted average cost of capital without enhancing the risk associated with debt finance too far.

2   ABC plc has a relatively complex structure with subsidiaries and overseas trade. The short-term fluctuations of cash requirements would need financing through overdraft facilities, possibly to be denominated in different currencies for certain subsidiaries.

3   ABC plc is exposed to exchange rate fluctuations in its foreign trade. The treasurer can be employed to minimise the transaction exposure through using forward rates offered by the bank. It is the role of treasurer to manage this risk and accept the best risk/cost relationship.

4   Monitoring and control of all of the bank accounts in each of the subsidiaries.

5   Investment of excess funds where there are short-term surpluses. This will require the investment in essentially risk free and liquid instruments. In a situation where there are permanent excess funds then the financing mix of the business must be considered.

A separate treasury function will have the following advantages:

1   *Better Skills* - Having a centralised and separate treasury function should ensure that employees with more specific skills to treasury are employed. This will have the impact of building a core of employees in the company who can offer specialised advice and assistance to each subsidiary.

2   *Better Control* - Centralising the funds of a business should lead to better overall control of cash, limiting the opportunity for fraud and ensuring that head office retains a key control in an otherwise decentralised business.

3   *Keener Investment and Borrowing Rates* - By borrowing and lending in larger amounts the company can take advantage of better rates offered by financial institutions. Transaction costs should be reduced as a result.

Advantages of the treasury department being:

1   **A profit centre**

   (a)   The treasury department will be encouraged to generate profits over and above simply covering costs. This should ensure that the department has more motivation as employees will attach 'value' to their contribution and not just be seen as a cost to the business.

   (b)   A more flexible response to hedging risk, where the department will be more inclined to accept low levels of risk if the return were sufficient to make it worthwhile.

        (c)   Offering of treasury services to other companies when facilities are greater than needed in-house.

        (d)   Becoming traders in options and forward contracts in their own right.

2   **A cost centre**

        (a)   Less costly because the treasury department will only generate cost data to control.

        (b)   Lower risk as the treasury department has no incentive to take on risk and is motivated to offer a simple low cost service.

        (c)   It reduces the treasury department to a facilitator for the rest of the business. This has the advantage that senior management do not need to monitor and manage a different and complex risk and can concentrate on the core business.

Answer 4

Inigo

(a)   Both a rights issue and a scrip issue involve offering new shares to existing shareholders in proportion to their existing holdings.

        Under a rights issue, the shares are issued to raise finance ie are offered in return for consideration. As with all equity issues, the principle is to raise long term finance. Rights issues are considerably cheaper than issues to the general public in terms of issue costs and advisory fees, as less advertising is necessary.

        The investor will be interested in what the company plans to do with the rights proceeds and the company must use the proceeds to invest in projects generating returns at least as good as those currently being offered by the company's existing activities. If any projects show declining returns, the issue will not prove popular, but such issues tend to be underwritten (insured) by merchant banks.

        An investor short of funds has the option under a rights issue to reject the rights offered and sell them on. In a perfect market this will not affect his wealth.

        A scrip issue involves issuing extra shares for nil consideration (ie free). This is done for two reasons.

        1   To reduce share price to make shares more marketable. Very few shares on the London stock exchange cost more than £10. Much above this and they appear 'expensive'. For example a company's shares may trade at £20. If the company does a one for one scrip issue, the number of shares will double, and in an efficient market, the share price will halve to £10 making them more marketable, and therefore attractive to investors.

        2   Following the above example, in a market which is not fully efficient, the market price may not fall as low as £10, but may stop at say, £11. This would mean that instead of having one share worth £20 someone now has two shares at £11 ie £22. This means £2 has been created from nothing. This will mean inefficiency in the market.

(b)

	£m
Current market value = 5m @ £1.6	£8.0
Issue 1 for 5 ie 1m @ £1.30	£1.3
	———
New MV	£9.3
	———
New shares	6m
Price per share	£1.55
	———

(i)   Takes up rights

	£
Before 10,000 @ £1.60	16,000
After 12,000 @ £1.55	18,600
NB paid 2,000 @ £1.30 for them	(2,600)
Net wealth	16,000

(ii)   Sells

Value of right = £1.55 – £1.30 = 25p

	£
Sell rights 2,000 @ 25p	500
NB shares now worth 10,000 @ £1.55	15,500
Net wealth	16,000

(c) $R = \dfrac{D_1}{MV} + g$

g = dividend growth

Dividend in 20X3 = 8p

Dividend in 20X7 = 12p

ie $8 \times (1 + g)^4 = 12$

$(1 + g)^4 = \dfrac{12}{8} = 1.5$

Therefore $1 + g = 1.5^{\frac{1}{4}} = 1.107$

$g = 10.7\%$

D_1 = next year's dividend

= 12p × 1.107

= 13.3p

$R = \dfrac{D_1}{MV} + g = \dfrac{13.3p}{160p} + 0.107$

= 0.083 + 0.107

= 0.19

ie Return = 19%

(d)   The market price of a share is determined by the future cashflows it generates. The more information an investor has about those cashflows, the more efficient the market.

If the market is strong form efficient, the share price reflects everything about the company, whether it is publicly know or not (ie a perfect market = perfect information).

As a result FDs of plcs will act in a manner which will increase shareholder wealth. This can only be done by increasing the cashflows that the company generates. In an inefficient market, the share price may not react (or not react quickly) to a bad decision, but in a strong form, the effect of incompetence will become immediately apparent.

Following on from this, FDs could not manipulate share price through accounting conventions (creative or not) as although profits may appear better, hard, measurable cashflows would not alter, and therefore neither would prices.

Answer 5

Bardsey

(a)

	£m	£m
Operating profit		60
Add back depreciation		8
Operating cashflow		68
Reinvestment	(10)	
Interest – 20X1	(15)	
Taxation – 20X0	(12)	
Dividends – 20X0	(20)	
		(57)
Net cashflow		11

(b) **Report on Bardsey plc's financial performance and health**

Points to be included:

(i)   Better than average pre-tax return on long-term capital

Bardsey   60m ÷ 383m*   = 15.7%   (after asset revaluation two years ago)

Industry sector   = 14.3%

(ii)   Better than average operating profit margin (Bardsey specialised in high quality items)

Bardsey   60m ÷ 150m   = 40%

Industry sector   = 26.2%

(iii)   Fixed asset to turnover ratio compares unfavourably with industry sector

Bardsey   150m ÷ 300m   = 0.5 times   (after revaluation)

Industry sector   = 1.2 times

(iv)   Return on equity below industry sector

Bardsey   33m ÷ 283m   = 11.7%   (but Bardsey is lower geared than industry sector)

Industry sector   = 15.3% post–tax

(v)   Gearing ratio is lower than industry sector

Bardsey capital gearing 100m ÷ 283m   = 35%

Industry sector   = 42%

(vi)   Liquidity – appears to be well managed

	Current ratio	*Quick ratio*
Bardsey	$\dfrac{200m}{117m} = 1.7$	$\dfrac{140m}{117m} = 1.2$

(vii)   Stock holding – 33% higher than industry standard

Bardsey $60m \div 90m \times 365$ = 243 days

Industry sector   = 180 days

(viii)   Debtor days (higher than average, but Bardsey deliberately offers generous credit)

Bardsey $100m \div 150m \times 365$ = 243 days

Industry sector   = 132 days

(ix)   Dividend cover is low

Bardsey $33m \div 20m$ = 1.65 : 1

Industry sector   = 2.1 : 1

The low dividend cover could reflect the policy requirement of dominant shareholders. There is however sufficient cash resource to improve the ratio if pressure demands.

(x)   Interest cover is above average

Bardsey $60m \div 15m$ = 4 times

Industry sector   = 3.2 times

This indicates that Bardsey could suffer a significant drop in profits without facing a liquidity crisis or profit crisis in paying interest liabilities.

Overall

The low P/E ratio of 11 awarded by the stock market appears to indicate that the market is not expecting substantial growth from Bardsey. This is unlikely to worry Bardsey shareholders who appear to be few but dominant. It would appear that Bardsey is profitable, and has good cash flow, but has returned a sluggish performance in a mature market.

(c)   Other possible uses of the increasing bank balance

(i)   Repay debentures (£100 million)

The consequence will be to save £10 million of interest cost. This option will effectively yield a return of 10% which is approximately equivalent to the return on equity, thereby maintaining the status quo but reducing indebtedness.

(ii)   Re-purchase shares

In certain circumstances UK companies are allowed to re-purchase a proportion of their shares on the market. This will reduce the base on which dividends will be payable in future years, but sends a signal to the stockmarket that the company has no options for growth.

(iii)   Acquisition of other companies

Acquisition by takeover is a method of growth but Bardsey may feel that the market is not indicating expansion and resist this method of cash employment.

(iv) Increase dividends

An increase in dividend payout would suppress the ratio of dividend cover further (currently 1.65 against industry norm of 2.1:1). A further problem is that Bardsey may not be able to live up to the new level of dividend payout in future years. The tax position and objectives of the few but dominant shareholders must also be taken into account.

Answer 6

Nismat and Kemp

(a) A traded investment is held for its returns (income or capital growth) and will be quoted on a capital market such as the London Stock Exchange.

The main types of investments are equity shares, preference shares, bonds (both government and corporate) and derivatives (such as futures and options).

The two principal factors to consider are risk and return which are closely linked. In general, a rational investor will require a higher return to compensate for a higher risk in investment.

Equity shares are risky investments for a number of reasons. Firstly the value of the investment will change over time and secondly, the return (dividend) will also vary depending on the company's fortunes. In the event of a collapse, the share will tend to be worthless.

Bonds are a form of debt and tend to be a lot less risky. A bond will pay a fixed level of return without variability (ie income is guaranteed). As a result, the price will tend to be more stable and can be predicted with more certainty. In a collapse, the bondholder is likely to recover at least part of their investment.

Derivatives are high risk, high return investments which tend to be used for hedging (protecting) other investments values.

The investor must also consider the liquidity of the investment, ie their ability to convert to cash at short notice.

(b) (i) Gross dividend

The dividend represents pay out of after-tax profits to a company's equity shareholders. It will be paid out equally on all shares ranking for dividend so a total dividend of £½m paid out across £1m shares would mean a gross dividend per share of 50p. This gross dividend received by the shareholder would then be liable to income tax.

In our case, to calculate gross dividends we will have to use the dividend yield.

$$\text{Dividend yield} \quad = \quad \frac{\text{Gross dividend}}{\text{Price per share}}$$

This reflects the income tax return generated by investing in a share, for example a 5p dividend on a 50p share means a 10% yield.

$$\text{Nismat yield} \quad = \quad \frac{\text{Dividend}}{\text{Price}}$$

Therefore Dividend	=	Price × Yield
	=	160p × 5%
	=	8p
Kemp	=	3.33% × 270p
Kemp dividend	=	9p

Although both companies pay a similar dividend, Nismat's dividend is higher relative to its share price.

(ii)   EPS   (earnings per share)

On a simplistic basis EPS = $\dfrac{\text{Profit after tax}}{\text{No. issued shares}}$

In other words, EPS is calculating the amount of profit attributable to each share in circulation. It therefore represents the amount of profit available for dividends. Any profits not paid out in dividend will be added to retained earnings (reserves) for reinvestment.

We will have to calculate EPS via PE ratio.

PE ratio	=	$\dfrac{\text{Price per share}}{\text{EPS}}$

Therefore	EPS	=	$\dfrac{\text{Price per share}}{\text{PE}}$

Nismat	EPS	=	$\dfrac{160p}{20} = 8p$

Kemp	EPS	=	$\dfrac{270p}{15} = 18p$

On its own, EPS is of limited use and figures are not directly comparable between companies. It is useful to compare the EPS with last year's EPS to assess growth (providing the number of shares has been constant).

(iii)   Dividend cover

This measures the level of profits relative to level of dividend. It is calculated as follows.

Dividend cover	=	$\dfrac{\text{PAT}}{\text{Dividend}}$	or	$\dfrac{\text{EPS}}{\text{Dividend per share}}$

Nismat	=	$\dfrac{8p}{8p} = 1$

Kemp	=	$\dfrac{18p}{9p} = 2$

Nismat is paying out all of its earnings as dividends. This would mean a lack of earnings for reinvestment, so future growth prospects would be limited.

Consequently share price growth will be limited. As a result, if the dividend cover of Nismat is representative of past years, investors in Nismat would receive their returns in the form of dividend income, not capital growth.

Kemp on the other hand pays out half of its' profit as dividend and reinvests the other half. Investors in Kemp would therefore expect to see capital growth as well as income.

Clientele theory suggests that investors will invest in companies whose dividend policy is relevant to their circumstances ie those preferring long term capital gains in companies with low dividend cover; those preferring long term capital gains should invest in companies with higher cover.

(c)   *Note.* In future, should the dividend growth model be required, the formula will be given.

$$MV = \frac{D_1}{R-g}$$

MV = market value

D_1 = next year's dividend

R = shareholder required return (= company's cost of equity)

y = dividend growth rate

To calculate g consider past dividends

1993   Dividend = 5.5p
1997   Dividend = 3p

Therefore	$3p \times (1 + g)^4$	=	5.5p	
	$(1 + g)^4$	=	$\dfrac{5.5p}{3p}$	= 1.833
	$1 + g$	=	$1.833^{1/4}$	
		=	1.164	
ie g		=	16.4%	
	D_1	=	next years dividend	
		=	this years dividend	
		=	$5.5p \times 1.164 = 6.4p$	

Therefore MV $= \dfrac{6.4p}{20\% - 16.4\%} = \dfrac{6.4}{0.036} = 177.8p$

Therefore   1,000 shares would cost

$$1,000 \times 177.8p = £1,778$$

(d)   Yield curve plots gross yield against number of years to redemption/maturity.

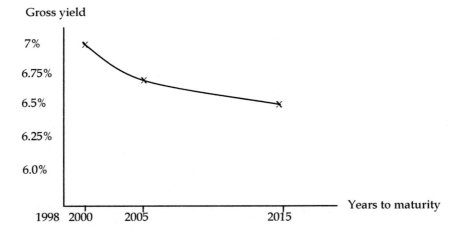

Gross yield

	Years to maturity	Gross yield
Treasury 8.5% 2000	0	7.0%
Exchequer 10.5% 2005	5	6.7%
Treasury 8% 2015	15	6.53%

Put simply, the yield curve plots the yield (return or cost of finance) against years to maturity (length of finance).

Normally longer-term finance costs more, as lending long-term is more risky (due to uncertain future returns) from a lender's point of view.

In this case, the yield curve above is showing the opposite. This means that investors believe that in the long term, interest rates will fall.

Answer 7

Newsam

(a)   Gearing $= \dfrac{\text{Long-term debt}}{\text{Shareholders' funds}}$ (as defined)

  (i)   Book values $= \dfrac{£5m}{£15m} = 33\%$

  (ii)   Market values

The debentures trade at £15 above par (100) and are thus worth £115 per £100 nominal block, ie $\dfrac{115}{100} \times £5m = £5.75m.$

Equity PE	$=$	$\dfrac{\text{Price}}{\text{Earnings per share}}$		
Therefore price	$=$	Earnings per share $\times$ PE	$= 6.7\text{p}^* \times 14$	$= 93.8\text{p}$
* Earnings per share	$=$	$\dfrac{\text{Profit after tax}}{\text{Number of shares}}$	$= \dfrac{£1.34m}{20m}$	$= 6.7\text{p}$
Total market value	$=$	$20m \times 93.8\text{p}$	$= £18.76m$	
Gearing	$=$	$\dfrac{£5.75}{£18.76m}$	$= 31\%$	

(b)   If we measure gearing based on long–term debt, Newsam appears to have some leeway as it is barely over 30% compared with the covenant of 50%.

Note. Market value gives us an idea of current gearing; book values are historical.

However, if we introduce the bank overdraft of £3 million as part of the debt the gearing ratio rises to 47% based on market value.

The overdraft should be included if it is used as a long term source of finance, ie is perpetually at around the £3 million mark.

The current ratio is currently 1.0. The industry average is currently 1.35 which gives us a range of 1.08 to 1.62 (1.35 ± 20%). Therefore Newsam is in breach of the covenant. This could be a problem given that cash makes up only 7% of current assets.

(c)   Financial gearing measures the risk the shareholders face through the way the company is financed. Debt finance attracts a fixed interest charge which a firm may struggle to cover should its profits fall.

When we assess Newsam's gearing we should also consider some comparisons, eg prior years and the industry averages; but this data is unavailable to us.

In trying to assess whether Newsam can meet its interest payments we should review interest cover (operating profit/interest) which is currently 3. Again this should be compared with prior years.

The key is to assess the future profitability of Newsam. Given that the company's sales have only grown at 2% per annum over the past 10 years, Newsam could be vulnerable to any increase in interest rates.

However the company's fixed assets appear to more than cover the long-term debt, although if they were used to repay the loans, the firm's long-term prospects would be in doubt.

Given that Newsam has breached its liquidity covenant, we need to know what the debenture holders plan to do (if anything).

(d)   (i)   Possible steps to improve gearing

- *Revalue land and buildings* – Given that the property was purchased 12 years ago, it is highly likely that the market value is greater than the book value. However this will be viewed as purely an accounting exercise by the City. This will also increase future depreciation and therefore reduce profit.

- *Leasing* – If Newsam has any finance leases, it could improve its gearing ratio by altering to operating leases. However this would mean that Newsam loses the risk and rewards of ownership of those assets, and the details would still be disclosed in the accounts.

- *Liquidity* – Newsam would be advised to better employ its current assets in order to pay off its overdraft.

  Possible methods would include more aggressive credit control, a just–in–time stock policy or a non–disclosed debt factoring arrangement.

- *Refinancing* – If Newsam were to issue more shares, the proceeds could be used to redeem some of the debt. However, the City would need to be convinced of the benefits of refinancing and in particular how this would improve rewards to the shareholders.

(ii)   Raising interest cover

The liquidity and refinancing ideas above would also help interest cover, but Newsam should be looking for a cheaper interest rate. The two alternatives are as follows.

- *Replace debentures with Eurodollar loan.* This would save interest at 10 percentage points (15%–5%) and greatly improve interest cover, but the risk has been shifted elsewhere. This is a foreign currency loan and therefore Newsam would be exposed to exchange risk as the loan is in dollars. If the exchange rate moves the amount owed in sterling terms will be more or less.

  Note. The information given in the question is suggesting that sterling will weaken against the dollar by 4% over the next year, increasing the loan from £5 million to £5.2 million in sterling terms, but this is outside the syllabus.

- *Refinance with a bank overdraft.* This would also increase interest cover as the rate is 9% against 15%; however this ignores the fact that the bank may well ask for more interest to reflect their increased exposure to Newsam. The interest rate here is likely to be variable so it could go up or down. There is also the fact that an overdraft is repayable on demand.

Answer 8

Cleevemoor

(a)   As a public entity, Cleevemoor objectives would probably be more society led. The main objective would have been to provide a safe water supply at a reasonable price. Although a 'return' would have been demanded, this would have been lower than that of the private sector because of longer planning horizons and lower risks.

In addition, both prices and capital expenditure would have been subject to government fiscal policy.

Once privatised NW's stakeholders would now include shareholders, who would demand a return to compensate them for the risk they have taken on by investing in the company. These returns would include dividend payouts and also share price growth.

Any new projects taken on would need to generate a return equal to or greater than this return demanded by the shareholders. This return would be greater than that needed whilst in the public sector meaning that many projects acceptable in the public sector would be rejected by the private.

(b) (i) **Shareholders**

As mentioned above, shareholders will want returns in the form of dividends and share price growth. By following policies to promote these requirements NW will maximise shareholder wealth.

Dividends

The dividend has risen from a proforma 7p in 20X1 to 20p in 20X7. This represents growth of approximately 19% year on year. EPS has grown at a similar rate and the payout ratio has remained steady at round about one third. This policy suggests that dividends are closely linked to profits, and the payout ratio should be compared with the rest of the industry.

Price

The issue was heavily staggered with prices reaching £1.60 immediately on flotation. Given the PE ratios, the underlying share prices were as follows.

	20X1	*20X3*	*20X5*	*20X7*
EPS		29p	47p	65p
P/E		7	8	7.5
Price	£1.60	£2.03	£3.76	£4.875

These figures imply annualised growth of 20% per annum since the issue. These figures again need comparison to both the industry and the stock market as a whole but appear to be healthy returns.

(ii) **Consumers**

Consumers will be interested in prices, which whilst no longer government defined will be laid down by the regulator (eg OFWAT).

We have information about the volume of the market (growing at 2% per annum) and can therefore measure the price rises by removing the volume growth from turnover.

	20X1	*20X3*	*20X5*	*20X7*
Turnover	£450m	£480m	£540m	£620m
		$\times \dfrac{1}{1.02^2}$	$\times \dfrac{1}{1.02^4}$	$\times \dfrac{1}{1.02^6}$
Turnover in 20X1 volume	450	461	498	550

We can see that after taking out the growth, prices have risen at approximately 3.4% per annum, which is above the rate of inflation for the period (1.4%).

Whether or not this is justified depends on factors such as where the money has been spent. Has it gone into capital expenditure (improving the supplies or preventing leaks) or has it been used to increase dividends?

(iii)   **Workforce**

The workforce has fallen by 2,000 from its 12,000 level in 20X1. Whilst it is possible that Cleevemoor was overstaffed, shedding over 15% of the workforce will have affected morale.

Average wages have risen from £8,333 to £8,600 over the period, a rise of just over 0.5% per annum. Had the workforce enjoyed pay rises in line with inflation they could have expected to earn £9,083 in 20X7. This means they are actually worse off in real terms. Without more information (eg skills mix of labour force, full/part time employees) it is hard to comment, but the increased profitability of NW does not appear to have been passed on to them.

At the same time, the directors' emoluments have nearly quadrupled. We could again do with more information such as the number of directors involved. Part of the increase will be to bring fees in line with the private sector and part of it could be linked in with the share price. However, their fees as a percentage of the whole wage bill have risen from 0.8% to 3.4% over the period.

The figures probably will not include other perks such as share options.

The directors may increasingly find themselves having to justify 'fat cat' salaries.

(iv)   **Government**

Price stability

♦   Prices have risen by 38% in the absolute and 22% in real terms, which will not be in line with price stability.

♦   Wages have been held down to less than the headline RPI, but at the same time directors' emoluments have risen sharply.

Economic growth

♦   Efficiency is difficult to measure without more details, but we could calculate various ratios such as ROCE or net margin to measure the situation. Both have shown improvement over the period.

	20X1	*20X3*	*20X5*	*20X7*
Net margin	5.8%	7.2%	10.2%	12.1%

♦   Capital expenditure has risen by 275% over the period, which combined with the multiplier effect would be expected to generate a knock–on growth elsewhere in the economy.

Answer 9

Burnsall

(a)   Additional financing is required for both fixed and current assets.

Working capital is expected to increase in line with sales (20%).

	£m
Stocks	16.0
Debtors	23.0
Cash	6.0
Creditors	(18.0)
Working capital at present	27.0
20% increase	5.4
Capital expenditure	20.0
Total funding required	25.4

This will come partly from retained funds and partly through external finance.

We need to focus on cashflow.

Expected cashflow

	£m
Sales (10m × £10 × 1.2)	120.0
Operating costs (£79m × 1.2) (W1)	(94.8)
	25.2
Tax (year end liability)	(5.0)
Dividend (£5m × 1.1)	(5.5)
Interest (£20m × 12%)	(2.4)
Internal funds generated	12.3

The funding will therefore be as follows.

Internal	12.3
External	13.1
Required	25.4

Workings

(W1) *Last year*

Sales	200
Other costs	(79)
Depreciation	(5)
Profit before interest and tax	16

(b) **Long–term financing options**

Equity

♦ Burnsall could raise extra share capital through a rights issue. This would be expensive to do and careful consideration needs to be paid to both pricing and timing issues. If existing shareholders cannot afford to take up any rights, they can theoretically sell theirs on the market although their control would be diluted.

♦ Venture capital would be another possible solution. Unless existing shareholders waived their pre-emption rights, another class of shares would need issuing. Venture capital tends to be expensive to finance however, and any venture capitalist would probably require board representation.

♦ Burnsall could also consider launching preference shares. However, any preference dividends need to be paid out before equity, and in effect this would raise gearing.

Debt

Burnsall could perhaps take on long-term debt, either through a secured bank loan or through a debenture issue. Its interest cover based on projected cashflows is healthy at 10.5 (25.2 ÷ 2.4) and its fixed assets appear to cover existing debt comfortably based on book values. Burnsall could probably easily absorb the extra £13.1 million required in debt without worrying the market.

Burnsall should also review its existing and required fixed assets. Any future capital investment need not be all up front. Capital expenditure could be financed through either leasing or hire purchase. The legal and tax considerations of each would need evaluating but these are effectively methods of hedging in that the capital flows would be spread over the project's life. Any surplus of fixed assets could be disposed of to raise finance and a further possibility would be to sell and leaseback any freehold property although this would involve losing title to the assets.

Burnsall should also explore the possibility of government grants or regional aid packages.

Answer 10

Phoenix

(a)   **20X0/X1**

Issued share capital is £70 million, which means 280 million shares of 25p each.

Since the dividend paid is 1.5p per share, this makes a total dividend of £4.2 million.

Profit available for distribution to ordinary shareholders

	£000
Operating profit	25,000
Interest	(700)
	———
Tax at 33%	24,300
	(8,020)
	———
Profit available for equity	16,280
	———

Dividend payout   = £4,200,000 ÷ £16,280,000 = 26%

or

Dividend cover   = £16,280,000 ÷ £4,200,000 = 3.9

20X1/X2

Total dividend is the 20X1/X2 dividend of £4.2 million plus a further £10 million, ie £14.2 million in total.

Profit available for distribution to ordinary shareholders

	£000
Operating profit	40,000
Interest	(700)
	———
	39,300
Tax at 33%	(12,970)
	———
Profit available for equity	26,330
	———

Dividend payout   = £14,200,000 ÷ £26,330,000= 54%

Dividend cover   = £26,330,000 ÷ £14,200,000= 1.9

This represents a fall in dividend cover, at the expense of paying out higher dividends in the reporting year, a policy that will be questioned by shareholders.

(b)   **Memorandum**

To: Finance Director

From: Financial Strategist

Subject: Use of cash surplus   Date: xx/xx/xx

Phoenix is in the position of having a substantial cash surplus to distribute. This has arisen due to the economic recovery fuelling demand for houses. Two options are available, a special dividend or redemption of loan stock.

Special dividend

Shareholder preferences need to be assessed here. Do they hold Phoenix shares for income (dividend) or growth (retentions)? If they hold our shares for long–term growth, a large dividend may well encourage them to invest elsewhere.

Linked to the preference is the shareholders' tax positions. The majority of personal investors will enjoy a capital gains annual exemption and therefore may prefer share growth, rather than dividend income. Institutional investors, such as pension funds, in the past preferred dividends, but owing to the abolition of ACT are now indifferent.

We also need to consider the market's reaction. The stock market does not like major changes in dividend policy as such a distribution would represent. In particular, we should be concentrating on a sustainable policy.

Although Phoenix is now in the comfortable position of having a cash surplus, its prospects very much depend on the strength of the economy. Another recession will be around the corner eventually, and in such a case, Phoenix may find itself facing a cash deficit.

Redeem loan stock

It is important to review the conditions attached to the debt, in particular any penalty clauses which may come into effect following early redemption.

Gearing will be reduced by the redemption. Currently it is $\dfrac{£10m}{£200m}$ = 5%

This will fall to zero, compared with the industry average of 45%. However this will improve earnings by £10m × 7% × (1 − 0.33) = £469,000, which would be available for dividend. We would also be getting rid of a relatively cheap source of finance.

As with a special dividend, we need to consider market reaction. Usually the effect of degearing has a positive effect on our share price, but as our gearing is already low, any such reaction may be negligible. However the extra earnings would improve our EPS.

Conclusion

Our primary consideration should be towards future outlook to ensure there will be no immediate market downturn before distributing the cash. It may also be worthwhile consulting any major shareholders before a decision is made. As things currently stand, I would suggest a special dividend rather than degear and lose the cheap debt.

Answer 11

Netherby

(a)

	0	1	2	3	4	5	6
	£000	£000	£000	£000	£000	£000	£000
Restructuring	(5,000)						
Cash benefit		2,000	2,000	2,000	2,000	2,000	
Tax at 33%		1,650	(660)	(660)	(660)	(660)	(660)
	(5,000)	3,650	1,340	1,340	1,340	1,340	(660)
Discount factor at 15%	1.000	0.870	0.756	0.658	0.572	0.497	0.432
Present value	(5,000)	3,176	1,013	882	766	666	(285)

NPV = £1.218m   therefore it is a good idea to restructure

(b)   Market efficiency is concerned with the amount of information in a share's price.

If the market is said to be semi-strong efficient, the market price reflects all past share price movements as well as all published information.

As a result, the market will react quickly to releases made by a company. It would only be possible to 'beat' the market by exploiting the time frame between information becoming public and the share price reacting to it or alternatively by having access to information not in the public domain.

As a company's value is determined by its cashflows, Netherby's share price will rise by the NPV of the restructuring (£1.218 m).

Normally new MV = Old MV + Finance raised + NPV generated by finance.

Old MV =

Number of shares × price

Number of shares $= \dfrac{£5m}{50p} = 10m$ therefore Old MV = 10m × £3 = £30m

New MV   = £30m + £5m + £1.218m

= £36.218

ie MV has risen by £6.218m.

The shareholders have contributed £5m themselves, so true increase in wealth = £1.218m or 12.18p per share.

(c)   The market price will be a weighted average of the shares in issue. Rights are issued at a discount on the market price to make them attractive to investors.

For example if we have 1m shares trading at £1 and perform a one for two rights issue for 70p, we will issue ½ m shares for 70p raising £350,000.

The total MV is now £1.35m, total shares 1.5m so new price is 90p.

Rights issue @ £1

Need to raise £5m ie issue 5m shares at £1. There are 10m shares already in issue, ie a one for two rights issue.

New MV = Old MV + finance raised + NPV

= £30 m + £5m + £1.218m

= £36.218

Number of shares   = £15m

Price per share   = £2.415

Rights issue @ £2

Must raise £5m ie issue 2.5m shares (one for four).

New MV = Old MV + finance + NPV

= £36.218 as before

Number of shares   = 12.5m

Price per share   = £2.897

(d)

Current profit after tax	£15m	
Current shares	10m	
EPS	£1.50	
Rights issue	£000	
Current profit after tax	15,000	
Benefits net of tax		
£2m × (1–0.33)	1,340	
	16,340	
Shares (see above)	12.5m	
EPS	£1.307	

Loan stock		*£000*
Current profit after tax		15,000
Cash benefit	2,000	
Interest	(600)	
£5m × 12%		
	1,400	
Tax @ 33%	(462)	938
		15,938
Shares		10m
EPS		£1.594

Note. You should consider the effect on gearing.

(e)   **Sources of risk**

♦   Political risk – how reliable is the supplier from Hungary? We should not pay for the product up front.

♦   Sensitivity analysis – we should undertake analysis on our cashflow estimates to see how sensitive the NPV is to change.

♦   Quality – we are already having quality problems. We will need to check the quality of the tents coming in from our Eastern bloc manufacturer.

♦   Time scale – the contract may be extended beyond five years, giving us further (if more distant) benefits.

♦   Exchange risk – we are purchasing in Hungarian currency. If the exchange rate moves against us we may well start to lose money.

Answer 12

PAS

(a)   The P/E ratio is calculated as follows:

$$\text{P/E ratio} = \frac{\text{Share Price}}{\text{Earnings Per Share}}$$

The relationship of share price to the earnings per share it is a measure of earnings growth. It compares the share price which is based on future earnings (dividend valuation model), to the earnings per share currently.

If the P/E ratio is high this suggests that the company will have high earnings growth in relation to current earnings.

Looking at the values given we see that Ply and Axis have similar P/E ratios of 13 and 14.2 but Spin has a P/E ratio 50% higher at 21.1.

Spin has higher earnings growth potential possibly because current earnings are depressed.

It is necessary to ensure that comparison is made by industry type, the growth potential of each industrial sector will differ.

(b) $$\text{Dividend cover} = \frac{\text{Earnings Per Share}}{\text{Dividends Per Share}}$$

		Spin	Axis
Earning Per Share = Share Price ÷ P/E Ratio			
Spin	201p ÷ 21.1 =	9.53p	
Axis	317p ÷ 13.0 =		24.38p
Dividend Per Share = Share Price × Dividend Yield			
Spin	201p × 2.3	4.62p	
Axis	317p × 2.1		6.66p
Dividend Cover = EPS/DPS			
Spin		2.06 times	
Axis			3.66 times

The significance of dividend cover is the proportion of earnings generated by the business which are returned to the shareholder in the form of dividends.

The higher the dividend cover, the lower the proportion of the earnings distributed to the shareholder. Some shareholders are concerned with high dividend payouts if they require an income from the shares, others look for little in the way of dividend and prefer capital growth instead.

(c) A company may only pay dividends in excess of earnings on a temporary basis. Dividends are paid out of retained earnings, these will be reduced year on year until exhausted.

A company may wish to pay out a dividend in excess of current earnings if it has a single poor year of trading or incurs excessive one-off costs in a single year. It is paid as a signal to the market that management expect to maintain a level of dividend in spite of current trading problems. It is taken as a key indicator of health of the business by the market.

The dangers of such an approach are that if a company is in trading difficulty, the dividend is a further outflow of cash taxing the cashflow of the business. In the longer term it may hasten the demise of the business.

Answer 13

AB Ltd

(a) **REPORT**

To:	The Bank	Date:	xx-xx-xx
From:	Mr A and Mr B		
Subject:	Forecast Financial Statements		

Forecast profit and loss account

	£000's
Sales	1,400
Less Cost of sales (60%)	(840)
Gross profit	560
Less Expenses (30%)	(420)
Net profit	140

Forecast balance sheet

	£000's		£000's
Fixed assets (60% of cap. emp.)		(60%)	300
Current assets			
Stock (1,400 ÷ 5.6)	250		
Debtors $(1,400 \times \frac{60}{365})$	192		
Sub-total	442		
Current liabilities			
Creditors $(1,400 \times 60\% \times \frac{60}{365})$	138		
Overdraft	104		
Sub-total (442 ÷ 1.83)	242		
Net current assets		(40%)	200
Total assets (capital employed)		(100%)	500

(b) **Assumptions**

1   Industry averages are representative of the business being considered.

2   Past data is representative of the future.

3   Year end values for debtors and creditors represent the average level for these balances during the year.

4   The managers must be assumed to be responsible and honest in their application.

5   External information regarding the potential market, customers, suppliers and competitors will assist in assessing the application.

(c)   Alternative sources of finance may include:

1   Extended credit from suppliers may be available particularly if the supplier is a long-term acquaintance from previous employment.

2   Debt factoring reducing the level of debtors that need to be financed otherwise.

3   Invoice discounting, using debtors as an asset.

4   Leasing of fixed assets from the provider of the fixed asset.

5   Issuing debt to the market.

6   Venture capital funding in the form of debt or equity invested by a third party.

7   Government grants.

8   Mortgage the assets of the business (or own home).

Answer 14

X and Y plc

(a) $\text{P/E ratio} = \dfrac{\text{Current Market Price}}{\text{Earnings Per Share}}$

The market price of a share is principally determined by future potential earnings. The earnings per share is the current (past) performance achieved by the business.

The P/E ratio is a measure of expected earnings growth. In the example given it is not surprising that Y has a higher P/E ratio because its earning growth is from such a low base.

(b) $\text{Earnings yield} = \dfrac{\text{Earnings Per Share}}{\text{Current Market Price}} \times 100$

ie the inverse of the P/E ratio.

It is very possible that Y has a lower cost of capital than X, this is due to the fact that Y has a higher level of gearing, debt is cheaper than equity normally, therefore, the weighted average cost of capital should be lower.

To assess the earnings yield as a cost of capital however is wrong, the earnings yield is the inverse of the P/E ratio relating the current earnings to a measure of future earnings (market price). In this situation the key reason for such a low earnings yield for Y is the very low current earnings which depress the current earnings per share in relation to future market expectations.

(c) $\text{Financial gearing} = \dfrac{\text{Debt}}{\text{Equity}}$

Higher financial gearing per se will not improve the P/E ratio, the relationship of current to future earnings. There are, however, reasons how the gearing may facilitate higher P/E ratios at a given time.

(i) Gearing tends to enhance the volatility of the earnings, in the circumstances of Y it is possible that an upturn in the economy is leading to higher potential for future earnings.

(ii) The riskiness of Y will be higher than X purely due to financial risk. As the level of earnings rise this could increase the level of retained earnings and hence value of equity. The level of gearing will fall reducing the level of financial risk. Reduced risk should lead to higher value being placed on the company.

(d) The nominal value of the shares are of little importance when comparing ratios. The fact that they differ does not invalidate the ratios calculated.

The comparison of ratios for X and Y are valid when they are in the same industry sector and similar in size and stage of development.

X and Y seem to be well suited to comparison despite some differences.

(e) The dividend yield to investors is not the only return a shareholder can expect to receive. Shareholders would also expect a capital gain as share prices rise.

It is true to say that the overall return on shares would normally be expected to be greater than that earned on a risk free investment such as a government bond.

Shares are riskier to hold than government debt because the return is less certain, therefore, they should offer higher compensation as a result.

It is very possible that for a given period of time the overall return of a share is lower than government debt, over the longer term this unlikely to be the case.

Answer 15

S plc

(a) **Conversion premium**

			£
Conversion 20 shares @ 400p	=		80
Issue price of debenture	=		100
Premium			20

The premium indicates that the share price must rise by 25% in order that the conversion is financially viable to the debenture holder.

The debenture holder has two potential returns, interest on the debenture and a potential capital gain on conversion. In return for this potential capital gain the debt-holder will accept a below average interest rate.

The coupon rate is 3% below (9% rather than 12%) the market rate or £3 interest foregone each year for five years. The lower the coupon rate the higher the market expectation of a substantial capital gain on conversion.

(b) At 10% growth rate

$$400p \times 1.1^3 = 532.4p.$$

Conversion value

$$= 532.4p \times 20 \text{ shares/debenture} = £106.48/\text{debenture}.$$

The market value of the convertible is likely to be in excess of this because it has a potential upside on conversion illustrated above. If, however, the share price falls the debenture would be retained with a guaranteed redemption value of £100.

A convertible therefore provides potential for high capital gain with a limited downside. In this particular example we would also expect the share price to rise beyond its current value based on 10% increase year on year to date.

(c) Dividend policy will be of considerable important to the debenture holder. It determines the amount of earning which are distributed and hence by implication the amount retain.

The holder of convertible debt will only benefit from the retained earnings being reinvested in the business, dividends will only be paid to existing shareholders.

The convertible debt may carry covenants that limit the level of dividends and hence project the interests of the debenture holder.

(d) A company issuing convertible debt is selecting a source of fiancé with the best of both sources of debt and equity.

In the short-term debt is held which does not dilute shareholders control and has the advantage of being tax efficient and probably cheaper to service. In the event of the company doing well and the share price rising then conversion to equity will take place, creating additional permanent capital necessary to a growing company. Existing shareholders' interest have been projected to some degree by the conversion premium. In the event that the company does less well conversion would not take place.

Convertible debt will be used by fast growing companies particularly where the share price may be considered to be undervalued. It allows the company to borrow relatively cheaply reducing cash outflows in the early years of a project.

Answer 16

CP plc

(a)   (i)   The stock exchange publishes the following list of advantages and disadvantages associated with floatation on the stock exchange.

Advantages

1   Access - Shareholders are given access to a wider market for their shares. The quoted shares are more liquid making their value increase.

2   Visibility - The company will generate considerable publicity in the financial community making it easier for the business to raise funds.

3   Prestige - The act of becoming quoted requires abiding by a high level of regulation. Any company able to hurdle these requirements will be held by the business community in higher esteem than other comparable private limited companies.

4   Growth - The listing of the company opens up new sources of finance (debt and equity) to the company allowing for faster growth of the business either through investment internally or by taking over other companies.

Disadvantages

1   Accountability – The directors are now accountable to a wider range of shareholders, decisions will have a direct and immediate influence on the share price of the business.

2   Regulation – The stock exchange requires ongoing compliance for listed companies.

3   Responsibility – Directors must act within the rules of the exchange providing price sensitive information in a timely and orderly manner to all shareholders.

Specifically with regard to CP plc the following concerns are pertinent:

1   The recent earnings of the company are fluctuating due to the problems associated with diversification. Maybe the company should put off the floatation for two or three years to ensure a better more consistent earnings recorded.

2   The shareholders must be careful not to lose control to new investors.

3   The costs of floatation must be considered, both floatation and ongoing compliance costs considerably more than those incurred by a private limited company.

(ii)   **Private placing**

The shares are sold to a merchant bank or stockbroker who places (sells) them with institutional investors and other large private investors.

Key advantage: Much the cheapest way to float the company for small issues.

Offer for sale at fixed price

Sale of shares direct to the public using merchant banks to advise and underwrite the issue. The price of the issue is normally at a discount to encourage take up.

Key advantage: Ensures a wider range of shareholders including individual rather than just institutional investors.

Offer for sales by tender

Sale of shares where potential investors are able to bid their own price for shares.

Key advantage: Particularly useful where a valuation is difficult to attach to the company.

In the circumstances of the company CP plc a private placing would probably be most appropriate providing the issue is for an amount within current restrictions.

(b)　　(i)　　**Merchant banks**

As an issuing house the merchant bank controls the offer of shares.

Firstly, it will offer advice on the timing of the issue, the valuation of the company and the type of issue. The merchant bank co-ordinates with accountants, lawyers (in-house or otherwise) and other consultants.

It will normally underwrite the issue, agreeing to purchase shares if not taken up by the market. The company therefore can rely on the issue generating the funds they originally expected.

The merchant bank markets the issue through advertisement and promotions to key institutional investors.

Stockbrokers

May be used in addition to merchant banks as a facilitator of the process of share issue. The broker is an agent and is usually used in marketing the issue to investors private or institutional.

Institutional investors

Institutional investors include pension funds and insurance companies who are key potential buyers of shares. They will be heavily canvassed on an issue and particularly their willingness to underwrite the issue.

Answer 17

4D plc

(a)　　The treasurer is purchasing marketable securities to generate a return. Acting rationally the treasurer will wish to maximise return but at the same time he will consider risk of each investment. We would normally expect a pay-off between risk and return, the higher the risk the higher the return.

The reason for holding the security will dictate the amount of risk the treasurer will accept, short-term investment requires minimal risk to ensure the funds are available when needed. Longer term investment will accept higher levels of risk in return for higher returns.

Over the short-term the liquidity of the investment is important. The ease with which the security can be converted into cash will determine its acceptability. Generally those assets with a wider ownership will be more liquid as there is larger potential market for the security.

(b)　　(i)　　The risk of the portfolio is the weighted average β of the individual components.

Investment	Proportion	β
UK Retailing Company	30%1.2	0.36
High Tech Growing Company	30%1.6	0.48
American Bank	20%1.0	0.20
Government Bonds	20%0	0
		1.04

Return – using CAPM

$R_s = R_f + (R_m - R_f) \, \beta$

$\quad\quad = 5\% + (12\% - 5\%)\, 1.04$

$\quad\quad = \underline{12.28}\%$

(ii)   **REPORT**

To:	The Bank		Date:	xx-xx-xx
From:	Mr A and Mr B			
Subject:	Forecast Financial Statements			

The company has 4 potential investments outlined:

1   Medium sized UK retailing company;
2   Small high tech UK company;
3   US Bank;
4   Government stock.

As a company with a low risk ($\beta = 0.8$) we would not be very interested in high risk investment (Investment 2). Secondly, the US Bank requires investment overseas in a foreign exchange, this introduces exchange exposure and difficulties of monitoring so is not appropriate. Securities 1 and 4 may both be appropriate to the company depending on their attitude to risk.

Other potential investment may include:

(i)   Local authority debt;
(ii)   Debentures;
(iii)   Preference shares;
(iv)   Ordinary shares;
(v)   Bills of exchange;
(vi)   Certificates of deposits.

Answer 18

Howgill

(a)   Sale and leaseback involves selling the freehold land or buildings to an institution such as a pension fund and at the same time entering into an agreement to lease it back from the institution. This will free up a large up-front cash advance to the vendor. On the downside, there will be a long–term commitment to rental payments and title to the asset has passed, which means that any future capital growth will be lost.

The financial substance is similar to that of a secured loan, and under FRS 5 it will be treated as such. The future liabilities will therefore be capitalised into long-term creditors.

Hire purchase involves buying an asset on credit. The payment comprises a capital repayment and interest charges, which are tax deductible. Legal title does not pass on till the end of the contract. However for accounting purposes the asset will be capitalised and for tax purposes capital allowances are available.

Finance leases are usually effected through a branch of a bank. For legal and tax purposes, title remains with the purchaser, but capital allowances are passed on to the user via lower rentals. The advantage is that the leasing company can buy assets in bulk and thus attract discounts. At the end of the lease, the user may be offered an option to buy. The rental payments are tax deductible for the user. However the accounting rules demand that the asset be capitalised along with future liabilities. Hence finance leases cannot (unlike operating leases) be used to disguise gearing.

All the three options are helpful to the capital rationed firm.

(b)   Howgill borrows at 15% pre tax. Post tax this approximates to approximately 10% (15% × 0.67).

	0	1	2	3	4	5
	£000	£000	£000	£000	£000	£000
Purchase	(20,000)					
Capital allowances (W1)		1,650	1,238	928	696	2,088
Discount factor 10%	1.000	0.909	0.826	0.751	0.683	0.621
Present value	(20,000)	1,500	1,023	697	475	1,297

Net present value = (£15,008) if purchased.

If Howgill leases out the asset to break even, the PV of post–tax rental must be £15.008 million.

Let annual rental be R. (*Note*. This is receivable in advance.)

Rental flows

Time	Narrative	£	Discount factor	Present value
0–3	Rental	R	1 + 2.487	3.487 R
1–4	Tax	(0.33R)	3.170	(1.046 R)
			Present value	2.441 R

So to break even:

2.441 R   = £15.008m

           = £6,148,000

Workings

(W1)

Time		Pool £000	Tax @ 33%	Reduce tax bill at time
	Purchase	20,000		
0	25% WDA	(5,000)	1,650	1
		15,000		
1	25% WDA	(3,750)	1,238	2
		11,250		
2	25% WDA	(2,813)	928	3
		8,437		
3	25% WDA	(2,109)	696	4
		6,327		
4	Zero proceeds	–		
	Balancing allowance	6,327	2,088	5

(c)   We are now looking at this from Clint's point of view. Clint borrows at 18% pre tax, ie 12% post tax.

(i)   Ignoring maintenance savings

Lease

Time	Narrative	£000	Discount factor 12%	Present value £000
0–3	Rental	(7,000)	1 + 2.402	(23,814)
1–4	Tax relief	2,310	3.037	7,015
				(16,799)

Net present value = £16.8m to lease

Purchase (cash flows as Part (b))

	0	1	2	3	4	5
	£000	£000	£000	£000	£000	£000
Purchase	(20,000)					
Capital allowances (W1)		1,650	1,238	928	696	2,088
Discount factor 12%	1	0.893	0.797	0.712	0.636	0.567
Present value	(20,000)	1,473	987	661	443	1,184

Net present value = (15,252) ie net present value = £15.252m to buy

This suggests that Clint should purchase the asset.

(ii)   If we take into account maintenance savings, under the lease option, Clint would save £750,000 per annum pre tax. The PV of these savings is as follows.

Time	Narrative	£000	Discount factor 12%	Present value £000
1–4	Savings	750	3.037	2,278
2–5	Tax @ 33%	(248)	3.605 – 0.893	(673)
				1,605

Therefore the net present value of leasing becomes:

		Net present value £000
Present value	Leasing flows	(16,799)
Present value	Savings	1,605
Net present value	Leasing	15,194

This appears marginally preferable to buying.

Note. In all cases we have ignored the finance package of buying, eg borrow £20 million over four years at 10%. The reason for this is as follows:

Time	Narrative	£000	Discount factor 10%	Present value £000
0	Borrow	20,000	1.000	20,000
1–4	Interest @ 10%	(2,000)	3.170	(6,340)
4	Repay	(20,000)	0.683	(13,660)
			Net present value	0

This will not therefore affect our decision.

Answer 19

Acme

(a)   **Finance lease**

A finance lease usually requires the payment of an initial deposit and then regular payments over the life of the lease agreement. At the end of the lease agreement the asset may continue to be leased at a nominal rent. Legally, the asset remains the property of the leasing company.

The constant cashflows over the lease agreement will assist the business in planning its cashflow requirements.

The lessee is responsible for the repair and maintenance costs of the asset over its life which will vary according to the use of the asset.

The lessee will be able to make taxation claims against the lease repayments rather than capital allowances that may be claimed against the full cost of the asset.

This may benefit the business where profits are insufficient to claim the full capital allowance but sufficient to claim the lease payments.

Bank loan

The bank loan will also require the repayment of cash over the life of the loan.

In contrast to a finance lease the interest rate may be variable and therefore the cashflow payments may vary over the life of the loan.

The company may also face increased uncertainty with variable interest rates and may gain or suffer depending on the interest rate movements.

A fixed interest rate may be agreed should the company wish.

The business will be able to claim capital allowances against the cost of the asset and tax relief on the interest payments made.

Where the company has sufficient profits and capital allowances are favourable this may have a beneficial effect on the company's taxation and cashflow position.

Cash deposits

Should the business decide to take the cash from deposits the company will lose out on the interest that it was receiving but will no longer suffer the tax on that interest.

As the interest rate on savings is often lower than that on loans or lease finance the cost is likely to be cheaper.

The company will suffer a significant cash outflow and must consider whether its position is able to cope with this. Will the cash be required for other activities and not just the purchase of the fixed asset?

The business will be able to claim capital allowances on the asset as with the bank loan scenario.

(b)   **Capital allowances (CAs)**

			Capital allowances	Tax benefit	Year of tax benefit
Year 1		£	£	£	
Cost	Cost (A at 25%)	120,000			
CA at 25%		(30,000)	30,000 × 0.3 =	9,000	2
WDV	WDV (A at 25%)	90,000			

Year 2

CA at 25%	(22,500)	22,500 × 0.3 =	6,750	3

WDV WDV (A at 25%)	67,500

Year 3

CA at 25%	(16,875)	16,875 × 0.3 =	5,063	4

	50,625

Year 4   (A at 25%)

CA at 25%	(12,656)	12,656 × 0.3 =	3,797	5

	37,969

Year 5

Sales proceeds Sales proceeds	0

Balancing allowance	37,969	37,969 × 0.3 =	11,390	6

Year	0	1	2	3	4	5	6
Savings		50,000	50,000	50,000	50,000	50,000	
Tax on savings			(15,000)	(15,000)	(15,000)	(15,000)	(15,000)
Asset	(120,000)						
Tax on CAs			9,000	6,750	5,063	3,797	11,390
Cashflow	(120,000)	50,000	44,000	41,750	40,063	38,797	(3,610)
Discount factor	1.000	0.870	0.756	0.658	0.572	0.497	0.432
Present value	(120,000)	43,500	33,264	27,471	22,916	19,282	(1,560)

NPV = £24,873

As the NPV is greater than 0, the company should acquire the machine.

The decision to acquire the machine is based on the company's cost of capital, ie the machine gives a good enough return to cover this.

Which type of finance?

Discount rate after tax = 13% × 0.7 = 9%

Ignore savings and tax on savings as these are common to both situations.

Buying the machine

Year	0	1	2	3	4	5	6
Cost	(120,000)						
Tax on current assets			9,000	6,750	5,063	3,797	11,390
Discount factor	1.000	0.917	0.842	0.772	0.708	0.650	0.596
Present value	(120,000)	--	7,578	5,211	3,585	2,468	6,788

NPV = (£94,370)

Leasing the machine

Time	Description	Payment £	Discount £	Present value £
0–4	Lease payments	(28,000)	4.239	(118,692)
2–6	Tax on lease payments (0.3 × £28,000)	8,400	3.890	32,676
			NPV	(£86,016)

Conclusion

The asset should be leased as the net present value of payments is lower under this method.

Note. Tax on lease starts in Year 2 because the first lease payment is at the start of the first year. This will be set against profits to end of Year 1 and therefore the tax saving arises one year later, in Year 2.

Answer 20

MRF

(a)   Key point: There are no tax implications to MRF.

PV cost of buying and financing by a bank loan = £22.5m.

(Note: The cost of capital is 12% representing the cost of borrowing, the interest charge is already incorporated in the cost of borrowing).

PV cost of leasing

Year	Cashflow	£m	D.F.W. 12%	Present Value £m
1–6	Lease payments	7.5	4.111	30.83
6	Foregone residual value	4.0	0.507	2.03
				32.86

Decision: Buy and finance with a bank loan, the cost is 10.36m less than leasing.

(i)   **REPORT**

To: Helen   Date: xx-xx-xx

From: Account Negotiator

Subject: Minimum cost of lease

Minimum cost will be the cost of the lease payments that equate to the net cost of purchasing the asset.

Year	Incremental Cashflow £m	D.F. @ 12%	P.V. £m
0	Purchase cost saved 22.5	1.000	22.5
1–6	Lease payment X	4.111	4.111X
6	Sales proceeds foregone (4.0)	0.507	(2.03)
		NPV	0

$\therefore$ 4.111 X = £20.47m

X = £4.98m

The annual lease payments must fall from £7.5m pa to £4.98m to make MRF indifferent between leasing and buying.

(ii)   Impact of lease payment of £4.98m on leasing company.

Key point: The leasing company is liable for tax and tax allocations.

Working: Capital allowances.

Year		£m	Tax relief @ 33%	Timing (no time lag)
1	Investment £22.5m × 0.8	18.0		
	WDA 25%	(4.5)	1.48	
2	WDV	13.5		
	WDA 25%	(3.38)	1.11	
3	WDV	10.12		
	WDA 25%	(2.53)	0.84	
4	WDV	7.59		
	WDA 25%	(1.90)	0.63	
5	WDV	5.69		
	WDA 25%	(1.42)	0.47	
6	WDV	4.27		
	Proceeds	(4.0)		
	BA	0.27	0.09	

NPV of project to leasing company

Time	Cashflow		D.F. @ 14%	Present Value
		£m		£m
0	Investment	(18.0)	1.000	(18.0)
1-6	Receipts (after tax)			
	£4.98m × 67%	3.34	3.889	12.98
1	Capital allowances	1.48	0.877	1.30
2	Capital allowances	1.11	0.769	0.85
3	Capital allowances	0.84	0.675	0.57
4	Capital allowances	0.63	0.592	0.37
5	Capital allowances	0.47	0.519	0.24
6	Capital allowances	0.09	0.456	0.04
6	Capital allowances	4.0	0.456	1.86
	NPV			+0.22

The project generates a marginal profit for the leasing company if the revised lease payments of £4.98m are accepted.

(iii)   *Other actions*

The leasing company may look to rescue the deal by looking at alternatives to competing solely on the cost of finance.

It is quite normal to incorporate maintenance and emergency callout contracts within the lease contract the benefit t the charity will probably outweigh the cost to the leasing company.

Alternatively, the leasing company may use its relationship with the company selling the asset to negotiate upgrades and replacements guaranteed into the future.

Finally, the leasing company must look to reduce its own cost of capital perhaps through financing the asset using debt finance which is tax deductible.

Answer 21

Investment and Risk

(a)   (i)   **Memorandum**

To: Finance Director

From: Financial Strategist

Subject: Use of cash surplus   Date: xx/xx/xx

Risk

Risk is measured in terms of total risk which may be described at the sum of systematic and unsystematic risk. Systematic risk is risk associated with the market as a whole which cannot be diversified away. Unsystematic risk is risk specific to individual investments that may be eliminated by holding a sufficiently diversified portfolio of shares.

The key to understanding portfolio theory is that unsystematic risk should not be suffered by investors and therefore it is not rewarded by a higher return.

Systematic risk is rewarded and the beta value of an individual investment reflects the level of systematic risk suffered in relation to market risk. Market risk has a beta value of 1.0, any security with higher risk will have a beta value of greater than 1.0. A risk free investment has a beta value of 0.

(ii)   **Director 1**

The first comment is correct as holding a portfolio will allow only systematic risk to be considered. The only consideration must be that the portfolio is sufficiently large (30+ investments) and diversified otherwise unsystematic risk will also arise.

Director 2

It is always prudent to acknowledge total risk in assessing investments. This may lead to the purchase of risk free securities such as government borrowing to reduce the overall level of risk. Total risk, however, is not fully compensated for as the unsystematic part of the risk attracts no additional return.

Director 3

It is acceptable to buy securities with a return lower than the market as a whole, in fact it is also possible that securities with a return lower than risk free return may be chosen. This is dependent on the security providing sufficient diversification to the portfolio to reduce the overall unsystematic risk.

(b)   Market efficiency suggests that the current share price incorporates all current information. Any change in the share price will only arise as a result of additional information.

The information provided could equally be good or bad therefore the next move of the share price may go up or down; this is described as the share as following a 'random walk'. From this we must agree that market efficiency in itself does not ensure accurate forecasting.

The use of a multiple regression model is the means of using past data that has a correlation with share prices to predict the future share prices of an investment.

The data probably includes economic information relating to share prices such as growth and market share. The suggestion is that a known relationship between such data and share prices will continue from the period from 1964 to 1994 on into the future.

It is unlikely that such a correlation will continue into the future, even if it is the case that the relationship holds true then prediction of the economic data into the future will be difficult.

The two statements are not contradictory, the first model being a description as to how the current share price is calculated, the second is a predictive model extrapolating past data to establish future prices.

Answer 22

Leisure International

(a) **Weighted Average Cost of Capital (WACC)**

Cost of equity

$$K_e = \frac{D_1}{P_0} + g = \frac{\text{Next Dividend}}{\text{Market Value}} + \text{Growth rate of dividend}$$

$$D_1 = D_0\,(1+g) = \text{Most recent dividend} \times \text{One period of dividend growth}$$

$$K_e = \frac{4p}{80p} + 12\% \qquad = 5\% + 12\%$$

$$= \underline{17}\%$$

Cost of preference shares

$$K_{ps} = \frac{\text{Dividend}}{\text{MV}} = \frac{\text{Dividend}}{\text{Market Value}}$$

$$K_{ps} = \frac{9p}{72p} = \underline{12.5}\%$$

Cost of debt

$$
\begin{aligned}
K_d \quad &= \quad \text{Coupon rate} \times (1 - \text{tax rate}) \\
&= \quad 14\% \times (1 - 0.35) \\
&= \quad 14\% \times 0.65 \\
&= \quad 9.1\%
\end{aligned}
$$

	Market Value *£m*		*Return* *£m*
Ordinary shares	8.32	(x 17%)	1.4144
10.4m × £0.8			
Preference shares	3.24	(x 12.5%)	0.405
4.5m × £0.72			
Debentures	5.00	(x 9.1%)	0.455
	———		———
	16.56		2.2744
	———		———

$$\text{WACC} = \frac{2.2744}{16.56} = 13.73\%$$

Alternative formula

$$\text{WACC} = \left(r_e \frac{E}{E + P + D} \right) + \left(r_p \frac{P}{E + P + D} \right) + \left(r_d\,(1-t)\, \frac{D}{E + P + D} \right)$$

E	=	Equity	r_e	=	Cost of equity
P	=	Preference shares	r_p	=	Cost of preference shares
D	=	Debt	$r_d\,(1\text{-}t)$	=	Post tax cost of debt

$$= \quad \left(17\% \times \frac{8.32}{16.56} \right) + \left(12.5\% \times \frac{3.24}{16.56} \right) + \left(9.1\% \times \frac{5}{16.56} \right)$$

$$= \quad 13.73\%$$

(b)   CAPM establishes the rate of return that the market would generate given a sufficiently diversified portfolio. This is based on the principal that the only risk an investor must suffer is systematic risk (ie, risk relating to the market as a whole).

The model also identifies a risk free turn based on purchase of government debt. The difference in return is the compensation for accepting risk and is given the beta value of 1.0.

For the cost of equity to be estimated the model must know the risk-free return and the market return. The final piece of information needed is the beta value for the individual share which reflects the level of volatility of the share relative to the market the beta value is calculated based on past data. The formula used is:

$$K_e = R_f + (R_m - R_f)\,\beta$$

(c)   There is some logic to this suggestion and it depends on the ability of the business to segment the activities of the business and the finances of the business.

The accepted investment appraisal methodology is to consider the business as a single legal entity which must achieve a given cost of capital described as the opportunity cost of capital. This may be further developed to adjust the cost of capital of the business to reflect the level of risk of a specific investment.

The other aspect to consider is that finance for a specific asset should be used as the cost of capital because of the direct linkage between the two.

Answer 23

GLC Ltd

(a)   **Working**

	2002 £000's	2003 £000's	2004 £000's	2005 £000's
Sales receipts				
10% Year 2	55	75	90	60
30% Current year	120	165	225	270
60% Year 0 (20%)	80	110	150	180
+1 (20%)	60	80	110	150
+2 (20%)	100	60	80	110
Total	415	490	655	770

Cash budgets

	2002 £000's	2003 £000's	2004 £000's	2005 £000's
Sales receipts	415	490	655	770
Payments	200	120	160	220
Materials	80	110	150	180
Labour	200	200	200	200
Fixed overhead	20	20	20	20
Interest	200		200	
Fixed asset				
Sub-total	700	450	730	620
Net cash flow	(285)	40	(75)	150
Balance bd	50	(235)	(195)	(270)
Balance cd	(235)	(195)	(270)	(120)

(b)   **Sources of finance**

The business will require a substantial increase in the level of funding to ensure the overdraft is reduced. This may be in the form of asset based finance over the medium term (2 - 5 years) or short term finance other than an overdraft of a more temporary nature.

Medium term finance

Normally asset specific using the asset to provide the finance company with security. Examples may include:

(i)   Hire purchase;
(ii)   Finance leasing;
(iii)   Variable rate loan.

Hire purchase is an agreement to hire an asset for a period of time (2 to 5 years) paying monthly premiums, on the payment of the final premium the title of the asset passes to the user. Hire purchase is a useful fixed rate source of finance to companies already indebted or with relatively low levels of fixed assets because security is primarily based on the asset being purchased.

Finance leases have a similar payment profile to hire purchase agreements and is often compared to them. The key difference is that the lease may offer tax advantages due to differing tax treatment of the asset. With a finance lease the title is never held by the lessee (the user), being retained by the lessor (the finance company) until the asset is sold to a third party.

Variable rate loans are again lent against the specific asset being bought. They tend to offer a keener rate due to the variable nature of the loan but of course may suffer from increases in premiums as interest rates rise.

Short-term finance

The use of short-term finance is normally made to cope with short-term fluctuations in cash positions, but could be used to fund a shortfall in funding over the longer term. They include:

(i)   Extending trade credit;
(ii)   Debtor factoring;
(iii)   Invoice discounting;
(iv)   Bank loans.

Extending trade credit would appear to be the most beneficial source of finance because of its negligible cost but if done without agreement with the supplier may lead to a loss of reputation and disruption of supply.

Debtor factor may have a financing element whereby the factoring company advances up to 80% of the debt. This is incorporated within debtor collection and credit insurance facilities all of which are normally taken together.

Invoice discounting is the use of debts as an asset against which cash may be borrowed. Unlike factoring invoice discounting relates to individual invoices instead of all debts. Again up to 80% of the debt is advanced by the factor to be repaid on receipt of the debt.

Banks have been encouraged to offer term loans by government (and competition from foreign banking groups) where the loan is guaranteed for a term of up to five years.

Answer 24

Long-Term and Short-Term

(a)   The use of short-term funding is normally for day to day fluctuations in the cash needs of the business. It includes the following sources:

(i)   Overdraft;
(ii)   Bank loans;
(iii)   Debtor factoring;
(iv)   Invoice discounting;
(v)   Trade credit.

Advantages

1   *Flexibility* - The amount of funding (eg, overdraft) can be raised to cover only the amount required reducing the need to have long-term funds available that may not be used.

2   *Cost* - Due to liquidity preference we would normally expect short-term funds to be less costly than long-term funds (transaction costs excluded). Provided that the level of security for the funding is similar and the funds are raised in conditions of constant market expectations short-term funds should be cheaper.

3   *Additional finance source* – In a business that has a high level of debt secured on existing fixed assets the use of short-term funds borrowed against (say) debtors provides a further source.

Disadvantages

More frequent replenishment – Short-term sources by their very nature will need to be replenished more frequently. If a supplier withdraws trade credit, an alternative source of finance must be available immediately.

High reliance on retail bank – Most short-term sources of finance are provided by the retail or clearing bank. The financing of the business is therefore dependant on the decisions of very few people.

(b)   The yield curve is an illustration of the yield to redemption of a security plotted in relation to the number of years until maturity. We would normally see that the yields to redemption increases as the term increases.

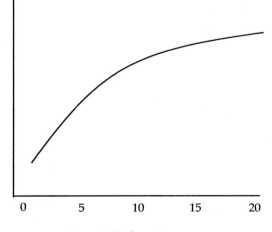

There are three theories that may be used to explain the shape of the yield curve:

(i) Liquidity preference;
(ii) Market segmentation;
(iii) Expectations.

Liquidity preference theory

Most investors would rather hold cash instead of have their money tied up in securities. The longer the cash is tied up (length of time to maturity) the less attractive the investment becomes. The investor is therefore compensated by offering a higher yield the longer the time to redemption.

Market segmentation theory

The suggestion that different investors have different uses for the yield curve. For example, in the short-term it is used by banks to protect the liquidity of its deposits whereas the longer-term is dominated by pension funds looking to match future long-term pension funding with available funds.

In this situation the short-term and long-term markets are quite distinct and behave differently.

Expectations theory

The theory that future market expectations on interest rates will have an impact. If the expectation is that interest rates will rise then the yield curve will rise in sympathy.

Download sloping yield curve

We would normally expect the yield curve to rise over time. In some circumstances, it does the opposite (in defiance of liquidity preference). It may arise due to expectations theory where future interest rates are expected to fall in relation to their current value.

Segmentation theory may also describe this situation. If the short-term interest rate reflects the current base rate but the long-term yield is determined by supply and demand for government debt. If a government is expected to repay debt even through the debt is in heavy demand for annuity financing of pensions the yield paid out will fall.

Answer 25

Interest Rates

(a) Time value of money reflects the fact that £100 (say) is worth more now than it would in one year's time. This arises for a number of reasons including:

(i) Risk;
(ii) Liquidity preference;
(iii) Inflation.

Risk is important due to the fact that the longer an investment is outstanding the more likely that the debt is to turn bad. You are at no risk if you hold £100 in cash but at some risk if you invest in commercial debt that it will not be repaid.

Liquidity preference simply reflects the desire for liquidity. The longer an investment, the greater the compensation to the investor for tying up the cash for the period.

Inflation has been a constant feature of the UK economy for almost fifty years. Inflation is the devaluation of money over time and can be identified by rising prices over time. The investor must be compensated for the loss of value of each individual pound by an increase in the time value of money.

Marketable securities reflect the time value of money by offering a yield or return to investors in return for tying up their funds in shares and debt instruments. Typically the longer the investor is willing to tie up his money the better the return to be earned.

(b)   The relationship between real and money rates is linked to inflation. The real rate of interest is the level of interest excluding inflation. The money rate incorporates inflation.

All investments are expressed in money or nominal terms including the inflationary element. This is because they are expressed in sterling (or other currency) which is susceptible to devaluation through inflation.

Real rate $r = 6\%$

Money rate $m = 2\%$

Inflation rate $i = ?$

$$(1+r)(1+i) = (1+m)$$

$$\therefore (1+i) = \frac{1+m}{1+r} = \frac{1.02}{1.06} = 0.962$$

$$\text{Inflation} = 0.962 - 1$$
$$= \underline{-3.77}\%$$

The difference between real and money interest rates is the inflation rate. We would normally expect this rate to be positive but in this example the inflation rate is negative suggesting deflation.

(c) $$\text{Flat Yields} = \frac{\text{Coupon Rate} \times \text{Nominal Value}}{\text{Current Market Value}}$$

Investment

(i) $\dfrac{8\% \times £100}{£108} \times 100 \quad = \quad \dfrac{£8}{£108} \times 100 \quad = \quad 7.41\%$

(ii) $\dfrac{4\% \times £100}{£90} \times 100 \quad = \quad \dfrac{£4}{£90} \times 100 \quad = \quad 4.44\%$

Gross redemption yields =

$$\text{flat yield} + \left[\frac{(\text{RedemptionValue} - \text{MV}) \div \text{No of years to redemtpion}}{\text{MarketValue}} \right] \times 100$$

Investment

(i) $7.41\% + \left[\dfrac{(100 - 108) \div 4 \text{ years}}{108} \right] \times 100$

$= 7.41\% - 1.85\% = 5.56\%$

(ii) $4.44\% + \left[\dfrac{(100 - 90) \div 6 \text{ years}}{90} \right] \times 100$

$= 4.44\% + 1.85\% = 6.29\% \quad \times \quad 5.5\%$.

The investor concerned solely with interest payments would invest in investment (i) however, if we incorporated the capital gain to redemption investment (ii) is more attractive.

Answer 26

Cash Discount: TLC company

(a)   **Working: Existing debtor days**

$$\text{Debtor days} = \frac{£0.833m}{£5m} \times 360 = 60 \text{ days}$$

			1% Discount	1.25% Discount
Number of days saved				
1%	- 60-20	=	40 days	
1.25%	- 60-10	=		50 days
Interest rate				
1%	$- \dfrac{0.01}{0.99} \times 100$	=	1.01%	
1.25%	$- \dfrac{0.0125}{0.9875} \times 100$	=		1.27%
n				
1%	$- \dfrac{360 \text{ days}}{40 \text{ days}}$	=	9	
1.25%	$- \dfrac{360 \text{ days}}{50 \text{ days}}$	=		7.2
Annualised interest rate				
1%	$- 1.0101^{9}$	=	9.47%	
1.25%	$- 1.0127^{7.2}$	=		9.51%

(b)   There are three alternatives to our present debtor policy:

(i)   Cash discounts;
(ii)   Debtor factoring;
(iii)   Cash on delivery.

Cash discount

The cash discount is a popular way of encouraging early payment. It generates early cashflows from some customers without compelling all customers to pay early. It does have downsides however, there is foregone revenue due to the discount and the uncertainty as to the level of take-up by customers. In practice further problems arise because customers may take advantage of the discount without paying early.

Debtor factoring

The use of a third party (a factor) to collect debt. Additional services the factor may provide include credit insurance and finance. The advantages of factoring are associated with these services, it reduces internal administration costs, provides protection against bad debt and most importantly in this situation provides finance in advance of collection.

The disadvantages of factoring include the cost (the factor wishes to profit out of the arrangement) and the stigma associated with using them. Traditionally, factors were used by failing companies.

Cash on delivery

A simple suggestion to eliminate all credit sales would improve the cost base of the business. Credit control cost could be saved and their would be no costs of financing outstanding debtors. It must be questionable whether our customers would accept such a change in credit policy. It is likely that substantial sales volume would be lost as we move away from industry norms.

Conclusion

Contrary to the suggestion in the question the overall level of debtor is relatively low at 60 days. The likely problem relates to a few problem accounts who always pay late or are delinquent and have no intention of paying.

The best policy to adopt in this cash is to change the credit policy (maybe to cash on delivery) for these customers and employ factors if we are unable to control the debtors ourselves.

(c)   Additional sources of short-term finance include:

      (i)   Overdraft;
      (ii)   Invoice discounting;
      (iii)   Trade credit;
      (iv)   Bank loans.

Overdrafts are traditionally the key short-term source of finance for business. Provided by banks they are flexible (you only pay for the indebted amount) but suffer from in theory being 'repayable on demand'.

Invoice discounting is where individual debts are used as collateral against which funds may be borrowed. The key to the debt is that the customers must have good credit rating, they are the security.

Trade credit is a key short-term source of finance. It represents the investment of funds by suppliers in the business in the way of deferred payment. Extending trade credit is endemic to trading relations in the UK. Excessive extension will lead to a poor reputation being earned in the longer term.

Bank or term loans have been encouraged by government in recent years to offer a more permanent form of financing to business. The loans have overtaken overdraft facilities in terms of their importance in funding terms.

Answer 27

BYO plc

(a)   In the event of a short-term cash surplus it is vital to use the funds in such a manner as to allow easy access. Uses could include:

      (i)   Short-term investment in government securities would generate a better return than is probably offered in the current account of the business. It offers good security with minimal risk of default and can be liquidated with ease due to the depth of the market.

      (ii)   Take up cash discounts reducing the overall cost base of the business. If we hold excess funds we should attempt to generate a return in excess of our cost of capital, if the annualised benefit of paying the cash discount is greater it should be taken up.

      (iii)   Purchase goods in bulk taking advantage of trade discounts if there is sufficient space available for storing the goods. It must be guaranteed that the stock will be used and will not have time to deteriorate or become obsolescent.

      (iv)   Offer special extended credit schemes to boost existing sales over a limited period. Allow the excess funds to be used to invest in our customers. The key to this being successful is that the extended credit is only offered to customers who pass stringent credit checks.

(b) **Miller-Orr model**

Formula

$$\text{Spread} = 3 \left(\frac{\tfrac{3}{4} \times \text{transaction} \times \text{variance of cashflows}}{\text{Interest rate}} \right)^{\tfrac{1}{3}}$$

$$\text{Return point} = \text{lower limit} + \frac{1}{3} \times \text{spread}$$

$$\text{Spread} = 3 \left(\frac{\tfrac{3}{4} \times 300 \times 9,000,000}{0.0004} \right)^{\tfrac{1}{3}}$$

$$= £110,979$$

$$\text{Return point} = £15,000 + \frac{1}{3} \times 110,979 = £51,993$$

(c) (i) Defer capital expenditure and only spend on time critical capital assets. In most business there is regular expenditure on assets that can be pushed back without drastically affecting the business. Examples may include upgrading and refurbishment of buildings and replacement of company cars.

(ii) Accelerating cash inflows by offering cash discounts and better credit control. The most important control in a company short of cash is the control of debtors. By encouraging early payment and ensuring prompt payment the company can go a long way to minimise cash shortages.

(iii) Reduce cash outflows through negotiation. In severe cash shortages it may become necessary to renegotiate debts to ensure solvency. Longer credit may be taken by arrangement of course this runs the risk of losing future supply. Dividends could be reduced even at the expense of upsetting shareholders. Corporation tax may also be deferred although at an interest cost and only for a limited time period.

Answer 28

Ewden

Part (a)

Note. The best way to answer this question is to use the classic approach of 'define and illustrate'.

Liquidity measures the amount of cash the company can expect to realise in the short term. In this case, Ewden's cash balance has fallen from £1.5 million in 19X2 to a net overdraft of £0.1 million, a decline in liquidity of £1.6 million. This is in stark contrast to the apparently healthy profit for the year, indicating that cash has been used to finance balance sheet assets.

Indeed, analysis of the balance sheet indicates that at least £3 million has been ploughed into fixed assets. It is not possible to say whether this investment has been in new technology, or perhaps some kind of acquisition, but the result appears to be that turnover has increased by 33%.

At the same time, the company's working capital has been funded, to the tune of £0.8 million in stocks and £1 million in debtors, probably at the expense of trade creditors who have lengthened by £0.5 million.

More significantly, no long-term finance has been raised which appears to be in conflict with the maxim that we should match the length of the finance with the length of the project.

This may be a case of overtrading where a company undergoes a rapid expansion without the support of long–term financing.

Growth here has been financed short term, at the expense of cash and creditors. As sales increase, so too do stock and debtors, leading to further liquidity problems.

We can now look at more specifics in the form of ratio analysis.

Current ratios

These have fallen from 2.3 to 2.0, but once we remove stock to give us the acid test ratio the fall is from 1.6 to 1.1 which may be significant if Ewden experiences bad debts and therefore severe short–term liquidity constraints.

Working capital cycle

Stock days have increased from 73 in 19X2 to 88 days in 19X3, almost three months; this appears high but should be measured against the industry average.

Debtor days have lengthened from 49 days to 59 days, almost two months, which will significantly pressure liquidity. Credit terms may have to be reviewed and enforced.

Creditor days have lengthened marginally from 78 to 80 days. Again this must be compared to the terms offered and industry averages, but any increase may result in a loss of goodwill from suppliers.

The net effect is that the working capital cycle has lengthened from 44 days to 67 days.

Return on capital employed

The ROCE (operating profit as a percentage of shareholders' funds and long–term loans) has in fact risen from 43% to 47%. This could be explained either by the net profit margin or by the asset turnover.

The net profit margin has remained stable at 42% versus 43%, which indicates firstly that the turnover increase is not due to price reductions, and secondly that ROCE has improved due to asset turnover by 1.04 versus 1.10. This has not lengthened too much in that the increase in turnover appears to have been asset backed.

In summary although liquidity is certainly a problem, the expansion does appear to be backed by fixed assets and therefore Ewden may not necessarily overtrade.

It would perhaps be advantageous to obtain long–term financing if Ewden is to maintain its growth.

Note. The following ratios have been used.

$$\text{Current ratio} = \frac{\text{Current assets}}{\text{Current liabilities}}$$

$$\text{Acid ratio} = \frac{\text{Current assets - stock}}{\text{Current liabilities}}$$

$$\text{Stock days} = \frac{\text{Stock}}{\text{Cost of sales}} \times 365$$

$$\text{Debtor days} = \frac{\text{Debtors}}{\text{Sales}} \times 365$$

$$\text{Creditor days} = \frac{\text{Creditors}}{\text{Sales}} \times 365$$

$$\text{ROCE} = \frac{\text{Operating profit}}{\text{Shareholders' funds + long-term loans}}$$

$$\text{Net profit margin} = \frac{\text{Operating profit}}{\text{Sales}}$$

$$\text{Asset turnover} = \frac{\text{Sales}}{\text{Shareholders' funds + long-term loans}}$$

If in doubt about using a ratio, always define the way you have calculated it.

Part (b)

Discount scheme

Current debtor days $\quad$ = $\quad$ 59 $\qquad$ Current debtors $\quad$ = $\quad$ £2.6m

Fifty% will pay in 10 days. The average collection period can be calculated as follows.

$\qquad$ (50% × 59) + (50% × 10) $\qquad\qquad$ = 35 days

New debtors would be: $\dfrac{35}{365}$ × £16m $\qquad$ = £1,534,000

This would generate an interest saving as follows.

Reduction in debtors (£2,600,000 – £1,534,000)		£1,066,000
		£000
Interest saved at 18%		192
Cost of discount (£16m × 50% × 2%)		160
		___
Net benefit		32
		___

Note. We could argue that we may only save interest on the first £200,000 of debtors as this is the overdraft figure. The interest saved would then be only £36,000 rather than £192,000.

Factoring

						£000
Revised debtors	=	$\dfrac{45}{365}$	×	£16m	=	1,973
Current debtors						2,600
						___
Reduction						627
						___
Interest saved at 18%						113
Admin savings						100
Service charge (1.5% × £16m)						(240)
						___
Net loss						(27)
						___

This suggests that the discount scheme is preferable, but obviously the decision will depend on the accuracy of the assumptions.

In particular, with any discount scheme, Ewden must ensure that only early payers claim the discount and not everyone. In any case a settlement period of just 10 days is a bold assumption.

Answer 29

Keswick

Part (a)

(i) $\quad$ Working capital is defined as current assets less current liabilities. It is therefore vital to a firm's liquidity and short-term cashflow.

$\qquad$ For a firm with no overdraft, trade creditors will make up the majority of current liabilities and therefore cash outflows in the short term.

A firm's working capital (or cash conversion) cycle is the time taken for cash to rotate through the business. It is given by the following formula.

Debtor days + Stockholding period – Creditor days

Where creditor days = $\dfrac{\text{Creditors}}{\text{Purchases}} \times 365$ = average time taken to pay creditors

As the stock holding period and debtor days are determined by the sales cycle, they are often difficult to control by the firm itself. On the other hand a firm can determine its creditor days by deciding when to pay its suppliers. The longer the period of credit taken, the faster cash would rotate through the business.

(ii)   Trade credit is essentially short–term borrowing, but from suppliers. It carries no interest charge but it is not free.

Withholding payments will result in surrendering discounts received. On an annualised basis this may well be an expensive source of financing.

There is also the goodwill issue. Taking extended credit will result in a loss of goodwill leading to any or all of the following problems.

♦   Low priority given to orders
♦   Cash demanded before orders
♦   Loss of reputation within the industry
♦   Refusal to supply

Part (b)

Keswick working capital: current system

		Days
Debtors	$\dfrac{£0.4m}{£10m} \times 365$	15
Stock	$\dfrac{£0.7m}{£8m} \times 365$	36
Creditors	$\dfrac{£1.5m}{£8m} \times 365$	(68)
		(21)

The profit and loss account has been simplified as follows.

	£m
Sales	10
Cost of sales	(8)
Earnings before interest and tax	2

This is clearly an efficient working capital cycle.

Proposed system

50% of creditors now on 15 days.

So average becomes (15 days × 50%) + (68 days × 50%) = 42 days

New cycle = 15 + 68 – 42 days = 41 days

Interest cover: current

$$\text{Current} = \frac{\text{Earnings before interest and tax}}{\text{Interest}} = \frac{£2\text{m}}{0.5\text{m}} = 4$$

Proposed interest cover

1   Half of cost of sales will now attract a 5% discount, ie 50% × £8m × 5% = £200,000

      Therefore cost of sales becomes £8,000,000 – £200,000 = £7.8 million.

      Therefore earnings before interest and tax become £2.2 million.

2   Interest paid will increase as the reduced credit taken will be financed via the overdraft.

      Effectively we will be borrowing an extra £3.8 million (£4m – £0.2m) for an extra 53 (68–15) days.

$$\text{Interest} = £3.8\text{m} \times 12\% \times \frac{53}{365} = £66,000$$

$$\text{New interest cover} = \frac{£2.2\text{m}}{£0.566\text{m}} = 3.9$$

Profit after tax

	£000
Currently	
Earnings before interest and tax	2,000
Interest	(500)
Profit before tax	1,500
Tax @ 33%	(495)
Profit after tax	1,005
Proposed	
Earnings before interest and tax	2,200
Interest	(566)
Profit before tax	1,634
Tax @ 33%	(539)
Profit after tax	1,095

Return on equity

$$\text{Current} = \frac{\text{Profit after tax}}{\text{Shareholders' funds}} = \frac{1,005}{2,000}$$

$$= 50.3\%$$

$$\text{Proposed} = \frac{1,095\text{k}}{2,000\text{k}} = 54.8\%$$

$$\text{Earnings per share} = \frac{\text{Profit after tax}}{\text{Number of shares}}$$

$$\text{Current} = \frac{£1,005\text{k}}{4\text{m}} = 25.1\text{p}$$

$$\text{Proposed} = \frac{£1,095\text{k}}{4\text{m}} = 27.4\text{p}$$

$$\text{Gearing} = \frac{\text{Debt}}{\text{Equity}} = 178\%$$

We can see that the proposal is beneficial to profitability but lengthens the gearing position and interest cover. Although Keswick is able to pay its interest bill, the bank must undoubtedly be worried about security. In the event of any problems, it would be unlikely to 'bale out' in full.

Answer 30

Ripley

Part (a)

Memorandum

To: Chairman and management board – Ripley plc

From: Management accountant

Subject: Finance strategies – fixed and working capital

The policy adopted at present is considered to be 'conservative'. In principle it matches the financing of long–term assets with long–term finance, and the financing of short–term assets by short–term methods (such as overdrafts and creditors).

It has two distinct advantages.

♦   It is safe in terms of liquidity in that there is little danger of sources of finance required long–term being withdrawn, involving the business in a liquidity crisis, as it seeks to find replacement for perhaps an overdraft now recalled or pressure from creditors.

♦   It takes advantage of the lower cost of finance available from long–term sources, and avoids the cost of paying continual set–up costs for short–term methods as overdrafts and short–term loans are continually renegotiated and replaced.

The proposed policy is considered to be 'aggressive'.

In principle it relies more on finance through short–term methods and the skill of management to obtain 'cheap or free' sources of finance in an attempt to balance the books.

Much higher attention will need to be paid to the comparative relationship between working capital items, in particular the minimisation of debtors and stocks and the maximisation of creditors. An advantage claimed for this theory is that it promoted the development of keen, entrepreneurial management. A disadvantage however is that it exposes the company to problems of illiquidity and possible business failure, if it cannot meet its financial obligations.

Before changing to an 'aggressive' approach the company should consider the following factors.

♦   Degree of expertise that has been demonstrated in the past in respect of our ability to accurately forecast cash inflows and outflows.

♦   Degree of expertise that has been demonstrated in the past in respect of our ability to successfully manage working capital.

♦   Degree of manoeuvrability in financing of fixed assets. How liquid are they, and can some be readily converted into cash?

♦   Adequacy of our information and forecasting systems.

♦   Reaction of the stock market, and of other finance providers.

Part (b)

Evaluation (separately) of costs/benefits from each of two options

Option 1 – sell security stocks

$$Q = \sqrt{\frac{2 \times 1.5m \times £25}{0.12}} \qquad = \qquad £25,000 \quad \text{Optimal proceeds per each sale}$$

£1.5m ÷ 25,000   =   60   Number of sale transactions required

	£
Sales transaction costs (60 × £25)	(1,500)
Interest earned on shot–term deposit (based on average held) (£25,000 ÷ 2) × 5%	625
Interest earned on portfolio over year (based on average level) (£1.5m ÷ 2) × 12%	90,000
	89,125

Option 2 – secured loan

	£
Interest charged (£1.5m × 14%)	(210,000)
Set–up fee	(5,000)
Interest earned on reinvested cash (based on average held) (£1.5m ÷ 2) × 9%	67,500
Interest earned on portfolio £1.5m × 12% (full amount – not sold)	180,000
	32,500

This makes Option 1 preferable in terms of profitability.

Note. Under Option 2, the portfolio would be used as security for the loan and sold off to repay the loan. This would therefore incur a transaction cost of £25 at the end of the year.

Part (c)

Limitation of simple cashflow model

♦ Assumes that cash is replenished from the sale of securities precisely at the moment when the cash balance drops to zero. In reality there is likely to be a buffer stock of cash which has been excluded from these calculations.

♦ Selling securities in small parcels may be uneconomic in terms of transaction costs for the sale. It may be more economic to have fewer sales but of a higher value of securities.

♦ The rate of return on the portfolio is subjective at 12%. Actual market and economic conditions will determine the actual return and in retrospect the return may be substantially different from the 12% used in the model. Interest rates also are subject to actual economic conditions.

Answer 31

Marton

Option 1

♦ Factoring with recourse
♦ Savings £200,000 – lower debtors days by 15
♦ Service charge of 1% of turnover (UK)
♦ Insurance against bad debts of £80,000

Option 2

♦ Terms – payment within 10 days of despatch – 3% (take up 20%)
♦ Terms – payment within 20 days of despatch – 1.5% (take up 30%)

Option 2a

♦ JIT with major customer (usually 90 days credit)
♦ Borrowing £0.5 million overdraft: five year life, 60 day settlement, premium 5% price/5% penalty

Overall

♦ Mixed business of UK and overseas customers
♦ All business on credit terms
♦ 20% of UK turnover with one firm
♦ Bank overdraft at 13% per annum
♦ Risk of foreign currency losses (all customers pay US$)

Part (a) Evaluation of two proposals for dealing with domestic debts

Option 1

	£
Savings in debtors days 15/365 × 20m × 13%	106,849
Administration savings	200,00
Service charge 1% turnover	(200,000)
Insurance against bad debts	(80,000)
Annual (cost)/benefit)	26,849

Current debtor days are $\dfrac{£4.5m}{£20m} \times 365$ = 82 days

Under Option 2 this would change to:

20% × 10 days + 30% × 20 days + 50% × 82 days = 49 days (a reduction of 33 days)

Savings would be as follows.

		£
Interest saved	$\dfrac{33}{365}$ x £20m × 13%	235,068
Cost of discount		
3% discount:	*20% × £20m × 3%*	*(120,000)*
1.5% discount:	*30% × £20m × 1.5%*	*(90,000)*
		25,068

Option 1 offers marginal benefit over Option 2 and should be recommended.

Part (b) Benefits from JIT arrangements

	Proposed position *£000*	
Annual depreciation £0.5m × 20%	100,000	Depreciation cost
20% turnover with one customer		
= 4,000 × 30 ÷ 365 × 13%	42,740	Interest saving
Premium price 5% × 4,000	(200,000)	Margin improvement
Guarantee =		
4,200 × 10% = 420 × 5%	21,000	Guarantee
Bank interest 500,000 × 13%	65,000	Interest cost
Net benefit	56,740	

Part (c) Benefits from a JIT agreement

(i)   Benefits in having a firm long–term order from a customer.

(ii)   Benefits in production scheduling and planning.

(iii) Benefits in being able to negotiate JIT arrangements from its own suppliers.

(iv)   Close relationship with customer may lead to other benefits, such as joint project research and development.

Part (d) Services provided by an overseas factor

(i)   Locally based debt collection
(ii)   Locally based finance advance
(iii) Locally based bad debt insurance
(iv)   Locally based credit vetting
(v)   Administration of accounts receivable.

Part (e) Worst outcome on exchange rates

(i)   Worst outcome when US$ falls against pounds sterling as on conversion Marton will receive less pounds sterling (£5m × 1.45 = $7.25m).

				£
Therefore worst outcome	=	$1.60 : £1	Converted as	4,530,000
Present rate	=	$1.45 : £1	Converted as	5,000,000
Exchange loss of				470,000

(ii)   Maximum opportunity cost of selling $ forward at $1.55 : £1

	£
Selling $7.25 million forward at $1.55	4,677,420
Most favourable rate would be $1.30	5,576,923
Maximum opportunity cost	899,502

(iii) Discuss whether Marton should hedge foreign currency risk

Businesses which wish to adopt a cautious policy towards foreign exchange should hedge. Knowing in advance the cost of hedging (transaction cost plus cost of hedge) may enable the business to reflect the cost in its selling price and thus be on an equal footing margin wise to UK business.

Businesses which adopt a less cautious approach will not hedge, they will work on the basis that there is as much chance of the exchange rate moving in their favour as there is against.

Answer 32

Wastell

Part (a)

(i)   *Early settlement discounts*

   Current collection period

   (5% × 30) + (28% × 45) + (10% × 60) + (30% × 75) + (16% × 90) + (11% × 120) = 70.2 days

   Year end debtors

   Sales net of bad debts   =£67.5m – £2m

                                    = £65.5m

$$\text{Debtors} = \frac{70.2}{365} \times £65.5m$$

$$= £12.598m$$

Early settlement

New debtor days $[(5\% + 28\% + 10\% + 30\%) \times 30] + (16\% \times 90) + (11\% \times 120) = 49.5$

New y/e debtors = $\frac{49.5}{365} \times £65.5$	£8.883m
Previously	£12.598m
Reduction	£3.715m
Interest saved at 12%	445,800
Discount 1% × 50% × £67.5m	(337,500)
Benefit	108,300

(ii)   *Debt collection*

Cost 1% × 67.5m	(655,000)
Bad debts saved 50% × £2m	1,000,000
Interest saved	
$\frac{20}{365} \times £65.5m \times 12\%$	430,700
Benefit	775,700

On financial grounds, Wastell should choose the factoring service.

Part (b)

Bank/Trade references

- ♦   In practice references can be sought from a potential customer's bankers and a couple of suppliers.
- ♦   Banks are hesitant to give a firm recommendation so as not to be liable for a duty of care.
- ♦   The trade referees chosen will be ones with whom the customer has a good relationship.

Credit agencies

Firms such as Dun and Bradstreet monitor credit details for all UK companies and will provide a credit reference for a fee. Firms like Equifax will do the same for members of the public.

Analysis of accounts

By analysing published accounts, liquidity and credit periods can be calculated, but these will be largely historical.

Word of mouth

In some close knit industries, competitors will be willing to share information about certain customers in the sector.

Part (c)

Invoice discounting works via a discounting company (usually a division of a bank). The customer receives advances from the discounter on an invoice by invoice basis, usually up to 90% of the invoice value. This is then treated as a loan with interest charged at base rate plus two or three percent. When the customer receives the cash from its own customer, the money (plus interest) received from the discounter is paid off.

This will improve short-term cashflow as cash is received in advance, but it will be at the expense of an interest charge. The company will try to collect its debts quicker to avoid interest charges from the discounter.

Bad debts remain a risk to the company and indeed the discounter only tends to advance money on customers with good credit ratings in the first place.

Answer 33

Fleming plc

	Nov	Dec	Jan	Feb	March	April
1 Production budget						
Sales			6,200	6,800	5,400	6,000
75% current			4,650	5,100	4,050	4,500
25% previous		1,550	1,700	1,350	1,500	?
		1,550	6,350	6,450	5,550	
2 Materials budget						
Production (units)		1,550	6,350	6,450	5,550	
× £/unit		× 4	× 4	× 4	× 4	
Production required (£)		6,200	25,400	25,800	22,200	
50% previous	3,100	12,700	12,900	11,100	?	
50% current		3,100	12,700	12,900	11,100	
	3,100	15,800	25,600	24,000		
Payment 1 month delay		3,100	15,800	25,600	24,000	
3 Wages budget						
Production (units)		1,550	6,350	6,450	5,550	
× £/unit		× 3	× 3	× 3	× 3	
Production required (£)		4,650	19,050	19,350	16,650	
75% current		3,488	14,288	14,513	12,488	
25% following			1,162	4,762	4,837	
		3,488	15,450	19,275	17,325	
4 Variable overhead budget						
Production (units)		1,550	6,350	6,450	5,550	
× £/unit		× 1.5	× 1.5	× 1.5	× 1.5	
Production required (£)		2,325	9,525	9,675	8,325	
40% current		930	3,810	3,870	3,330	
60% following			1,395	5,715	5,805	
		930	5,205	9,585	9,135	

5 Fixed overhead
   budget

Cost per month (£)	4,000	4,000	4,000	4,000	4,000
30% current	1,200	1,200	1,200	1,200	1,200
40% following	-	1,600	1,600	1,600	1,600
	1,200	2,800	2,800	2,800	2,800

Cash Budget

	December £	January £	February £	March £
Receipts -	12,369	45,987	59,666	
Payments (excluding materials)				
Wages	3,488	15,450	19,275	17,325
Variable overheads	930	5,205	9,585	9,135
Fixed overheads	1,200	2,800	2,800	2,800
	5,618	23,455	31,660	29,260
Net cashflow for month				
(excluding materials)	(5,618)	(11,086)	14,327	30,406
Balance b/d	30,000	21,282	(5,604)	(10,000)
Balance c/d (before materials)	24,382	10,196	8,723	20,406
Payment to materials creditors	3,100	15,800	18,723 max	30,406 max
Balance c/d	21,282	(5,604)	(10,000)	(10,000)

Notes

Payments for February	=	18,723 which leaves 25,600 – 18,723 = £6,877 unpaid
Payment for March	=	£6,877 still owing from February + 24,000
	=	£30,877, but the maximum amount payable = 30,406 which leaves £471 unpaid

Answer 34

Credit Management

(a)   Small companies face more acute problems than other businesses due to the following reasons regarding credit management:

   (i)   Limited sources of finance

           A small business has limited access to funds, normally restricted to the bank and personal funds. If the company is growing this tends to manifest itself as a shortage of working capital where the funds available are insufficient to pay bills as they fall due.

   (ii)   Lack of credit control

           Small businesses are normally unable to support the services of a dedicated credit controller; lacking that credit control can easily be too lax leading to extended credit periods and excessive bad debt.

(iii)   Lack of power to enforce payment

Larger companies may take advantage of the relationship to pay late on a regular basis. There are limited sanctions if an ongoing relationship is sought.

(iv)   Lack of focus from management

Managers tend to concentrate on sales or other parts of the business and hence do not give the controller of credit sufficient attention.

Actions to minimise the problem:

♦   Formal in-house procedures.
♦   Limit growth to the funds available or access new sources of finance.
♦   Use external credit control facilities to enhance debt collection eg factoring.

(b)

REPORT

To:	**The Credit Manager**
From:	**The Management Accountant**
Date:	**XX/XX/XX**
Subject:	**Credit Control Policy**

Credit Control Policy

The adoption of an effective credit control policy is normally key to the success of the company. The receipt of cash will be determined by the effective operation of the policy and in extreme circumstances an inappropriate policy may lead to insolvency and business failure.

The policy must include all aspects associated with credit control from terms offered through to the more prosaic aspects of individual responsibilities.

An effective policy should assist the company in the following ways:

1   Confidence in the system to generate cash in time for use within the organisation.

2   Better selection of a customer base that is solvent ensuring lower bad debt.

3   An encouragement to all employees to identify the importance of completing the process of selling through collection of debt.

4   Lower requirements on working capital due to better control of cash.

Cash Discounts

The introduction of a cash discount allows (but does not compel) customers to pay early. The cost to the supplier is that a discount on revenue is given, in return the shorter credit period will save financing costs. The effective interest rate cost may be given below:

$$\frac{1\%}{99\%} \times \frac{365\,\text{days}}{20\,\text{days}} = 18.4\%$$

Advantages

1   Early receipt eliminates uncertainty regarding bad debts.
2   Quicker payment reduces the cost of financing debtors as the level of working capital falls.
3   May reduce the workload to credit control as the amount of debtors to be monitored is reduced.

Disadvantages

1   No compulsion means only those who can and wish to pay will, this will probably not have much effect on bad debt.

2   In practice the customer may take the cash discount even though they do not pay early.

3   The level of take-up is difficult to predict before the event, the discount may be more or less generous than it needed to be.

4   The effective interest rate may be considered too high.

Answer 35

EFT Miller

(a)

Advantages of an electronic funds transfer system

◆   Reduction in the amount of paperwork.
◆   Limited opportunity for errors given the original transaction was correct.
◆   Lower clerical costs as receipt requires monitoring but no action.
◆   No postal costs.
◆   May lead to better terms being offered to customers.

(b) *(i)*

REPORT

To:	**The Treasurer**
From:	**Accountant**
Date:	**XX/XX/XX**
Subject:	**Cash Management Models**

Advantages of cash management models

A means of managing cash through use of a specific template of action. The model reduces the process to a series of mechanical responses that may be delegated to junior staff. Most models are imposed to manage cash more efficiently (by minimising the costs of operation) or to minimise the cost of operation.

Use by a local authority

As a non-profit-making organisation cash management may have differing priorities to other companies. That said, the efficient use of funds is probably just as important. Use of cash management models should be just as applicable.

(b) *(ii)*

Miller-Orr Model

Formula (not needed in **this** question).

$$\text{Spread} = 3 \left[\frac{\frac{3}{4} \times \text{transaction cost} \times \text{variance of cashflows}}{\text{Interest rate}} \right]^{\frac{1}{3}}$$

= £26,820.

Diagrammatic Representation

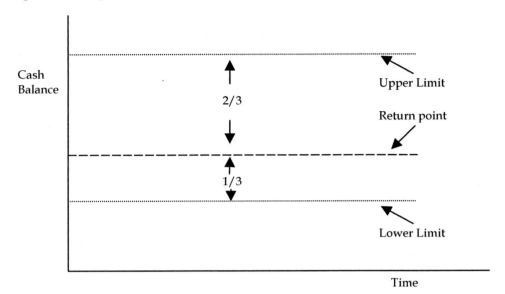

The Miller-Orr Model identifies upper and lower limits for the cash balance. Between these two points, cash is allowed to move up or down without control action. If they are reached the amount of cash is brought back to the return point by either encashing or investing in short term securities.

In the example we must hold a minimum level of cash of £15,000, the lower limit.

The upper limit will be given by adding the spread to the lower limit (15,000 + 26,820) = £41,820.

The return point is 1/3 of the spread from the lower level (15,000 + 26,820 × 1/3) = £23,940.

The key to the Miller-Orr Model is the manner in which control action is minimised, limiting the amount of work required of the management team.

Answer 36

XYZ plc

(a)

Cash discount

Credit sales = £4.85m × 70% = £3.395m

Debtor days (existing) = $\dfrac{£0.85m}{£3.395m} \times 365 = 91.4$ days

Revised debtor days (weighted average)

50% × 91.4 + 50% × 10

= 50.7 days

Cost/benefits of cash discount £

Reduction in interest cost

$$£3.395m \times \frac{91.4 - 50.7}{365} \times 10\%$$ 37,857

Reduction in bad debt 50% × 48,000 24,000

Cost of discount £3.395m × 1.5% × 50% (25,463)

_____

Net benefit 36,394

_____

Revised overdraft = (565) + 378 + 38 = (149)

↑ ↑ ↑

Original   Additional funds   Reduction in
Overdraft   received   interest paid

Financial ratios

	Existing	*Revised*
Current ratio	$\dfrac{1,305}{1,115}$	$\dfrac{1,305 - 377}{550 + 149*}$
	= 1.17	= 1.33
Debtor days (from above)	91	51

Debt factoring

Costs	(i)	Commission
	(ii)	Finance charge

Benefits	(i)	Interest cost reduction
	(ii)	Admin saving

Cost/benefits £

Commission £3.395m × 2% × 90% (61,110)

Finance charge
£850,000 × 11% × 90% (84,150)

Reduction in interest cost
£850,000 × 10% × 90% 76,500

Admin savings 65,000

_____

Net cost (3,760)

_____

Financial ratios

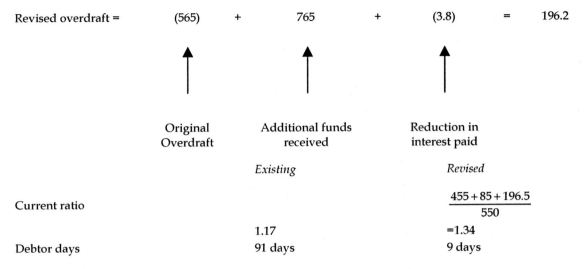

Revised overdraft = (565) + 765 + (3.8) = 196.2

Original Overdraft → (565)

Additional funds received → 765

Reduction in interest paid → (3.8)

	Existing	*Revised*
Current ratio		$\dfrac{455 + 85 + 196.5}{550}$
	1.17	=1.34
Debtor days	91 days	9 days

Ignore secured mortgage option.

Recommendation

The cash discount option generates the higher net benefit. All else being equal this option should be chosen.

The accounting ratios calculated do not indicate a major difference between the options with the exception of debtor days which reduce dramatically when using the factor (not surprisingly).

Answer 37

V plc

(a)

REPORT

To:	**Credit Control Manager**
From:	**The Management Accountant**
Date:	**XX/XX/XX**
Subject:	**New Order**

Net (cost)/Benefit of order

Receipt of payment – expected value

	Cashflow	Probability	
Payment by customer	22,500	0.6	13,500
Received from agency	10,750	0.4	4,300
(22,500 × 0.5) – 500			
			17,800

PV of order

YR	0	1
Inflows	2,500 (deposit)	17,800 (ev of balance)
Material cost	(12,600)	
70% × £3,600 × 5		(5,400)
30% × £3,600 × 5		
	(10,100)	12,400
DF @ 16%	1.000	0.862
	(10,100)	10,689

NPV 589

(b) *Other factors*

(i) The expected value of the cash inflow is simply a weighted average value. It would be more informative to consider the potential upside or downside of the venture. Alternatively further research of the ability of the customer to pay could be undertaken.

(ii) A further consideration may be to arrange alternative payment terms or credit insurance for this transaction to guarantee payment on time.

(iii) Are there alternative uses for the capacity and funds utilised.

(iv) What are the future prospects with this customer; do we expect repeat orders leading us to be willing to accept a measure of risk in return for a potential future return.

(c) *Measuring creditworthiness*

Creditworthiness may be considered by:

♦ Use of a credit rating agency.
♦ Use knowledge via the grapevine from the sales department.
♦ Analyse the financial statements published by the company.
♦ Use bank references to gain underlying assurances of the viability of the business.
♦ Use trade references.
♦ A site visit will often yield a valuable feel for the relative size and stability of the business.

Answer 38

Sprinter plc

(a) Forward contracts are used to eliminate exchange rate exposure. The contract is entered into when the transaction is undertaken in order that cashflow in another currency may be exchanged at a fixed rate determined today. This ensures that for a particular trade we may be certain of the revenue we may receive in sterling terms.

(b) Working capital cycles

		UK (days)		Total (days)	
Debtors	$\dfrac{\text{Debtors}}{\text{Sales}} \times 365$	$\left(\dfrac{1,300}{6,500} \times 365\right)$	73	$\left(\dfrac{3,221}{9,290} \times 365\right)$	127
Stocks					
– raw mats	$\dfrac{\text{RM stock}}{\text{Purchases}} \times 365$	$\left(\dfrac{812.5}{3,900} \times 365\right)$	76	$\left(\dfrac{1,404}{6,720} \times 365\right)$	76

- WIP	$\dfrac{WIP\,stock}{Cost\,of\,sales}\times 365$	$\left(\dfrac{568.75}{5,525}\times 365\right)$	38	$\left(\dfrac{980}{8,130}\times 365\right)$	44
- finished goods	$\dfrac{FG\,stock}{Cost\,of\,sales}\times 365$	$\left(\dfrac{650}{5,525}\times 365\right)$	43	$\left(\dfrac{1,120}{8,130}\times 365\right)$	50

Less

Creditors	$\dfrac{Creditors}{Purchases}\times 365$	$\left(\dfrac{448}{3,900}\times 365\right)$	(42)	$\left(\dfrac{773.3}{6,720}\times 365\right)$	(42)
			188 days		**255 days**

(c)

The working capital cycle will obviously replace the market in which the company is operating. Here we are comparing domestic sales to those overseas. Looking at the cycles in part (b) we see that creditor and raw material periods are relatively similar periods at about 76 days and 42 days respectively. The other areas differ considerably.

WIP period	UK 38 days	Total 44 days

The increase in WIP of about 16% may reflect the additional packaging required for export products. It is also possible that export products are more sophisticated requiring additional time to produce.

Finished goods period	UK 43 days	Total 50 days

The finished goods stock is higher for total sales which may reflect the wider range of products, held in larger amounts, to fulfil the export market.

Debtor period	UK 73 days	Total 127 days

Including the export sales has extended the overall debtor period by 54 days. This may be due to differing credit periods offered and more difficulty with chasing up delinquent stock. A further key reason for the difference is the length of time for delivery to take place together with the exchange of foreign currency.

(d)

The profit impact associated with the longer working capital cycle will amount to the following.

Additional days required for export sales.

Total sales	=	100%
UK sales	=	70%
Export sales	=	30%

WIP

	Days		*Additional funds required*
Total	44	100%	
UK	38	70%	
$\therefore$ Export =	$(44 - 38 \times 0.7) \div 0.3 = 58$ days		
	Additional funding = 20 days		
	$=$ (Total stock – UK stock) $\times \dfrac{20}{58}$		
	$= (980,000 - 568,750) \times \dfrac{20}{58}$		$= £142,000$

Finished goods

	Days	*%*
Total	50	100
UK	43	70

$\therefore$ Export = $\quad$ (50 – 43 $\times$ 0.7) $\div$ 0.3 = 66 days

Additional funding $\quad \Rightarrow$ 66 – 43 = 21 days

$$= (1{,}120{,}000 - 650{,}000) \times \frac{21}{66} \qquad = £150{,}000$$

Debtors

	Days	*%*
Total	127	100
UK	73	70

$\therefore$ Export = $\quad$ (127 – 73 $\times$ 0.7) $\div$ 0.3 = 253 days

Additional funding $\quad \Rightarrow$ 253 – 73 = 180 days

$$= (3{,}221{,}000 - 1{,}300{,}000) \times \frac{180}{253} \qquad = £1{,}367{,}000$$

Total funds required

= 142,000 + 150,000 + 1,367,000	=	£1,659,000
Cost of funds @ 12%	=	£199,080

Answer 39

Delcars

(a)

Days to banking of cash

Days	*Existing*		*New*
	2nd Hand	*Servicing*	*All*
M	$\varnothing$	2	$\varnothing$
Tu	5	1	$\varnothing$
W	4	$\varnothing$	$\varnothing$
Th	3	1	$\varnothing$
F	2	$\varnothing$	$\varnothing$
Sa	1	3	$\varnothing$
Su	-	-	-
Sum	15	7	$\varnothing$
Average ($\div$ 6)	2.5 days	1.17 days	$\varnothing$

Total borrowing required

£

2nd Hand £6.25m $\times \dfrac{2.5}{365}$ 42,808

Servicing £3.75m $\times \dfrac{1.16}{365}$ 12,021

         54,829

Interest saved

£54,829 $\times$ 8.5% = £4,660.

(b)

Advantages of centralisation of a treasury department

(i)   Expertise – only by centralising the role of treasury can an organisation afford to retain specialist staff who deal with treasury on a permanent basis.

(ii)   Economies of scale – the overall investment on treasury may be reduced by the elimination of duplication and taking advantage of size of funds in banking investing or obtaining finance.

(iii)   Portfolio effect – allows for the netting of surplus and deficit balances held within the organisation.

(iv)   Strategic planning – centralisation should lead to a more strategic view of treasury to be taken particularly with regard to funding cash requirements.

(v)   Cash balance – the overall need for cash should fall as a result of the portfolio effect.

(vi)   Cheaper credit facilities – banks will provide a better service to what would be perceived a larger and hence more important client.

Disadvantages of centralisation

(i)   Local managers will be able to take advantage of local financing opportunities.

(ii)   The services provided to the unit will better reflect the need compared to a more centralised approach where the inclination is to offer all parts of the business a uniform 'one size fits all' approach.

(iii)   Delegation of responsibility may improve the control of cost as local managers are more motivated to perform.

(iv)   A centralised service may lead a greater bureaucracy of operation.

ANSWERS TO PILOT PAPER

PILOT PAPER ANSWERS

Answer 40 (1 of Pilot Paper)

Multiple choice questions

40.1 C

Since the investor must be compensated for the increased risk in lending his money for a longer period of time, the normal shape of the yield curve is for longer-term financial assets to offer a higher yield than short-term financial assets.

40.2 D

From tables, $k_e = \dfrac{d_o(1+g)}{P_o} + g$

$= \dfrac{3 \times 1.15}{150} + 15\%$

$= 2.3\% + 15\% = 17.3\%$

40.3 B

$\text{P/E ratio} = \dfrac{\text{Share price}}{\text{Earnings per share}} = \dfrac{290p}{20p} = 14.5$

45.4 D

Where a company already has a wide spread of shareholders, an active market can be assured simply by recategorising the existing shares as publicly quoted shares. This is known as an introduction.

40.5 A

It is the lessor (who owns the asset) who receives the capital allowances.

40.6 C

From tables, $k_e = R_f + (R_m - R_f)\ \beta$

$= 6\% + (11\% - 6\%) \times 1.4$

$= 13\%$

40.7 C

Certificates of deposit are issued by banks and can then be sold (ie negotiated) by the holder in the market. They are therefore **negotiable** instruments.

40.8 C

Capital employed	=	$\dfrac{£760,000}{2.5}$	=	£304,000

∴ Fixed assets = 70% × £304,000 = £212,800

∴ Working capital (ie current assets – current liabilities)

= £304,000 - £212,800

= £91,200

So: CA – CL = £91,200

and $\dfrac{CA}{CL}$ = 1.5, ie CA = 1.5 CL

1.5 CL – CL = £91,200

∴ 0.5 CL = £91,200

∴ CL = £182,400

CA = 1.5 × £182,400 = £273,600

40.9 C

$$EOQ = \sqrt{\dfrac{2C_oD}{C_h}} \quad = \quad \sqrt{\dfrac{2 \times £185 \times 2,500}{£25}}$$

$$= \quad \sqrt{37,000}$$

$$= \quad 192 \text{ units}$$

Each week $\dfrac{2,500}{52}$ = 48 units are required,

so each order of 192 units will last $\dfrac{192}{48}$ = 4 weeks.

40.10 B

BACS is typically used by a business to process the payment of the payroll to each individual employee. The business supplies a tape or disk to BACS which carries out the instructions.

(Note that CHAPS enables banks to make same-day payments between each other, while SWIFT enables international transfers to be made.)

40.11 A

The strong form implies that shares are priced fairly. If an economic slump is predicted, it is possible to predict that share prices will fall.

40.12 C

A higher P/E ratio between comparable companies implies that the company has better prospects.

40.13   D

From tables, spread between lower and upper limits

$$= \quad 3\left[\frac{0.75 \times £20 \times £250,000}{0.00025}\right]^{1/3}$$

$$= \quad 3 \times (1.5 \times 10^{10})^{1/3}$$

$$= \quad 3 \times 2,466.2$$

$$= \quad £7,400$$

Lower limit = £1,000, so upper limit   =   £1,000 + £7,400

                                       =   £8,400

40.14   C

Dividend per share	=	$\dfrac{50p}{2.5}$	=	20p
Dividend yield	=	$\dfrac{\text{Dividend}}{\text{Share price}}$	=	3.2%
∴ Share price	=	$\dfrac{20p}{3.2\%}$	=	625p

40.15   D

New profit and loss account would show:

	£000
Operating profit (100 + 18)	118
Interest (40 + 0.05 × 140)	(47)
	71

So interest cover is now $\dfrac{118}{47}$ =   2.51

40.16   D

9% pa = $\dfrac{9}{12}$ % per month   =   0.75% pm

After 3 years (= 36 months), £1,700 will have grown to:

$$£1,700 \times 1.0075^{36}$$

$$= \quad £1,700 \times 1.3086$$

$$= \quad £2,225$$

40.17 B

Credit insurance is insurance against domestic debts going bad. Export credit insurance is available against overseas debts going bad.

40.18 C

Warrants are worthless once they have expired.

40.19 C

From EOQ formula, optimum amount $\quad = \quad \sqrt{\dfrac{2 \times £20 \times £1.26m}{0.08}}$

$$= \quad \sqrt{6.3 \times 10^8}$$

$$= \quad £25,100$$

40.20 B

Venture capital organisations provide finance for a price. They will offer loan finance and/or equity finance provided that the terms and the price are satisfactory.

Answer 41 (2 of Pilot Paper)

KM plc

(a) The two main aspects of financial management within a business are the treasury function and the financial control function. The treasury is the **external** aspect, concerned with the relationship between the business and those stakeholders outside the business, ie shareholders, providers of loans and taxation authorities. In comparison, financial control is the **internal** aspect, concerned with the relationship between the business and those stakeholders within the business, ie customers, employees and suppliers.

The key responsibility of the treasury department is therefore ensuring sufficient appropriate sources of finance are available for the operations of the business to proceed smoothly. This will include:

♦ advising on the type of capital to raise
♦ arranging short-term borrowing
♦ foreign currency management
♦ banking
♦ collections
♦ investment of surplus funds

It is clear that the treasury will have an impact on each of the levels of management within the business. Strategic management can be advised on the capital structure of the business and on the level of dividends to be paid. Tactical management can be advised on the investment of surplus cash and on the hedging of currency and interest rate risk. Operational management can be advised on cash transmission procedures and banking relationships.

In large businesses, a centralised treasury department is often established at the head office, while financial control is delegated to controllers in each business unit. In this way the treasury can enjoy the economies of scale of a single large operation, while the controllers can benefit from a close face-to-face relationship with their customers and suppliers.

In recent years the skills expected of a treasurer have increased, as the role has become more professionally recognised. Now it is common for the corporate treasurer to be involved in all aspects of capital raising, from liaising with merchant banks and planning capital issues required, to risk management by derivatives, to advising on the taxation implications of possible approaches.

The advantages to KM plc of having separate treasury and financial control departments include the following:

♦ Individuals can specialise in the fields that they are most interested in. As the range of possible capital instruments becomes more diverse, it is no longer possible for a part-time manager with general skills to excel as a corporate treasurer. The role needs full-time dedicated staff in a large business.

♦ The treasury department can be operated as a profit centre (see part (b)) in order to generate additional profits for the business.

♦ The reason why companies fail is that they run out of cash. The existence of a treasury department constantly monitoring this most vital of assets should lessen the risk of failure. A separate treasury can afford the latest computer technologies and software to manage cash resources.

♦ A separate treasury should be able to act quickly to deal with opportunities and threats, rather than the matter languishing in a queue of matters to be dealt with by a general manager.

♦ The treasury will monitor all the units of the business, including the overseas operations. It will therefore offer a fertile training ground for the senior managers of tomorrow. Other areas cannot offer the breadth of experience covering the whole group.

(b) It is possible for the treasury department to be operated as a profit centre rather than a cost centre. This would involve the treasury charging the various business units for its services provided.

The advantages of such an approach are:

♦ the treasurer is motivated to carry out activities that actually add value to the group, which are recognised by the individual units as being of value.

♦ the individual business units will be aware of the value of the services provided to them, so that their reported total operating costs are more realistic.

♦ the treasury department will report a profit or loss, like all other operating departments in the group.

The disadvantages of such an approach are:

♦ additional paperwork and administration time.

♦ the potential for time-wasting arguments between the treasury and unit managers over the pricing of services provided.

♦ treasurers may be unwilling to keep up-to-date with technical reading since this is non-chargeable time.

♦ treasurers may be tempted to take risks, eg by speculating on currencies and interest rates, in a high-risk attempt to generate additional profits. If such activities are not controlled properly, there is the possibility of disastrous losses.

Answer 42 (3 of Pilot Paper)

SF Ltd

REPORT

To: The board of directors

From: External consultant

Date: X-X-20XX

Subject: Cash budget for the year ahead

Introduction

You have asked me to advise on possible actions that you could take to improve the budgeted cashflow for the year ahead. The bank has stated that it is not willing to increase the company's overdraft facility beyond the current £50,000 limit. The cash budget as currently prepared exceeds this limit from August to November, so you should consider the following proposals.

Receipts from debtors

Customers are currently granted an average of two months credit. If it were possible to reduce this period by urging customers to pay sooner, this would ease the cash position. However two months does not seem excessive, and may be the norm for the industry you operate in. Encouraging debtors to pay earlier by offering discounts is possible but is generally an expensive approach.

Another possibility is to factor the debts which would yield immediate cash and could offer savings in sales ledger administration costs, but the factor would charge interest and usually an annual service fee.

Investment

I note that you are budgeting to receive a £10,000 dividend from an investment in June. Perhaps part of this investment could be sold to eliminate the cash shortage. I do not know the current value of the investment, but assuming a typical dividend yield of, say, 4%, the value could be around $\frac{£10,000}{0.04}$ = £250,000. Realising £50,000 from selling part of this investment might therefore be the easiest way to improve the cashflow. However if this is a critical strategic investment that cannot be realised without endangering the company's future strategy, then it should not be sold.

Payments to creditors

The company is already taking 90 days credit, which seems a long period, so it is unlikely to be possible to delay payments still further without endangering a good relationship with suppliers. I note that production is even throughout the year while sales are seasonal. It might be possible to reduce the volume of production in the Spring when sales are low in order to save some cash then.

Payments for fixed assets

These four payments are all for fairly small amounts, so are not critical in the big picture. The progress payment on building extensions is likely to be contractual so cannot be avoided. However if the other payments can be deferred or rescheduled (eg buying the car on hire purchase rather than outright), then some cashflow advantage can be achieved.

Dividend

Whether the £25,000 dividend payment due in April can be reduced or deferred depends on the attitude of the directors and the main shareholders. If they are independently wealthy, they may be happy to forgo this dividend to avoid a cashflow problem for the company. However if they depend on this dividend to fund their personal commitments, it will not be possible to reduce or defer it.

Tax payment

A £30,000 tax payment is due in September. Presumably this is the company's annual corporation tax charge, payable nine months after the balance sheet date. It would be possible to be late in paying this liability, preferably with the consent of the Inland Revenue. An interest charge would be payable, but the interest rate would probably be lower than the rate charged by the bank on overdrafts.

Other possibilities

It is generally advisable for capital expenditure to be financed by long-term sources of finance. The company is planning new capital expenditure, but does not seem to be planning any new issue of capital. The current shareholders may be willing to increase their investment by subscribing for new shares. Alternatively a new shareholder could be introduced, or a long-term loan raised. The profitability of the company is not described in the question, but a tax bill of £30,000 suggests that profits are being earned, which should be attractive to potential investors.

Final points

The budgeted cashflow statement does not contain any interest payments at present, to increase cash balances in hand, or to be charged on overdrafts. Overdraft interest will make the position rather worse than is shown in the current statement.

The cash surplus at the start of the year could be put to more profitable use than leaving it in the bank account. For example it could be transferred into a bank deposit account to earn interest, or could buy gilts or treasury bills that are close to redemption.

Please contact me again if I can be of any further help to you in this or any other matter.

Answer 43 (4 of Pilot Paper)

D plc

(a) (i) Gearing ratio $= \dfrac{\text{Prior charge capital}}{\text{Total capital}}$

Using book values

Gearing ratio $= \dfrac{8m + 1m}{10.65m + 8m} \times 100\%$

$= 48.3\%$

(ii) **Using market values**

The debentures have a market value of 8m × 80%	=	£6.4m
The ordinary shares have a market value of 8m × £1.35	=	£10.8m
The preference shares have a market value of 1m × £0.77	=	£0.77m
Total market value of capital = 6.4 + 10.8 + 0.77	=	£17.97m

Gearing ratio $= \dfrac{6.4m + 0.77m}{17.97m} \times 100\%$

$= 39.9\%$

(b)   **Cost of equity**

$$k_e \quad = \quad \frac{d_0(1+g)}{P_0} + g$$

$$= \quad \frac{10p \times 1.09}{135p} + 9\%$$

$$= \quad 17.1\%$$

Cost of preference shares

$$k_{pref} \quad = \quad \frac{d}{P_0} \quad = \quad \frac{7p}{77p} \quad = \quad 9.1\%$$

Cost of debt

$$k_d \quad = \quad \frac{i(1-t)}{P_0}$$

$$= \quad \frac{9(1-0.3)}{80}$$

$$= \quad 7.9\%$$

$\therefore$ WACC $\quad = \quad \left(\frac{10.8}{17.97} \times 17.1\%\right) + \left(\frac{0.77}{17.97} \times 9.1\%\right) + \left(\frac{6.4}{17.97} \times 7.9\%\right)$

$$= \quad 10.3\% + 0.4\% + 2.8\%$$

$$= \quad 13.5\%$$

(c)   Debentures offer several significant advantages over preference shares as a means of raising finance:

(i)   debenture interest is allowable against tax in the company's annual corporation tax computation, while preference dividends are not allowable against tax. Preference dividends are an appropriation of post-tax profits (like ordinary dividends).

(ii)   debentures can be secured on the company's assets, thus reducing the risk faced by investors, who will therefore be happy with a lower return. Preference shares cannot normally be secured on a company's assets.

(iii)   on a winding-up of the company, debenture holders are repaid in priority to preference shareholders. Again this implies that investors in debentures are exposed to less risk, so will be happy with a lower return.

(iv)   debenture interest must be paid each year, while preference dividends can be passed. Although this might seem a disadvantage, it again means that investors in debentures are exposed to less risk and will accept a lower return.

The effect of (i) to (iv) above is that, to the company, the annual cost of servicing debentures will be lower than the cost of preference shares. For example, the company in the question is paying a cost of capital of 9.1% on its preference shares and only 7.9% on its debentures.

(d)   A merchant bank is likely to be involved before the finance is raised, during the raising of the finance, and after the finance is raised.

Before the finance is raised, the bank will advise on the best source of finance for the sum that is required, for example new equity, preference shares or debentures. Once debentures have been chosen, the precise terms of secured/unsecured debentures, redeemable/irredeemable debentures, the coupon rate and issue price can be decided. It may be appropriate to issue warrants with the debenture as a 'sweetener' for the issue.

When the finance is raised, the bank can be actively involved in marketing the issue to its investor clients. The bank can also advise on legal and regulatory requirements that must be complied with, such as lodging official returns and paying appropriate taxes.

After the finance is raised, the bank can monitor debenture price movements to ensure the price is stable. If the company is worried about interest rate risk exposure, the bank could advise on derivative products to hedge this risk.

The relationship between the company raising the finance and the merchant bank should be close if the raising of the finance is to have the greatest chance of success.

Answer 44 (5 of Pilot Paper)

ABC Ltd

(a)   Factoring organisations will typically offer the following services:

      (i)   advancing of finance, usually at a percentage of debtors invoiced. For example the factor might pay 80% of debts immediately that the goods are invoiced, and charge interest on this loan secured on the debtors.

      (ii)   administration of the sales ledger. The factor could run the whole function of credit checking, sending out invoices, maintaining the ledger and chasing collections.

      (iii)   bad debt insurance. For a fee the factor will insure the company against non-payment of invoices by credit customers.

      (iv)   confidentiality. Historically, factoring was seen as a symptom of financial distress, so the factoring agreement was designed so that customers would not be aware of its existence. This is less necessary today now that factoring is seen as a more legitimate and sound source of finance, especially for smaller companies.

(b)   Annual sales   =   £400,000 × 12   =   £4.8m

The annual net cost of factoring is as follows:

	£
Service fee (2% × £4.8m)	96,000
Interest (75% × £4.8m × 10% × $\frac{40}{365}$)	39,452
Savings (£5,000 × 12)	(60,000)
	75,452

(c)   The company is offering a 2% discount for paying at 10 days rather than 40 days, ie paying 30 days early.

The interest rate over a 30 day period is given by:

        98 × (1 + r)   =   100

        ∴ r   =   2.04%

Over a whole year, there are $\frac{365}{30}$ = 12.17 30-day periods.

So the annualised cost is given by $(1.0204)^{12.17} = 1.2786$

ie, an annualised cost of 27.86%.

(d) The factoring proposal brings in cash immediately that sales are invoiced, rather than having to wait 10 days under the discount proposal. Since the company is suffering cashflow difficulties and is already at its maximum overdraft facility, this is a point significantly in favour of factoring.

Factoring will enable the company to benefit from the factor's expertise in credit control and chasing overdue accounts. However there will be a loss of direct contact between the customer and the company, which could prevent possible sales leads from being exploited.

The annual cost of offering the discount (at 27.86%) seems very high, considerably higher than the cost of a bank overdraft or bank loan. There are some industries in which discounts are an accepted practice, so ABC Ltd would have little choice other than to offer discounts if it operated in such an industry. But this appears not to be the case, since the company has not offered discounts before.

Offering discounts can lead to problems, since some customers will take the discount but still pay late. Is it worth endangering the relationship with the customer to press for the discount amount to be paid? The decision is often taken that it is not worth the bother.

On balance, the factoring option seems more attractive, avoiding the very high cost of offering the discount as currently proposed.

Answer 45 (6 of Pilot Paper)

KB plc

(a) (i)

Current EPS	=	$\dfrac{£1.2m}{6m}$	=	20p
P/E ratio	=	$\dfrac{\text{Share price}}{\text{EPS}}$	=	12
$\therefore$ Share price	=	$12 \times 20p$	=	£2.40

(ii)

Number of shares to issue	=	$\dfrac{£5.04m}{£1.92}$	=	2.625m

We therefore have:

	Shares		Value £m
Current	6m	£2.40	14.4
Rights issue	2.625m	£1.92	5.04
	8.625m		19.44

Theoretical ex-rights price = $\dfrac{£19.44m}{8.625m}$ = 225.4p

In practice the post-rights price might not equal this theoretical ex-rights price for the following reasons:

♦ the general level of share prices might have changed in the period between announcing the terms of the rights and issuing the new shares. For example, a surge in share prices generally would mean that the actual post-rights price would be higher than the 225.4p calculated above.

♦ shareholders may believe that the new investment is of a different risk profile to the company's existing activities. For example, if it is believed that the new investment is more risky, the shares will be marked down.

♦ the increased number of shares and lower share price after the rights issue may make the shares more marketable and therefore more attractive to the market at large. However, the increased number of shares might lead current investors to worry that the future dividend per share might be cut from its existing level.

♦ if the rights issue is a failure, with many shares left in the hands of the underwriters, this will have a depressing effect on share performance for several months, as the underwriters offload their shares whenever there is any indication of positive movement in the share price.

(iii) In a deep-discounted rights issue, the offer price for the new shares available in the rights issue is set well below the current market price for the shares. For example, if the current share price is £5, a rights issue offering new shares at a 20% to 40% discount (ie at any price between £3 and £4) would be described as a deep-discounted rights issue.

Note that UK company law prohibits shares being offered at below their nominal value, so this places a lower limit on the offer price in a rights issue.

The advantage of a deep-discounted rights issue is that there is less chance that the market price of the share will fall below the offer price while the rights are available. Such a fall would mean that the rights issue would fail and the shares would be left with the underwriters, since investors would find it cheaper to buy new shares in the market rather than to take up their rights. In a period of share price volatility, therefore, one would expect to see discounts on rights issues increase.

(b) (i) At any time before conversion of the loan stock, there is likely to be a difference between the cost of buying ordinary shares in the market, and the cost of acquiring ordinary shares by buying the loan stock and converting it into ordinary shares.

Since the loan stock pays interest as well as having the conversion rights, you would expect there normally to be a conversion **premium**, so that it is more expensive to buy the shares via the loan stock than it is to buy the shares direct.

Using the data in the question:

	£
Cost of buying 1 share via loan stock $\dfrac{£100}{35}$	2.86
Cost of buying 1 share direct (from part (a) (i))	2.40
Premium	0.46

The conversion premium is usually stated as a percentage of the current share price ie:

$$\frac{0.46}{2.40} \times 100\% = 19.2\%$$

(ii) The company will have the following advantages of issuing convertible loan stock rather than a rights issue:

♦ Loan stock interest is allowable against tax, whereas ordinary dividends payable are not allowable against tax. The company will therefore pay a lower tax bill if it issues loan stock rather than equity.

♦ The cost of servicing loan stock each year will be lower than the cost of servicing the ordinary shares issued in the rights issue. The facts that the loan stock is convertible, can be secured on the company's assets and is repayable before equity on a winding up, mean that investors will be happy with a lower annual return for holding debentures than equity since the risks are lower.

♦ It is generally cheaper to issue loan stock than conduct a rights issue, since the regulatory requirements are less stringent.

♦ New loan stock will not dilute the existing shareholders' reported earnings per share or proportion of the company controlled.

♦ Issuing loan stock now means that the option of conducting a rights issue in the near future remains a possibility. Companies are unable to carry out rights issues at very frequent intervals.

May 2001 Exam Answers

Answer 46 (Answer 1 of Exam Paper)

46.1   D

The current ratio will decrease as the level of creditors increases, the cash operating cycle will also decrease as more days will be financed by creditors.

46.2   B

The perpetuity is calculated by dividing the amount per annum by the interest rate.

PV of a perpetuity = $\dfrac{£10,000}{10\%}$ = £100,000

In this situation the perpetuity commences in Year 2 and not Year 1 we must discount the value above for one year at 10%.

PV   =   £100,000 × 0.909

     =   £90,909

46.3   B

The suggestion is that there will be an increase in financial risk leading to a higher cost of equity in compensation for that risk.

46.4   D

46.5   C

46.6   C

46.7   D

Working

P	1.01^{12}	=	1.1268	$\Rightarrow$	12.68%
Q	1.02^{6}	=	1.1262	$\Rightarrow$	12.62%

46.8   D

It reduces the level of investment in working capital due to the reduction in the debtor balance as a result of customers paying early.

46.9 A

The suggestion is that no new information is made available at the point at which the dividend is paid, therefore, no change will occur to the price.

When the share goes ex dividend the share price will drop to reflect the loss of that specific dividend to any new purchaser of the share.

46.10 B

All rational investors are risk averse, this means they require a higher level of return to compensate for additional risk.

46.11 B

Inflation rate	=	$\dfrac{1+m}{1+r}$	-1	
Year 1	=	$\dfrac{1.09}{1.04}$	-1	= 4.8%
Year 2	=	$\dfrac{1.10}{1.05}$	-1	= 4.76%
Average	=	$\dfrac{4.80+4.76}{2}$		= 4.78%

46.12 A

	£	
Cost of sales	60,000	
Δ In stock	(2,000)	Decrease
Cost of production (purchases)	58,000	
Δ In creditors	(8,000)	Increase
Payment to suppliers	50,000	

46.13 C

46.14 A

Machine 1

Purchase cost

Year		Cashflow £000's	D.F. @ 10%	PV £000's
0	Investment	(100)	1.000	(100)
5	Residual value	10	0.621	6.21
				(93.79)

Lease cost

Year		£000's	D.F. @ 10%	£000's
0-5	Rentals	(20)	1.000 + 3.791	(95.82)

Decision: Purchase

Machine 2

Purchase cost

Year		Cashflow £000's	D.F. @ 10%	PV £000's
0	Investment	(48)	1.000	(48)

Lease cost

Year		£000's	D.F. @ 10%	£000's
2-6	Rentals	(14.5)	4.355-0.909	(49.97)

Decision: Purchase

46.15   C

46.16   D

Sales

Receipts in February	£000's
(i) Debtors from January	43.65
(ii) Cash sales from February 60 × 1.1	66.00
	109.65

46.17   D

46.18   B

$$P_o = \frac{D_1}{K_e - g}$$

We know:

Po (in 1 years' time)	=	£10	×	1.1		
	=	£11	=	11.00p		
K_e	=	10%				
g	=	5%				

$$P_o = \frac{D_1}{K_e - g}$$

$$\frac{P_o}{D_1} = \frac{1}{K_e - g} \quad \Rightarrow \quad \frac{D_1}{P_o} = K_e - g$$

$$D_1 = (K_e - g) P_o$$

$$= (0.1 - 0.05)1100$$

$$= 55p$$

46.19   B

46.20   A

$$P_o = \frac{D_1}{K_e - g}$$

$$D_1 = D_o(1 + g) = 20p \times 0.98$$

$$= 19.6p$$

$$K_e = 8\%$$

$$g = -2\%$$

$$P_o = \frac{19.6p}{0.08 + 0.02} = 196p$$

Answer 47 (Answer 2 of Exam Paper)

James Williams

Cash budget for 6 months to 30/06/2002

	Jan £000	Feb £000	Mar £000	Apr £000	May £000	June £000
Receipts						
Sales (W1)			20	64.2	113.2	128
Payments						
Variable cost (W2)	56.25	112.5	93.75	84.38	93.75	103.12
Fixed o/h	5	5	5	5	5	5
Fixed assets	150					
Sub total	211.25	117.5	98.75	89.38	98.75	108.12
Net cashflow	(211.25)	(117.5)	(78.75)	(25.18)	14.45	19.88
Balance b/f	250	38.75	(78.75)	(157.5)	(182.68)	(168.23)
Balance c/f	38.75	(78.75)	(157.5)	(182.68)	(168.23)	(148.35)

WORKINGS

(W1)

	Jan	Feb	Mar	Apr	May	June	July
Sales (£000)			100	125	125	150	150
20% current month			20	25	25	30	30
Sub-total			80	100	100	120	120
Bad debts 2%			(1.6)	(2)	(2)	(2.4)	(2.4)
Sub-total			78.4	98	98	117.6	117.6
50% month +1				39.2	49	49	58.8
50% month + 2					39.2	49	49
Add back cash sales			20	25	25	30	30
Total			20	64.2	113.2	128	

(W2)

	Jan	Feb	Mar	Apr	May	June	July
Cost of sales (75%)	112.5	112.5	75	93.75	93.75	112.5	112.5
Wages (50%)	56.25	56.25	37.5	46.88	46.88	56.25	56.25
Materials (50%)		56.25	56.25	37.5	46.87	46.87	56.25
	56.25	112.5	93.75	84.38	93.75	103.12	

MEMORANDUM

To:	**Mr J Williams**
From:	**An Advisor**
Date:	**XX/XX/XX**

Subject: Cash Management and Financing Needs

The company will need additional financing to the cash injection of £250,000 by you. From the cash budget it appears that up to £200,000 of additional funding is necessary on current predictions. It would be prudent to ensure a larger credit line in case of excess funds being required at a later date.

Type of Finance

The additional finance will be borrowed from a financial institution (probably a retail or clearing bank) and will require security. You may borrow in the short-term using an overdraft facility. The key advantage of an overdraft is that only that amount of money which is needed at any point in time will be borrowed; this will minimise the cost of financing.

The use of a bank loan may also be considered. This form of finance is more permanent and does not need to be repaid over the short-term. It is normally prepared for a period of between one and five years.

In your circumstances it appears that with no further investment it will take about a year to repay the amount outstanding (based on May and June values).

Average payback per month

$$= \frac{£14,450 + £19,880}{2 \text{ months}}$$

$$= £17,165.$$

Amount to be repaid (from above) $= £200,000$

Total time $= \dfrac{£200,000}{17,165}$ $= 11.7$ months.

This would suggest that some of the funds required at least should be more permanent. Maybe it would be prudent to finance half by overdraft and half over one year with a term loan.

Improving Working Capital Management

A further way to ensure that funds are sufficient is to reduce the amount of working capital required. This may be attempted in the following ways:

1   *Reduce the level of stocks* - The level of stock is at present £225,000 which appears excessive. It is a major drain on working capital and should be reduced if possible.

2   *Cash discounts* -   We may encourage additional cash sales by offering a discount for cash.

3   *Extend trade credit* - By agreement with suppliers extend the period over which payment may be made.

Answer 48 (Answer 3 of Exam Paper)

Deaton plc

(a)   **Weighted average cost of capital**

Cost of equity

Growth rate $\qquad\qquad 1 + g = \left(\dfrac{d_0}{d_n} \right)^{1/n}$

g   -   growth rate

d_0 -   most recent dividend $\qquad\qquad$ 45p

d_n -   dividend n periods ago $\qquad\qquad$ 35.64p

n   -   number of periods $\qquad\qquad$ 4 years (1997 to 2001)

$1 + g = \left(\dfrac{45}{35.64} \right)^{1/4} = 1.2626^{\,0.25}$ $\qquad\qquad = 1.06 \Rightarrow 6\%$

$K_e = \dfrac{D_0 (1 + g)}{P_0} + g$

$\quad = \dfrac{D_1}{P_0} + g$

D_0 = most recent dividend $\qquad$ 45p
P_0 = current market price (ex dn) $\qquad$ 550 – 45 = 505p
D_n = next dividend $\qquad$ 45p × 1.06 = 47.7p

$K_e = \left(\dfrac{477}{505} + 0.06 \right) \times 100$ $\qquad\qquad = 15.45\%$

Cost of debt

Year		Cashflow	D.F.W. 10%	Present Value
0	Market value	(98)	1.000	(98)
1	Interest	8	0.909	7.27
1	Capital repayment	100	0.909	90.9
2	Tax saving	(2.4)	0.826	(1.98)
				(1.81)

Year		Cashflow	D.F.W. 8%	Present Value
0	Market value	(98)	1.000	(98)
1	Interest	8	0.926	7.4
1	Capital repayment	100	0.926	92.6
2	Tax saving	(2.4)	0.857	(2.1)
				(0.1)

Estimated cost of capital

$$= 8\% + 2\% \times \frac{(0.1)}{(0.1) - (1.81)} = \underline{7.9\%}$$

Weighted average cost of capital

Working	Value	% Age
Equity $(5.5 - 0.45) \times 12m$	£60.6m	83.2%
Debt $\frac{98}{100} \times £12.5m$	£12.25m	16.8%
	£72.85m	100%

WACC

	Cost of Capital	Proportion	%
Equity	15%	83.2%	12.48
Debt	7.9%	16.8%	1.33
WACC			13.81

MEMORANDUM

To: The Chairman   Date: xx-xx-xx

From: The Finance Director

Contents: Cost of capital for Japanese contract

The weighted average cost of capital (WACC) may be used for appraising new investments given the following assumptions:

1   The weighted average cost of capital reflects the long-term cost of capital and the capital structure (gearing) is not expected to change.

2   New investments are financed within the current funds available to the business and do not materially affect the WACC.

3   The cost of capital reflects the marginal cost of capital.

The Japanese contract is not to be financed in proportion to the debt and equity elements of the business, it is to be financed solely by a bank loan. In addition, the investment presents a considerable business risk, probably higher than that of the existing business.

The introduction of additional debt will enhance the level of gearing and hence increase the level of financial risk.

The project is occurring overseas which further enhances the risks associated with the investment, revenues and costs will be generated in terms of Yen which may increase or decrease in proportion to sterling.

Comments

1   Use of the WACC may be appropriate if the investment is marginal and does not materially affect the WACC. In this circumstance, it can be argued that this is not the case.

2   To discount the investment at interest cost is to muddle financing with investment appraisal. The company must generate a return to cover both debt and equity and reflect the level of risk of the project. The level of risk in this project is higher than that currently suffered, this must be reflected by enhancing the discount rate.

3   I agree with your use of the risk premium, by redeeming debt with earnings we would suffer from two problems:

(i)   Gearing will fall and the proportion of equity will rise increasing the weighted average cost of capital.

(ii)   Shareholders may be unhappy with the change in the dividend policy leading to a fall in the share price.

Answer 49 (Answer 4 of Exam Paper)

Stokko

(a)

Product LXX

Demand (d)	14,400 units
Transport charge (Co)	£500/delivery
Annual holding (Ch)	£400 × 25% = £10/unit/annum

$$Q = \sqrt{\frac{2\,Cod}{Ch}} \quad = \sqrt{\frac{2 \times 500 \times 14,400}{10}}$$

$$= 1,200 \text{ units}$$

Product GYY

As above but demand is 3,600 units.

$$Q = \sqrt{\frac{2\,Cod}{Ch}} \quad = \sqrt{\frac{2 \times 500 \times 3,600}{10}}$$

$$= 600 \text{ units}$$

The difference in the order quantities reflects the lower demand for the year for product GYY. The demand is one quarter of the other product (LXX) and the order quantity is the root of this at half the order quantity of LXX.

(b)   *Level of stock*

	Product	
	LXX	GYY
Demand (units)	14,400	3,600
Price	£40	£40
Cost of sales	£576,000	£144,000
or stocks (¼) (in value)	£144,000	£36,000
(in units)	3,600 units	900 units
Average stock using EOQ	600 units	300 units

The average level of stock will be considerably higher than the level of stock using the EOQ. The methodology in this instance is far simpler than that using the EOQ and requires less assumptions regarding certainty of orders and constant usage that underpin the EOQ.

(c)

(annual demand = 3,600 units)

	Order quantity		
	499	*600*	*720*
Average stock	249.5	300	360
Number of orders pa	7.21	6	5
	£	£	£
Stockholding cost (10.025:10:9.975)	2,501.24	3,000	3,591
Ordering cost (£500)	3,605	3,000	2,500
Purchase cost (40.1:40:39.9)	144,360	144,000	143,640
	150,466.24	150,000	149,731

Optimal order quantity = 720 units.

Answer 50 (Answer 5 of Exam Paper)

Rump

(a)   *Option 1* - Equity (2 for 5 rights issue)

$$\text{Offer price} = \frac{\text{Finance required}}{\text{Number of rights shares}}$$

$$= \frac{£24,000,000}{4,000,000*} = £6/\text{share}$$

*(10,000,000 existing shares $\times \frac{2}{5}$ = 4,000,000)

$$\text{Theoretical ex-rights price} = \frac{£6.60* \times 10,000,000 + £6 \times 4,000,000}{14,000,000}$$

$$= £6.43/\text{share}$$

(b)   *Option 2 – Debt Issue*

Value of shares post issue

	£000
Funds available	9,000
Less interest	(1,800)
£24m × 7.5%	
Dividends	7,200
Shares in issue	10,000
Dividend per share	72p
Market value of a share	$\dfrac{72p}{10\%}$
	£7.20

(c)

To: The Directors

From: An Accountant

Date: XX/XX/XX

Subject: Raising new finance

_____

(i)   When raising such a large amount (in proportion) of finance the impact on existing shareholders will be substantial. It is vital to ensure that such financing will not adversely impact the operational aspects of the business. There are two main considerations.

   (a)   Risk

   The level of operating risk will be determined by the level of fixed costs invested in. If this level changed significantly, this would change the return required by shareholders. The higher the risk, the higher the return required by shareholders.

   A further aspect of risk – financial risk – must be considered. Financial risk considers the level of gearing (debt). A company with no debt has no financial gearing since in the event of low earnings it would be possible to defer or stop dividend payouts. Interest on debt needs to be financed regardless of the profitability of the business.

   (b)   Cost

   The cost of financing must also be a consideration. Debt will normally be cheaper than equity financing. This is because of two factors. Firstly debt is tax efficient because it is paid as an appropriation of profit after tax.

   Secondly debt is less risky to the investor because it offers a fixed return and security in relation to liquidation of the company.

   Other considerations include the level of restrictive covenant associated with the debt financing. Debt finance may incur significant issue costs, equity finance issue costs will be substantial.

(ii)   Equity issues

   Placing. Handled through an issuing house, normally a merchant bank, who purchases the shares and sells or places the shares with selected, probably institutional, investors. Issue costs will be minimised due to the lack of advertising and promotion needed. The key potential problem is that the shares may be concentrated in relatively few hands passing a high degree of control to institutional investors.

Offer for sale. The issuing house sells the shares to the public either via a prospectus or by tender. The issuing house would underwrite the issue. The cost of the issue would be substantial due to the underwriting and advertising costs however the spread of shareholders will be wider.

Public offer for subscription. An offer made directly by the company to the public. A prospectus is issued offering shares at a fixed price. Issuing costs will be substantial. It only differs from an offer for sale insomuch as the shares are not sold in the interim to the issuing house.

The accountant.

Answer 51 (Answer 6 of Exam Paper)

Imlico

(a) $$r = R_f + (R_m - R_f)\,\beta$$

Aztaz $\quad r = 5\% + (15\% - 5\%) \times 0.7 = 12\%$

Borran $\quad r = 5\% + (15\% - 5\%) \times 1.4 = 19\%$

(b) Imlico

$$17\% = 5\% + (15\% - 5\%) \times \beta$$

$$\beta = 1.2$$

(c) **MEMORANDUM**

To: The Chairman	Date:	xx-xx-xx

From: The Finance Director

Contents:	(i)	CAPM Limitations
	(ii)	Share Price Fluctuations

CAPM

A model that adopts Portfolio Theory and separates risk into two elements, systematic and unsystematic. Unsystematic risk is specific to individual investments and is not suffered if a portfolio is diversified sufficiently.

Systematic risk is the underlying risk associated with the market and cannot be diversified away. Systematic risk is the only risk that need be borne by the investor.

The market risk may be incorporated with a risk-free investment such as government debt. The mix of risk-free to market portfolio investments gives what is called the capital market line, a straight line that indicates the pay-off between risk and return.

Individual investments may be more or less risky than the market as a whole. The market has a beta value of 1.0. An investment with a higher beta value would rise or fall more than the market in proportion to the beta value.

Limitations of CAPM

1   CAPM is a single period model which cannot easily be modified to incorporate changes over time.

2   Transaction costs of investments are not considered.

3   Betas are calculated on out of date data which may not reflect current conditions.

4   The market return and risk-free return change over time.

5   CAPM assumes an efficient market.

Share Price Fluctuations

The share price has appeared to have reacted counter-intuitively to the information published. The company has made a loss and the share price has then risen.

An explanation for this could be that the loss would already have discounted (included) in the share price before the event. Share prices are less concerned with the past and more concerned with the future expectations of performance. As the loss has occurred the market may expect for an improvement in performance.

November 2001 Exam Answers

Answer 52 (Answer 1 of Exam Paper)

52.1 C

52.2 B

This is the most likely answer, although special terms may be attached to preference shares. Normally warrants (effectively an option to buy shares) will have no value if a company does badly and preference shares (being a form of equity) will rank after unsecured loans.

52.3 A

52.4 C

Theoretical ex-rights price $2.8 $\quad = \dfrac{10m \times \$3 + x}{12.5m}$

$\$35m = \$30m + x$

$x = \$5m$

52.5 A

It is the only value which will increase to redemption (the gross redemption yield being greater than the flat or coupon yield).

52.6 A

52.7 C

Ke	$= Rf + (Rm - Rf)\ \beta$
15.6%	$= 6\% + (x - 6\%)\ 1.2$
9.6%	$= (x - 6\%)\ 1.2\ (-6\%)$
8%	$= (x - 6\%)\ (\div 1.2)$
x	$= 14\%$

52.8 B

52.9 A $\quad 100 \times 1.1^{-10} = 39.55$ or $100 \times 0.396 = 39.6$

52.10 D

52.11 B $100,000 \times 0.857 \div 0.583$

52.12 A

52.13 D (say) current assets = £15m

current liabilities = £10m

new ratio = $\dfrac{15-3}{10-3} = \dfrac{12}{7} = 1.71$

by observation an increase of less than 30%.

52.14 D

Total cost of stock bought will be credited to stock account on sale, therefore stock is unchanged. No change in cash.

52.15 D

52.16 B

52.17 B

52.18 C

Stock period	$^6/_{28.8}$	$\times 365 =$	76
Debtor period	$^8/_{36}$	$\times 365 =$	81
Less: Creditor period	$^3/_{28.8}$	$\times 3.65 =$	(38)
			119

52.19 A $Q = \sqrt{\dfrac{2Cod}{Ch}}$

$= \sqrt{\dfrac{2 \times 10 \times 36,000}{2}} = 600$ units/order

No of orders pa $= \dfrac{36,000 \text{ units}}{600 \text{ units / order}} = 60$ orders

---

52.20 C

Fixed assets are not part of working capital. Cash received from sale will increase cash which is part of working capital.

Answer 53 (Answer 2 of Exam Paper)

XYZ plc

(a)   After tax cost of debt

YR		£	Discount Factors @ 6%	Discount Factors @ 4%	Present Values @ 6%	Present Values @ 4%
0	Issue value	90	1.000	1.000	90	90
1 – 10	Coupon $(6 \times (1 - 0.3))$	(4.2)	7.36	8.111	(30.91)	(34.07)
10	Redemption value	(100)	0.558	0.676	(55.8)	(67.6)
					3.29	(11.67)

$$\text{IRR} = 4 + (6 - 4) \times \left(\frac{11.67}{11.67 + 3.29} \right)$$

$$= 5.56\%$$

(b)   It is important to make a distinction between the investment decision and the financing decision: the investment decision being whether or not to make the investment, the financing decision being how that investment should be financed.

The investment decision should be based on the company's own cost of capital, normally the weighted average cost of capital. If the investment has a different risk profit to that of the company this should be factored into the rate used.

The use of the after tax cost debt is appropriate as a measure of the financing decision.

(c)

MEMORANDUM

To:	The Directors	Date:	XX/XX/XX
From:	The Accountant		
Subject:	Factors in a financing decision		

(1)   Cost

The primary consideration when financing an investment will always be the cost of the financing. In most circumstances the lowest cost option in terms of interest or other charges will be chosen.

(2)   Term

The length of the funding will often depend on the ability of the company to finance the investment. Long-term debt is more costly due to liquidity preference. However it will take higher repayments of capital each month over a shorter term.

(3)   Security

The level of security required tends to increase with the term. The company will attempt to have as little security attached to each debt instrument.

(4)   Covenants or restrictions

With longer-term borrowing it is quite normal for further restrictions on say dividends or financial ratios to be applied to the company being financed. With more asset specific financing this form of restriction is unlikely to occur.

Types of finance suggested

(1)   Issue of debt

A long-term source of finance general to the business as a whole. No covenants are required however the debt is secured against both specific and general assets.

(2)   Long-term lease

A lease over the long-term is very inflexible and would not be easily cancelled once undertaken without substantial penalty. The key advantages of the long-term lease would be possible tax advantages and off balance sheet financing.

(3)   Short-term lease

A flexible lease agreement probably considerably cheaper in overall terms than the other forms of financing. Downside of the short-term lease being the substantial payments to be made compared to the longer term sources.

Answer 54 (Answer 3 of Exam Paper)

OVR Ltd

(a)

	30/09/01	30/09/00
Stock Turnover		
$\dfrac{\text{Year End Stock}}{\text{Cost of Sales}} \times 365$	$\dfrac{2,400}{6,000} \times 365$	$\dfrac{1,600}{4,000} \times 365$
	= 146 days	= 146 days
Debtor Turnover		
$\dfrac{\text{Debtors}}{\text{Sales}} \times 365$	$\dfrac{3,300}{12,000} \times 365$	$\dfrac{2,200}{8,000}$
	= 100 days	= 100 days
Creditor Turnover		
$\dfrac{\text{Creditors}}{\text{Purchases}} \times 365$	$\dfrac{1,000}{6,800 \times 50\%} \times 365$	$\dfrac{500}{4,400 \times 50\%} \times 365$
	= 107 days	= 83 days

(Working

Purchase = cost of sales + closing stock – opening stock.

50% of this figure is taken because wages are not usually subject to credit.)

Comments

Stock turnover

The level of stock would appear excessive except that the question already states that this is company policy. The level of stock is constant in relation to year end sales. The analysis may be improved by the use of average stock values rather than year end measures and the stock were better analysed into raw materials, work in progress and finished goods. A final concern is that the stock level in September is unlikely to be representative of the stock levels for other months.

Debtor turnover

The level of debtors is constant in relation to sales. At present customers are taking just over three months to pay. The debtor turnover does not reflect the manner of payment, we are told that instalment credit is offered suggesting that part of the credit is outstanding for a longer period than this. This period appears excessive but is suggested to be short for the type of industry which normally takes twice the period. Offering extended credit is likely to increase the overdraft above that currently negotiated with the bank.

Creditor turnover

Creditor turnover has increased appreciably during the year suggesting either that the company has negotiated extended credit terms or more likely that it will have difficulty paying over existing credit terms. The importance of this analysis is that the company is having difficult paying its bills and has extended its credit line (overdraft included) to a maximum. These are classic symptoms of 'overtrading' and should be acted on immediately to avoid insolvency. The measure of creditors turnover uses purchases as the numerator at 50% of cost of sales.

(b)

MEMORANDUM

To: The Board   Date: XX/XX/XX

From: The Accountant

Subject: Alternative working capital measures

To manage working capital more effectively we may use:

(i)   Working capital cycle
(ii)   Economic order quantity
(iii)   Miller-Orr Model
(iv)   Baumol Model

(i)   Working Capital (Operating) Cycle

Calculated by taking the creditor period from the sum of the debtor period and stock period. An important overall measure of working capital that identifies the period of time taken for funds to circulate in the business. All these being equal the control of the cycle should control the level of investment of working capital. This measure does not take into account level of activity. However an increase in sales would also increase the level of working capital required if the operating cycle were constant.

(ii)   Economic order quantity

A measure of stock that minimises the cost of stock (holding and ordering) by placing an order for a specific number of units of material. This is calculated by a statistical formula and gives an optimal value that should always be ordered. Its shortcomings are that it requires assumptions to be made regarding certainty of volumes and costs which do not necessarily hold true in practice. The formula used is:

$$Q = \sqrt{\frac{2C_o d}{C_h}}$$

Q   – Economic order quantity

Co   – Cost per order

Ch   – Cost of holding one unit per annum

d   – Annual demand

(iii)   *Miller-Orr Model*

A model of cash management that attempts to control cash at minimum cost by allowing the cash balance to fluctuate within a predetermined range. If the balance remains in this range then no action need be taken minimising the level of management intervention. If the upper limit is reached too much cash is held and a predetermined amount is invested in short-term securities. If too little cash is held and the lower limit breached then an amount of short-term securities is encashed. A statistical formula is used to determine the spread between the upper and lower limits.

(iv)   *Baumol Model*

The application of the EOQ model for use in cash management. An amount of cash is determined that is to be encashed each time to minimise the cost of financing cash.

Answer 55 (Answer 4 of Exam Paper)

AEF plc

(a)

(i)   Price per share

$$Po = \frac{Do(1+g)}{Ke-g}$$

$$g = 4\%$$

$$Do = \frac{3m}{2m} = £1.5$$

$$Ke = 10\%$$

$$P = \frac{£1.5 \times 1.04}{1.1-1.04} = £26$$

(ii)   Earnings per share

$$\frac{£12m}{2m} = £6 \text{ per share}$$

(iii)   Dividend cover

$$\frac{£12m}{£3m} = 4 \text{ times.}$$

(iv)   Price earnings ratio

$$= \frac{Pr\,ice}{Earnings} = \frac{£26m}{£6} = 4.33$$

(v)   Gearing

$$\frac{Debt}{Equity} = \frac{£70m}{2m \times £26m} \times 100 = 135\%$$

(b)

MEMORANDUM

To: The Directors   Date: XX/XX/XX

From: The Accountant

Subject: Financial Impact of New Project

---

1   The value of the company

Existing share value = £26/share.

Revised share value =

$$Po = \frac{Do(1+g)}{Ke-g}$$

g = 7%

Ke = 12%

Do = £1.5/share

$$Po = \frac{£1.5 \times 1.07}{1.12-1.07} = £32.1/share$$

2   Risk profile of the company

Existing gearing = 135%

Revised gearing

Total shares = 2m + $\frac{1}{4} \times 2m$ = 2.5m

$$\frac{Debt}{Equity} = \frac{£70m}{2.5m \times £32.1} \times 100 = 87\%$$

3   Earnings per share of the company

Existing EPS = £6/share

Revised EPS = $\frac{£12m}{2.5m}$ = £4.8/share

Comment

The value of the company is expected to rise as a result of the investment. This is due to the increase in the required return being outweighed by the increase in dividends. If the growth rate can be maintained at 7% as suggested, then the value of each share will increase from £26 to £32.1 consequently the overall value of the company will increase due to both an increase due to the number of shares in issue and the value of each share.

The risk profile of the company will fall in terms of gearing as the level of gearing falls from 135% to 87%. Financial risk has therefore fallen reducing the overall risk of the business. Taking on an additional project of such size in relation to the existing business and of a high risk nature will increase the overall riskiness of the company. This is reflected by the increase in required return of the shareholder from 10% to 12%.

Earnings per share has fallen as a result of the same level of earnings spread over more shares. This should be a temporary phenomenon which will change and improve as earnings from the new project start arising. Although investors may consider the earnings per share in their evaluation of a project, shareholders base their valuation of a share on future earnings potential rather than past earnings.

Answer 56 (Answer 5 of Exam Paper)

CF Ltd

(a)

	January $000	February $000	March $000	April $000	May $000
Receipts					
Sales	ø	9.36	28.44	40.32	66.24
Payments					
Purchases	16.8	25.2	33.6	67.2	67.2
Fixed assets	250.0				
Rent	6.0			6.0	
Wages	4.0	4.0	4.0	4.0	4.0
Overheads - current	3.0	3.0	3.0	3.0	3.0
- month +1		3.0	3.0	3.0	3.0
Sub-total	279.8	35.20	43.60	83.20	77.20
Net cash flow	(279.80)	(25.84)	(15.16)	(42.88)	(10.96)
Balance b/d	200.00	(79.80)	(105.64)	(120.80)	(163.68)
Balance c/d	(79.80)	(105.64)	(120.80)	(163.68)	(174.64)

	Dec	Jan	Feb	Mar	Apr	May	Jun
Sales (£000)		24	36	48	96	96	96
Receipts							
40% month + 1 (97.5%)			9.36	14.04	18.72	37.44	37.44
60% month + 2				14.4	21.6	28.8	57.6
		ø	9.36	28.44	40.32	66.24	95.04
Sales units (000)		2.4	3.6	4.8	9.6	9.6	9.6
Purchases– month –1 (×7)	16.8	25.2	33.6	67.2	67.2	67.2	
Payment month +1		16.8	25.2	33.6	67.2	67.2	67.2

Fixed assets

(b)

MEMORANDUM

To: Mr and Mrs Topper   Date: XX/XX/XX

From: The Accountant

Subject: Bank Financing

When borrowing funds from the bank you must be aware of the transaction from the perspective of the bank in order that we can best address them.

Screening of applicants

The key concern for banks when offering funds is the ability and likelihood of the customer to repay the amount borrowed. They screen the application in a number of different ways to ensure as far as possible that the debt is repaid. They include:

1   Previous trading record – normally a bank is only willing to lend to a company with at least three years' trading or more.

2   Future earnings potential – the bank will consider the business plan in relation to the repayments required on the loan.

3   Security – the bank will wish to secure the borrowing against good quality fixed assets either owned by the company or through personal guarantees from the owners (often secured against their property).

4   Individuals – you would also be scrutinised to establish your own personal creditworthiness particularly in relation to county court judgements (CCJs).

The amount offered to you and the type of finance will depend on the needs of the business. You only wish to borrow sufficient for your needs thereby minimising the costs associated with financing the business.

Looking at the cash budget it appears that the business is expected to generate cash overall and as such the need for funding is temporary. Temporary funding may be offered in the form of an overdraft facility.

The funding will be used to finance acquisition of fixed assets and as such it may be safer to contemplate borrowing some of the funds over a longer period of time – the medium term. These sources of finance may be general such as a bank loan or provided via the bank's finance house in an asset specific manner such as hire purchase or leasing.

Answer 57 (Answer 6 of Exam Paper)

DF Ltd

(a)   Annual equivalent rate of interest = $\left(\dfrac{100}{97}\right)^{\frac{365}{80}}$ = 1.149

$\Rightarrow$ 14.9%

Factors to be considered:

1   The cash position of the business – a business with a desperate need for cash as DF Ltd would consider using the discount even if the cost is relatively high.

2   The availability of other cheaper sources of finance – it is possible that extending the overdraft is not possible.

(b)

REPORT

To: The Wongs   Date: XX/XX/XX

From: Your Accountant

Re: Financing Current Assets

When considering funding current assets the key concerns will be cost, term and flexibility.

1   Bank loan – a medium term source of finance that may be used to provide the permanent or underlying finance invested in current assets. It is normally provided over a period of three to five years and is not flexible. The cost of the loan is similar to that of an overdraft with perhaps a small premium. Some measure of security will be required by the bank and the interest rate should be around 3% to 6% over base rates depending on the level of security and size of the business.

2   Overdraft – the traditional funding medium for current assets. The overdraft is theoretically repayable on demand but in practice they are normally agreed up to 18 months into the future. The key advantages of the overdraft are its flexibility where only the amount needed is borrowed and its relatively low cost. Part of the funding requirement is likely to be in this form.

Debt factoring

More than just a financing tool, debt factoring is where the company gives up its own credit control function and instead allows its debt to be collected by the factor. The factors are owned by the high street banks and offer financing (typically 80% of the debts outstanding) and credit protection services. Debt factoring offers a source of finance in addition to those offered above at a cost slightly higher than the bank overdraft. Drawbacks of debt factoring include the loss of control of debtor collection and a loss of reputation, factoring being associated with failing companies.

Invoice discounting

A single or a selected few invoices are used as security against which funds may be borrowed. Its key advantage over factoring is that no-one need know and hence the reputation of the company will not suffer.

May 2002 Exam Answers

Answer 58 (Answer 1 of Exam Paper)

> **Tutorial note:**
>
> **Required** - Simply tick-a-box answers required.
>
> **Not required** - No need to explain your answers, although some explanation is provided here to help you understand the answers.

1.1 A value for money audit is 'an investigation into whether proper arrangements have been made for securing economy, efficiency and effectiveness in the use of resources'. (CIMA)

- ♦ Earnings are profits, usually, referring to Earnings per Share.

- ♦ Equity is a claim to ownership of an asset (or assets), usually referring to the owners' stake in a firm ie net assets.

- ♦ Evaluation is any exercise that analyses past performance or information connected with a decision about future use of resources.

Hence D is correct

1.2 A major benefit of a quotation is the ability of the owners to trade their holdings on a wider market.

- ♦ A condition of quotation is *greater* disclosure of information.

- ♦ After quotation, the firm may *choose* to pay higher dividends, and there may well be pressure to do so from institutional shareholders. However, there is no *requirement* to do so.

- ♦ A plc is any firm whose shares can be publicly traded without the permission of the directors. It need not be quoted on a 'major stock market'.

Hence C is correct

1.3 P/E ratios differ for a variety of reasons, especially the perceived growth prospects of the firm, and its degree of risk. In an efficient market, share prices respond to the arrival of new information. If the content of the financial statements carries new information, then the share price will respond. However, many firms leak out key information about their accounts that analysts incorporate into the ruling share price. Thus, the share price **might** move on publication of the financial statements.

Hence D is correct

1.4 $1,000 accumulates over 10 years to the following Terminal Value (TV) or Future Value (FV):

$$\text{TV} = \$1,000 \times (1.1)^8 \times (1.05)^2 = \$2,363$$

Hence B is correct

1.5   Dividend cover is calculated as Earnings Per Share divided by net dividend per share.

It 'indicates the number of times the profits available to the equity shareholders cover the actual net dividends payable for the period'. (CIMA)

- ◆   Answer (a) is thus the inverse of dividend cover and indicates the payout ratio.

- ◆   Dividend per share divided by retained profit per share (b) simply measures the relative size of these two magnitudes.

- ◆   Answer (d) is just the inverse of the figure in answer (c).

Hence B is correct

1.6   The theoretical ex-rights price is given by:

$$\frac{(\text{Value of holding before issue}) + (\text{Sum required to exercise the right})}{\text{Number of shares held post - issue}}$$

$$= \frac{(3\,\text{shares} \times \$4\,\text{share price}) + (2\,\text{new shares} \times \text{exercise price of } \$2)}{3 + 2}$$

= [\$12 + \$4]/5 = \$16/5 = \$3.20 per share.

Hence D is correct

1.7   The PV of the lease rentals is the discounted value of a series of five \$10,000 payments beginning now.

PV   = \$10,000 + (\$10,000 × 4 year annuity factor @ 10%)

= \$10,000 (1 + 3.17) = (\$10,000 × 4.17) = \$41,700.

Hence D is correct

1.8   The cashier is removing a given sum every week and replacing an equivalent sum in each succeeding week, resulting in a permanent shortfall of the amount removed in week 1. This is known as 'teeming and lading' (or 'lapping' in the USA).

The OUP *Dictionary of Business* defines this as:

'…… the fraudulent practice of concealing a shortage of cash by delaying recording of cash receipts …. essentially, the cashier conceals the theft of cash received from the first customer by recording the cash received from the second customer as attributable to the first, and so on with subsequent customers. The cashier hopes to be in a position to replace the cash before the dishonesty is discovered'.

This practice involves no fraudulent payments as such, as in the case of paying a bogus supplier for non-existent deliveries of goods, and although cash is removed, there is no substitute entry in the books – it is simply a case of permanent delay in the recording receipts.

Advance fee fraud is where a bogus lender requires an up-front 'arrangement fee' 'to cover expenses' before (not!) advancing the loan principal. Commonly perpetrated by means of an unsolicited, faxed communication.

Hence A is correct

1.9 In the Gordon Growth Model, the annual rate of earnings and dividend growth is found by multiplying the proportion of earnings reinvested (b) by the rate of return on the projects financed by reinvested earnings (R).

Here $(b \times R) = (70\% \times 15\%) = 10.5\%$.

Hence C is correct

1.10 The risk of a portfolio can be reduced by adding new components so long as the returns have a correlation of less than +1. Risk-averters are prepared to tolerate risk so long as they are suitably compensated by an acceptable increase in expected return.

Hence A is correct

1.11 Normally the term structure of interest rates is upward sloping as the time to maturity of the bond lengthens, mainly because people prefer liquidity now and because liquidity risk increases with time. An 'inverse yield curve' contradicts this normal relationship, and is downward sloping.

Hence B is correct

1.12 Debt factors undertake all the services listed apart from actually taking customers' orders and invoicing. This remains part of the sales function of the client firm.

Hence A is correct

1.13 Under inflationary conditions, rational investors demand a higher nominal rate of interest to compensate for erosion of the purchasing power of the nominal sums they lend. In most overdraft arrangements, the interest charged is independent of the sum borrowed. The bank specifies an upper limit to the amount of the client's permitted borrowing.

Hence C is correct

1.14 Due to the discount, the fall in trade creditors (the full amount invoiced) is more than the increase in the overdraft. The firm borrows, say, $95 in order to pay down a debt of $100. Taking working capital to mean net working capital, this will increase – there is a net fall in current liabilities ($5) and no change in current assets. Thus, the current ratio will also increase.

Hence D is correct

1.15 Interest rates affect the holding costs of stock which appear in the denominator of the EOQ formula so a rise in interest rates will increase holding costs and lower the EOQ. Sales appear in the numerator of the expression, so a higher sales volume results in a larger EOQ.

Hence C is correct.

1.16 The optimal amount to be transferred is given by the formula:

$$\sqrt{\frac{[2 \times \text{switching cost} \times \text{annual demand}]}{\text{interest rate pa}}}$$

$$= \sqrt{[2 \times \$30 \times (12 \times \$20{,}000)]/0.05}$$

$$= \sqrt{[14.4\text{m}]/0.05} = \$16,971, \text{ or } \$17,000 \text{ to the nearest } \$100$$

Hence D is correct

1.17   If fixed assets are sold on credit, this increases (non-trade) debtors.

♦   Receipt of the full amount invoiced simply replaces one current asset (debtors) with another (cash) – no net change occurs.

♦   Payment of a creditor simply lowers current assets and increases current liabilities by the same amount – no net change occurs.

♦   Purchase of stock increases both current assets (stocks) and current liabilities (trade creditors) by the same amount – no net change occurs.

Hence B is correct

1.18   Writing off a bad debt is a book entry and will not affect cash or overdraft balances.

♦   A direct debit is paid direct from the current account so it would increase an overdraft.

♦   If the investment is made by writing a cheque, this will increase an overdraft (and also increase current assets to the same extent).

♦   Bank charges are simply added on to the amount already outstanding.

Hence B is correct

1.19   Expected cash receipts in May are:

(May cash sales of $20,000 plus 2%) + (97% of April credit sales)

$$= (\$20,000 \times 1.02 \times 40\%) + (0.97 \times \$20,000 \times 60\%)$$

$$= (\$8,160 + \$11,640) = \$19,800$$

Hence C is correct

1.20   The current ratio is all current assets including stocks divided by current liabilities, while the acid test is the current asset figure *less stocks* divided by current liabilities. These can only be equal if a firm carries no stock.

Hence B is correct

Answer 59 (Answer 2 of Exam Paper)

DB plc

Tutorial note:	
Required	- A straightforward question, testing calculation of gearing ratios, and knowledge of forms of long-term finance. Another chance to calculate a TERP!
Not required	- Analysis of the relevant theory.

Requirement (a)

(i) At book values:

Debt/Equity = ($150m/$120m) = 125%

(*Examination tip* – remember that reserves form part of equity!)

(*Examination tip* – also the answer could be incomplete as there may be short-term debt lurking in the current liabilities component of net current assets. Some observers also include the whole of current liabilities as part of 'debt'. Examiners like a word or two of such qualification).

(ii) At market values:

Value of debt = [($90/$100) × $150m] = $135m

Value of equity = 100m shares of stock × share price

= (100m × $4) = $400m

Hence, debt/equity = ($135m/$400m) = 33.75%

(*Examination tip* – do not double count reserves ie a common mistake is to value equity at market prices, then add the reserves figure).

Requirement (b)

Weaknesses

Book values

The balance sheet values can be misleading because:

♦ The balance sheet is only valid at a particular point in time and may be well out of date when inspected.

♦ Fixed assets may not have been recently revalued, if ever, and, especially in the case of property assets, may understate market values.

♦ Many assets are excluded from the balance sheet eg key personnel and various intangibles.

♦ Important liabilities eg warranty obligations, debts of subsidiary firms, may not appear on the balance sheet.

♦ The amounts of R&D capitalised (75% of total fixed assets) may overstate the market value of this expenditure.

(*Examination tip* – this item could occupy a whole exam question, so do not go overboard with points – the whole of section (b) only carries 6 marks).

Market value

♦ Subject to everyday volatility in share prices, often driven by 'external' factors which affect all share prices.

♦ Affected by the liquidity of the market in the firm's stock.

♦ To be valid, it requires an efficient market in the firm's stock ie shares 'correctly' priced.

♦ Market value of debt may understate the true liability to repay principal.

♦ Falling confidence in the firm leads to falling loan stock values which may lower the gearing ratio, making the firm look safer than it really is (although equity values will also fall).

(ii)   Benefits

Book value

- Has the virtue of prudence – asset values tend to fall in distress situations.

- In consequence, using market values for equity may artificially downgrade the gearing ratio, and lull management into a false sense of security.

- Restrictive covenants are usually based on book values.

Market value

- By definition, more up to date, therefore capturing the market's assessment of the firm's prospects. Especially relevant where share price is falling – gearing at book value may not change, but the market value measures will increase.

- Cross section comparisons of firms may be more meaningful.

(*Examination tip* – try to give a modicum of explanation. Mere bullet points would probably only gain half a mark per valid point.)

Requirement (c)

Proceeds of rights issue   = issue price × number of shares

$$= (\$2.50 \times 50m) = \$125m$$

(*Examination tip* – usually there are issue costs to net against the gross proceeds, mention of this may gain credit).

Theoretical ex-rights price $= \dfrac{\text{Cost of one new share} + \text{value of existing holding}}{\text{Number of existing shares} + 1}$

$$= \frac{\$2.50 + (2 \times \$4)}{3} = \$10.5/3 = \$3.50$$

Theoretical ex-rights value of equity = TERP × new number of shares = $3.5 × (100m + 50m) = $525m.

(*Examination tip* – the key word here is 'theoretical' – the actual share price will depend on the uses to which the firm plans to put the proceeds. An alternative approach would be to add the proceeds of the rights issue to current market value: £125m + £400m = £525m.)

Book value of debt after the rights issue = ($150m nominal less $125 nominal value) = $25m.

Assuming an unchanged market to book discount of 10%,

Market value of debt = (90% × $25m) = $22.5m.

Hence, gearing at market value = ($22.5m/$525m) = 4.3%.

(If the firm's credit rating improves, the debt may increase in market value, thus increasing the gearing ratio somewhat. However, this effect could be swamped by the change in the equity value).

(*Examination tip* – try to indicate your assumptions, if you think more than one answer might apply viz above point about issue expenses).

Requirement (d)

Advantages

- The reduction in debt and hence gearing (with debt representing ($22.5m/$547.5m) = 4% of long-term financing) will mollify the markets, if high gearing really is the root of DEB's problems. However, gearing at market value of 33.75% does not look excessive.

♦ The reduction in debt may replenish credit lines for future use.

♦ If covenants are under pressure, this may offer breathing space.

♦ If DEB has exceeded its critical gearing ratio, debt retirement may lower its WACC, according to traditional views of gearing.

Disadvantages

♦ Issue costs of new equity can easily amount to 3% of gross proceeds.

♦ Debt interest offers a tax shield to the profitable firm. If DEB is profitable, it is foregoing tax savings of (8% × $125m =) $10m × the tax rate. With tax at 40%, the annual saving is ($10m × 40%) = $4m.

♦ Markets do not always like rights issues, although the reception depends on the information released concurrently. But using new equity simply to retire debt may emit the wrong signals.

♦ The coupon rate on the debt is only 8% compared to the yield in the market of ($8/$90) = 9%, the rate DEB would have to pay for new debt finance. The plan thus involves retiring low cost debt that may soon have to be replenished by higher cost borrowing.

♦ Although the effect is purely cosmetic the fall in share price due to earnings dilution may have an adverse psychological effect on the market. (The EMH would refute this).

(*Examination tip* – as in section (c), try to give a modicum of explanation. Mere bullet points would probably only gain half a mark per valid point).

Answer 60 (Answer 3 of Exam Paper)

STF plc

Tutorial note:
Required — A very clear question, with opportunities to score well on parts (a) and (b).
Not required — CAPM theory in (a).

Requirement (a)

The CAPM formula for the required return on a portfolio is:

$K_P = R_F + [R_M - R_F] \beta_{portfolio}$

Portfolio Beta = $(1/3 \times 0.9) + (1/6 \times 1.50) + (1/2 \times 1.2) = (0.30 + 0.25 + 0.60) = 1.15$

Hence $R_P = 5\% + 1.15 (10\% - 5\%) = 10.75\%$

(*Examination tip* – remember that the bracketed term in the CAPM formula is the risk *premium* (5%) on the market portfolio, *not* the overall market return of 10%).

Requirement (b)

The types of marketable security are arranged in ascending order of risk.

Treasury Bills

Very short term (mainly three months) government securities, traded in a highly liquid market. New bills are sold at a discount to face value by weekly tender organised by the Bank of England. No interest payable as such, but redeemed at par to offer a capital gain.

Government stock

Long-term and medium-term securities issued by the state to raise money to finance its spending plans. The coupon rate is fixed but the actual yield varies depending on the market price of the stock, and it increases with the term to maturity. Easily traded on the capital market. Virtually free of default risk in advanced economies but subject to interest rate risk if sold before maturity.

Local Authority Bonds

Issued by local authorities and backed by the Treasury, thus offering minimal default risk. Less marketable than government securities. A variety of terms to maturity is available on both short- and long-term stock, and the yield varies with market prices.

Certificates of Deposit (CDs)

CDs are issued by banks to certify that funds have been deposited and are earning interest. Traded on the money market, allowing bearers to convert them into cash at any time. Maturities range from three months to five years. Highly liquid and low in risk, as they carry a bank guarantee.

Commercial Paper

Promissory notes (IOUs) issued below face value by larger firms direct to financial institutions and other corporates with cash surpluses. Restricted to firms with a Stock Exchange listing, and net assets exceeding £50 million. With maturities of 7 to 364 days, they are sold in minimum denominations of £500,000. No interest as such is payable, but they are redeemed at face value. Highly liquid and relatively low in risk.

Bills of Exchange (BOEs)

A BOE is an unconditional order by one firm to pay another party a given sum at a specified future date. Tradable, usually with a short maturity. Some are issued to support trade and are thus backed by the underlying transaction, and others (bank bills or acceptance credits) are issued by corporate borrowers using their credit worthiness as security. Bank bills give the firm the right to draw down on its bank account. Both forms are highly marketable, but risk depends on the issuer's credit worthiness.

Corporate Bonds

These offer higher yields than government stock of similar maturity due to higher default risk. Tradable in the capital market, with liquidity depending on the size of issue made. Underlying risk depends on the riskiness of the issuer and is assessed by credit agencies such as Standard & Poors. Can easily collapse in value if the firm's fortunes suffer.

(*Examination tip* – obviously, the question requires only five alternatives, but a couple extra are given here for completeness. Again, do not overkill. Only one mark is available per item mentioned, so two or three key points per item should win the mark. The question does say 'briefly describe', so a mere listing of alternatives is unlikely to score).

Requirement (c)

(*Examination tip* – remember your report format!)

MEMORANDUM

To: **Members of STF plc Board**

Subject: **Investment of Short-Term Funds**

From: **Management Accountant**

Date: **21 May 2002**

---

1   Introduction

The three key factors to consider when investing surplus funds are:

♦   the return expected
♦   the risks involved
♦   liquidity ie how easily the investment can be sold at minimal cost.

In our case, the critical aspects are the ability to liquidate our holdings to realise the sums required to pursue our strategic expenditures ie risk of loss and liquidity considerations are more important than expected returns. It is essential that we have easy access to a predictable amount in order to position ourselves to exploit acquisition opportunities.

2   The Finance Director's Comments

The FD correctly observes that diversification can lower risk. However, shareholders can achieve similar benefits by forming their own portfolios. We are operating a building firm not an investment trust. Moreover, the degree of risk reduction obtained in a three security portfolio is small, leaving substantial exposure to the risk of general market movements ie systematic risk. This portfolio, with Beta of 1.15, has above average exposure to general market movements. Despite above average expected turn, short-term investment in relatively risky equities is inappropriate in circumstances where we need to minimise risks and safeguard liquidity.

3   The Chairman's Comments

The chairman correctly emphasizes the need for protection against risk and for easy access to funds. Many of the suggested investment types are highly liquid, especially Treasury Bills, CDs and commercial paper but they carry varying degrees of risk. It is important to clarify the various sources of risk. These are:

♦   **Default risk.** The risk of outright default in the short-term with any of these investments is small, but markets do price in the risks of future default in debt service obligations. Consequently, securities issued by governments are inherently less risky than those issued by financial institutions and other businesses.

♦   **Liquidity risk.** This is the risk of inability to liquidate our funds easily at minimum loss. Local authority bonds and Bills of Exchange have a rather less ready market than, say, Treasury Bills and CDs.

♦   **Interest rate risk.** This refers to the effect of changing interest rates on the value of our holdings – generally, as interest rates rise, the capital value of fixed interest securities falls, and vice versa. Of course, interest rates may fall, but there is downside risk with traded bonds. Some of the other vehicles eg CDs, offer flexible interest rates and so their capital value is fixed, or are sufficiently short-term in nature eg Treasury Bills and commercial paper, to enable us to hold to maturity without loss.

♦ **Foreign Exchange Risk.** If we invest in foreign markets, we become exposed to the risk of loss if sterling appreciates against the currency of the country concerned. But the reverse is also true, besides if we are contemplating an overseas acquisition, investing in the target's home currency may give a hedge against foreign exchange risk.

4   The Marketing Director's Comments

Substantial holdings of cash and short-term securities will depress the firm's overall Return on Investment, as their yield is modest. They may also carry exposure to the risk of acquisition by a bidder offering to use the liquid resources more productively.

However, an exceptional payment to shareholders needs careful consideration. These investors have selected STF's shares expecting a particular stream of dividends. Suddenly raising the dividend may encourage expectations of similar future increases, and could trigger unwanted tax complications for owners.

If indeed we do require finance in the future to fund our strategic ambitions, we will have to incur not inconsiderable issue costs for a new equity issue, possibly when market conditions are weak ie unreceptive to rights issues. Retaining these funds will reserve for us the flexibility to pursue selected opportunities without the worry of raising new finance. In other words, the short-term cost in terms of lower returns may be justified by the pay-offs from exploiting possibly fleeting market opportunities.

I hope you find these comments useful. On balance, I would recommend a mixture of Treasury Bills, CDs and commercial paper of varying periods to maturity.

Signed: Management Accountant

(*Examination tip* – no recommendation is required, but you will surely gain credit for giving one.)

Answer 61 (Answer 4 of Exam Paper)

WCM Ltd

Tutorial note:	
Required	- Knowledge of working capital management procedures required here.
Not required	- Discussion of using short-term finance vs long-term finance.

Requirement (a)

INT is advancing payment of $98 per $100 invoiced, by 30 days, at a discount cost of $2. The implied interest rate offered is approximately:

(Cost of discount/Amount net of discount) × No of 30 day periods in a year × 100

= ($2/$98 × 365/30 × 100) = 24.83%

More precisely, this is:

$(1.02041)^{365/30} - 1 = 27.87\%$

(*Examination tip* – two levels of answer could be given here – the 'simple' answer and the more precise answer. With three marks available, the inference is that the examiner requires the precise answer for full marks but will award 1-2 marks for the approximation. Both are given in this answer).

Requirement (b)

Debtors are unchanged at:	$50,000
Stocks fall by $150,000 (as no purchases are made) to	$150,000
As no purchases are made, the overdraft will fall to	$400,000
Remaining trade creditors relate to April deliveries of	$150,000

Hence, current ratio = $\dfrac{\text{Current assets}}{\text{Current liabilities}} = \dfrac{\$200,000}{\$550,000} = 0.364{:}1\ (36.4\%)$

Requirement (c)

(*Examination tip* – remember your report format).

MEMORANDUM

To:	**Members of WCM Ltd Board**
Subject:	**Working Capital Management**
From:	**Management Accountant**
Date:	**21 May 2002**

1 Introduction

You have asked me to report on ways to reduce WCM's overdraft by changing working capital policies. Scope for doing this is limited due to limited flexibility in debtors policy, and other proposals carry major dangers, as explained below.

2 Policy towards paying suppliers

INT plc

The policy of paying early to access the cash discount damages liquidity, but the substantial implied return of 28%, well above the cost of our overdraft, offers a worthwhile increase in profitability. The question is whether it is worth foregoing the profit benefits in return for a one-off reduction in the overdraft to improve liquidity and reduce net interest payable?

GRN Ltd

Taking 40 days credit from GRN will technically breach their terms of sale and is likely to damage our relationship with a long-standing supplier. GRN, being smaller than WCM, may acquiesce in this, although under new legislation, it has the right to charge interest on overdue accounts. This really depends on our importance to GRN eg how easily it can find alternative customers.

GRN could retaliate in other ways eg by applying higher prices/lower trade discounts, delaying further deliveries until outstanding accounts are settled, cutting our credit limits by value. Moreover, if it becomes generally known that we are unilaterally delaying payment, this could damage our reputation, and eventually, our credit ratings elsewhere.

3 The proposed JIT system

Benefits of JIT include holding lower stocks, resulting in lower storage costs, reducing interest financing costs, and lower costs of wastage and shrinkage. Moreover, it should be possible to lower purchasing costs by making a long-term supply arrangement with designated suppliers, whose own costs may fall. Against this, the organisation's requirements are substantial. We need to receive more, but smaller, deliveries, possibly on a daily basis. Above all, we need to have utmost trust in the ability of our suppliers to deliver the correct quantities, of suitable quality, and at the right time. This requires close and ongoing liaison at all times, which itself is costly.

Our present policy is a 'just-in-case' policy, giving the benefits of safety. The more predictable the demand for our products, the less safety stock required. At present, we hold two months supplies – this seems excessive. Nevertheless we distribute a wide range of different tools, and a certain minimum stock seems necessary, if we wish to avoid periodic stock-outs in some lines, and hence, lost sales.

Moving directly to JIT is risky in our situation. It is more suitable for process industries where input requirements are more predictable, rather than distributive trades, where daily and weekly demand is erratic. Perhaps we can arrange *quicker* delivery, say on a fortnightly basis, rather than the bi-monthly deliveries implied by our present policy.

4 Assessment

Currently, our working capital is negative, and we have a sizeable overdraft. The proposed changes actually threaten to worsen liquidity ie the current ratio would fall from 50% to 36%. Negative working capital is not necessarily a problem, often, as in our case, reflecting the ability to trade largely in cash terms, and utilise the monies received by investment in other assets. In effect, we receive cash before we pay for supplies – an enviable position. Rather than use potentially dangerous ways of tightening liquidity to lower the overdraft, it may be more appropriate to raise money in other ways eg by asset sales, or by raising long-term finance, possibly by converting the overdraft into a term loan. At the very least, we should consult our suppliers rather than unilaterally changing our policies, as they may offer alternative terms in order to protect their own businesses.

Signed: Management Accountant

Answer 62 (Answer 5 of Exam Paper)

WEB plc

Tutorial note:	
Required	- Quite a lot of overlap with Question 2, as it deals with analysis of capital structure again. Clearly, this is likely to be a much examined issue.
Not required	- 'Advanced' capital structure theory.

Requirement (a)

The cost of equity is given by:

$$k_e = \frac{D_1}{P_0} + g = \frac{\$1(1.04)}{\$10.40} + 0.04 = (0.10 + 0.04) = 0.14 \text{ ie } 14\%$$

The cost of debt, R, is found from the IRR expression:

Current market price = sum of discounted post-tax future returns

$$\$100.84 = \frac{\$9[1-30\%]}{(1+R)} + \frac{\$9[1-30\%]}{(1+R)^2} + \frac{(\$9[1-30\%]+\$100)}{(1+R)^3}$$

At 6%, $\$100.84 \approx \$5.94 + \$5.61 + (\$5.29 + \$83.96)$

Hence cost of debt = 6%

(***Examination tip*** – a high degree of precision is not required in the IRR computation. Do not waste time in repetitive iterations).

Market value of equity = 100m × $10.40 = $1,040.00m (83.8% of the total)

Market value of debt $= \$200m \times \dfrac{\$100.84}{\$100} = \$201.68m$ (16.2% of the total)

Hence, WACC $\qquad = (83.8\% \times 14\%) + (16.2\% \times 6\%)$

$\qquad\qquad\qquad\qquad = 11.73\% + 0.97\% = 12.7\%$

Requirement (b)

Cost of equity

Since WEB is already quite highly geared (at book value), the most likely effect is to increase the cost of equity. Owners will require higher returns because:

♦ A higher proportion of profits is now pre-empted by interest, a prior charge, so residual equity earnings from which dividends are paid, become riskier.

♦ The risk of default on debt interest increases, and thus financial distress is more likely.

Cost of debt

Although gearing is modest at market values, lenders tend to look more at book value measures, especially when imposing debt covenants. Lenders look also at the fixed asset backing for their loans. Net assets at $150m are already only 75% of debt (ignoring any short-term borrowing). The proposed bank loan will add $30m to borrowings and increase debt/equity, and lower interest cover, initially at least. As it is difficult to sell aircraft at book value given the massive over-capacity in the industry, lenders will be concerned at WEB's ability to repay debt in a crisis.

Consequently, the proposal is likely to increase the cost of debt because:

♦ The chances of financial distress have increased.
♦ The likelihood of full repayment in a liquidation is lower.

The WACC

The impact on the WACC is ambiguous. An increase in debt, even at high gearing levels, can still lower the WACC because debt is invariably cheaper than equity, especially when tax relief on interest is allowed for. Although the costs of both equity and debt are likely to rise, the net effect is uncertain, given the relative cheapness of debt. It really depends how sharply owners react to an increase in gearing, and whether WEB is beyond the critical gearing ratio. If its gearing already exceeds the level at which the WACC is minimised, or if the proposed increase propels it beyond this point, this will certainly raise the WACC. Any beneficial effect of cheap debt will be outweighed by the shareholders' adverse reaction.

(*Examination tip* – a diagram might be useful here to show the WACC profile with increases in gearing.)

Requirement (c)

Debentures

In law, a debenture is any written acknowledgement of a debt and consequent obligation to repay, but the term is usually applied to secured loan stock. The loan may be secured on specific assets (fixed charge) or on the firm's assets in general (floating charge).

They normally specify a fixed interest rate and a repayment date eg 2007 or time interval eg 2007-9, when the principal will be repaid. Debentures are usually issued to several investors, but a prospectus is required for public issues. Once issued, they can be traded on secondary markets eg via the Stock Exchange if the firm is listed.

Bank loans

A bank loan is usually a contract with a single lender, although large loans can be syndicated to spread risks. Bank loans are not traded, although in recent years, some banks have securitised their loan portfolios to sell them on the financial markets as Asset-Backed Securities, resembling debentures in many ways. The interest rate is usually fixed, although it may be tied to LIBOR, and the loan is subject to a strict schedule of interest and capital repayments.

Why their costs differ

♦   The yield on the existing debentures is 6% after tax, which represents the cost of raising new debentures, while the bank loan carries an interest rate of 8% pre-tax ie 5.6% post-tax.

♦   The issue costs of a debenture eg admin etc are usually higher than the arrangement fees typically charged by banks.

♦   A bank has a wider portfolio of clients over which it can spread risks. This may enable it to charge a lower rate of interest.

♦   A bank is better able than debenture holders to monitor the performance of borrowers and thus the safety of its capital. It may pass on lower monitoring costs to its borrowers.

♦   A disparity in the range and severity of loan covenants applied by lenders may explain different interest charges. Again because the bank can more easily monitor its client, it may impose less onerous covenants.

♦   Against this, the comfort of imposing more covenants may induce lenders to accept lower interest rates.

♦   Usually, the loan outstanding will decrease over time, thus pushing up the effective interest rate.

♦   Because debentures are marketable, investors may accept a lower interest rate in return for greater liquidity.

(*Examination tip* – A lot could be said here, but only four marks are going, so avoid spending too much time. This answer here is too extensive – allow a mark apiece for the definitions, plus a couple for reasons why the rates differ.)

Answer 63 (Answer 6 of Exam Paper)

PRT Ltd

Tutorial note:
Required   - A very focused question, with clear requirements.
Not required   - FRS 3 format for part (b).

Requirement (a)

Cash operating cycle = [stock days plus debtor days less trade creditor days]

Stocks:

Raw materials: $\dfrac{(55+80)/2}{850} \times 365$ = 29 days

plus

Finished goods: $\dfrac{(185+185)/2}{1,830} \times 365$ = 37 days

 = **66 days**

Debtor days: $\dfrac{(114+200)/2}{1,996} \times 365$ = 29 days

Creditor days: $\dfrac{(50+70)/2}{850} \times 365$ = (26 days)

Overall cycle time: **= 69 days**

(*Examination tip* – the question asks for the figures for 2002, so you can work in terms of start- and end-year averages, as shown in the answer. You might lose a mark or two for using end-year figures only.)

Requirement (b)

Cash generated from operations ($000):

Sales:		1,996
Less increase in debtors (200 – 114)		(86)
Less cash expenses:		
Cost of sales	(1,830)	
Plus increase in trade creditors	20	
Less increase in stocks (0 + 25)	(25)	
Less admin expenses	(65)	(1,900)
Net cash flow from operating activities		10

(*Examination tip* – it is worth pointing out that no mention is made of depreciation. The answer here assumes there has been no provision for depreciation made before arriving at cost of sales.)

Requirement (c)

(*Examination tip* – the issues raised in this question blend financial and marketing considerations.)

MEMORANDUM

To:	**Members of PRT Ltd Board**
Subject:	**Cash and Working Capital**
From:	**Management Accountant**
Date:	**21 May 2002**

Introduction

PRT's strategy has resulted in rapid growth in capacity, 50% pa on average, by purchasing new premises. This has imposed severe strain on cash resources, as shown by our widening overdraft, which has more than doubled this year. To date, we are not reaping the sales benefits – this year's increase being only around 18.5%. Obviously, it takes time for new investments to pay off, possibly due to:

- new outlets being smaller than existing ones
- newer outlets being sited in less attractive locations
- introductory offers at new premises to get them established
- 'cannibalisation' of sales from existing premises.

Clearly, this situation needs careful monitoring and argues for a breathing space in our expansion, as it appears that we are over-trading.

Our inability to obtain long-term external finance means growth has necessarily been financed from internal resources. But because sales growth is lagging, cash flow from operations is far too low to finance growth, hence the increase in the overdraft. In effect, we have financed acquisition of long-term assets by short-term finance, violating the 'Golden Rule' of finance. Should the bank require us to curtail the overdraft, we may be unable to liquidate these assets quickly without loss.

Cash management

Clearly, we cannot keep increasing the overdraft at this rate, nor can we easily repay the overdraft in a hurry. Hence, we need to maintain good and close banking relations. This requires:

- supplying monthly management accounts in timely fashion
- informing the bank in advance of any additional cash needs
- directors pledging personal security if required to support extra finance.

Meanwhile, as well as putting a moratorium on further expansion to allow us to consolidate, we should look in other directions to generate more cash, for example, working capital management.

Working Capital Management

Working capital management can be used to 'fine tune' the cash flow position, but will not totally solve our problems. Moreover, one must bear in mind that the balance sheet figures are not totally reliable – they can hide seasonality, unusually high or low transactions towards the year end might have been 'window-dressed'. Nevertheless, there appears to be scope for improvement.

Debtors

The 29 day average collection period hides the mix of cash and credit sales. Given that individual customers pay cash, the credit period taken by business customers is rather longer, and can be shortened by offering discounts for early, or cash, payment. Alternatively factoring or invoice discounting, although costly, can be used to advance cash flows. However, it is important to consider customer goodwill here – if we suddenly impose more onerous terms that are out of line with competitors' offerings, we might lose business, especially in the newer locations.

Creditors

We seem to be paying suppliers very quickly – quicker than our business customers pay us. Are we exploiting early payment terms at the expense of liquidity, or are we losing our credit lines as word travels about how we are over-trading? Again, if we unilaterally decide to lengthen the payment period, goodwill with suppliers may suffer.

Stocks

Our business is a mixture of made-to-order jobs and sales from the stock we hold. Materials bought for immediate use on bespoke jobs are held very briefly, so other items must sit in stores for more than the 29 day average. Similarly, stocks of finished goods if bespoke jobs are excluded, are carried for much longer than the 27 day average. There is scope for rationalisation here, eg quicker movement of stocks between receipt of delivery and use. More careful examination of demand patterns will be needed.

Conclusion

The main priority is to stop the overdraft growing. This means restraining or ceasing growth and concentrating on realising sales and cash flow benefits from recently opened premises. Tighter management of working capital offers limited benefits and may offend customers and suppliers. We must look therefore at fixed assets to raise cash – can we dispose of under-performing shops, or franchise them? Is it possible to sell prime sites to financial institution via sale and leaseback? Although we forego future capital appreciation, this may be the price of survival.

Signed: Management Accountant

November 2002 Exam Answers

Answer 64 (Answer 1 of Exam Paper)

Objective test questions

64.1 C

64.2 B

64.3 D

64.4 A

If the rights issue is of the form 1 : x (ie 1 new share for every x shares owned) then the theoretical ex-rights price is given by:

$$\frac{£10x + £6}{x + 1} = £9$$

Rearranging:

£10x + £6 = £9x + £9

£1x = £3, thus x = 3

The rights issue is thus 1 : 3

64.5 C

$2/3 \times K_e + 1/3 \times 5\%$	=	8%
$\Rightarrow 2/3 \times K_e = 8\% - 5/3\%$ =	19/3%	
$\Rightarrow K_e$	=	9.5%

64.6 B

The shares will go ex-rights and thus will fall in value; total equity will be increased by the rights proceeds.

64.7 C

Asset 1   PV of lease rentals:

Time	£	df	PV £
0 – 9	12,000	1 + 5.759	81,108

It is better to buy at a PV of £80,000.

Asset 2   PV of lease rentals (on an opportunity cost basis):

Time	£	df	PV £
1 – 5	14,000	3.791	53,074
5	40,000*	0.621	24,840
			77,914

As buying has a comparative PV of £81,000, it is better to lease.

*Lost residual value.

64.8 B

Higher growth expectations lead to increased market price; higher risk expectations lead to a lower market price.

64.9 B

$$\text{Interest cover} = \frac{\text{Profit before interest and tax}}{\text{Interest}} = \frac{£50m}{£10m} = 5 \text{ times}$$

64.10 B

Converting each rate to an equivalent annual rate:

A $(1.016)^4$ $- 1 = 0.06556 = 6.556\%$
B $(1.035)^2$ $- 1 = 0.07123 = 7.123\%$
C $(1.052)^{12/9}$ $- 1 = 0.06993 = 6.993\%$
D $= 7.000\%$

64.11 A

64.12 C

	Effect on WC
Increase in debtors	24,000
Increase in creditors	(18,000)
Decrease in stock (purchases £18,000 less COS £19,200)	(1,200)
	4,800

64.13 C

Monthly sales	240,000
Decrease in trade debtors	12,000
	252,000

64.14 A

An example scenario where the cash in question is 5:

	Existing	*Transaction 1*	*Transaction 2*
Stock etc	10	10	10
Debtors	20	15	20
	30	25	30
Creditors	5	5	5
Overdraft	10	5	5
	15	10	10
Current ratio	2.0	2.5	3.0

64.15 C

Delaying payment to creditors increases cash (asset) and increases creditors (liability) leaving net working capital unchanged.

64.16 A

64.17 B

64.18   C

The amounts raised under each price are as follows:

£5 × 0.5m	=	£2.5m
£4.50 × (0.5 + 0.8)m	=	£5.85m
£4 × (0.5 + 0.8 + 0.2)m	=	£6m
£3.50 × (0.5 + 0.8 + 0.2 + 0.1)m	=	£5.6m

64.19   D

30 + 38 – 44 = 24 days

64.20   C

Answer 65 (Answer 2 of Exam Paper)

AAD Ltd

(a)   **Budgeted cash receipts from debtors**

(for (b))

Class	Sales		Receipts £000			Drs	Overdue
	Month	£000	Nov	Dec	Jan	£000	days
A	Oct	100		50	30	20	30 – 60
	Nov	150			75	75	0 – 30
	Dec	200				200	-
	Jan	300				300	-
B	Oct	60	36	15	6	3	>60 (BD)
	Nov	80		48	20	12	30 – 60
	Dec	40			24	16	0 – 30
	Jan	50				50	-
			36	113	155		

(b)   **Budgeted age analysis of debtors at 30 January 2003**

Using the information from the table in (a):

Class		Age of debt (days overdue)			
		-	1 – 29	30 – 60	>60 (bad debt)
A	£000	500	75	20	
B	£000	50	16	12	3
Total	**£000**	**550**	**91**	**32**	**3**

(c)   An age analysis of debtors in general provides useful information to management about the creditworthiness of their customers and the effectiveness of their debt collection procedures. It gives an indication of the level of credit risk to which the organisation is exposed at any time – with the older debts being more likely to go bad.

In addition, historic age analysis may be used for prediction of future cash receipts from debtors for cash flow forecast purposes and may be used as a basis for testing the potential effects of new credit policies.

An age analysis analysed by individual debtors gives more specific information about the particular customers that are potentially going to cause problems and most likely to lead to bad debts. Once these have been identified from the analysis, action should be taken to reduce the risk attached to the debts. Such action would commonly follow the route of:

Reminder letter/statement – phone call – visit – refusal of further orders – employ debt collection agency – threaten legal action – take legal action.

Answer 66 (Answer 3 of Exam Paper)

STK Ltd

(a)   **Optimal order size with SSS plc as sole supplier**

$$EOQ = \sqrt{\frac{2C_oD}{C_h}}$$

where C_o =   Cost of placing an order = £200

          C_h =   Cost of holding one unit in stock for one year
                     = £4 + 3% (£400) = £16

          D =   Annual demand = 10,000 units

Thus EOQ = $\sqrt{\dfrac{2 \times £200 \times 10,000}{£16}}$ = 500 units

(b)   (i)   This will be tackled by comparing the minimum annual costs associated with purchasing, ordering and holding stock from the two suppliers.

        SSS plc

(Ordering 500 units at a time)		*£000*
Purchase cost	£400 × 10,000	4,000
Order costs	$\dfrac{10,000}{500} \times £200$	4
Holding costs	$\dfrac{500}{2} \times £16$	4
		4,008

        RRR Ltd

First we must determine the EOQ:

C_o =   Cost of placing an order = £500

C_h =   Cost of holding one unit in stock for one year
                 = £4 + 3% (£398) = £15.94

D   =   Annual demand = 10,000 units

Thus EOQ = $\sqrt{\dfrac{2 \times £500 \times 10,000}{£15.94}}$ = 792 units

We are restricted to ordering a minimum of 1,000 units and the fact that the EOQ is lower than this indicates that total costs will be minimised, subject to this constraint, by ordering 1,000 units 10 times a year.

		£000
Purchase cost	£398 × 10,000	3,980
Order costs	$\dfrac{10,000}{1,000} \times £500$	5
Holding costs	(600 + 1,000/2) × £15.94	17.534
		4,002.534

Total annual costs are minimised by ordering from RRR Ltd giving a cost saving of £5,466.

(ii) The supplier decision should not be made on financial grounds alone. Other factors to consider will include:

- **Uncertainty/risk** – supplies from RRR Ltd are subject to a greater level of uncertainty in terms of lead time, and there is greater risk of stock-outs, even with buffer stock.

- **Location** – SSS plc is close to STK and emergency deliveries in the case of unexpected demand or faulty supplies will be far easier to arrange.

- **Reputation** – STK will need to check out each supplier's reputation for reliability, quality, after sales service, etc.

- **Forex risk** – it is not clear whether STK is to be invoiced in sterling or foreign currency by RRR Ltd. If the latter, consideration will need to be made of the need for hedging forex risk, with the additional costs this will involve.

(c) **MEMORANDUM**

To: Managing Director, RRR Ltd

From: Consultant

Date: XX/XX/XX

Re: Financing working capital for STK contract

The provision of sufficient working capital is of particular importance when supporting export trade, due to the additional uncertainties involved:

- Lead times are long and uncertain leading to variable additional working capital tied up in stock.

- Dealing with overseas customers is generally slower and we have less local knowledge of creditworthiness, etc leading to longer collection periods and increased chance of bad debts.

- Depending upon whether we invoice in domestic or overseas (UK) currency, we may have to incur additional risks/costs in forex management.

- Additional delays may be caused by export/import regulations, etc.

Methods of financing the working capital include:

Bills of exchange

A bill of exchange is a promise to pay a certain sum of money at a given future date – in effect, a post-dated cheque. You, as exporter, can send a bill of exchange for the value of goods shipped through the banking system for payment by STK on presentation. Goods will only be released on STK's acceptance of the bill. You can then either wait for STK's bank to pay on the bill or discount it at your bank to get the cash (albeit slightly less) earlier.

Documentary Letters of Credit (DLC)

A DLC is a facility set up by the importer upon which the exporter can draw in their own country provided they deliver the documents proving the satisfactory shipment of goods ordered.

This provides security to both parties – the importer knows that payment will only be made once the order has been properly fulfilled and the exporter knows that payment will be promptly forthcoming after shipment.

DLCs can, however, be expensive in that the importer may require a better price in exchange for its use. There is also a lot of paperwork involved and the process can be time consuming. This method is best used where you may have serious doubts about STK's ability to pay.

Forfaiting

Forfaiting is a form of medium-term financing of overseas trade that would involve the purchase by a bank (the forfaiter) of a series of promissory notes, usually due at six month intervals for three to five years, signed by STK in favour of RRR. They should be guaranteed ('avalised') by STK's bank and you can then sell them to a bank at a discount without recourse.

Thus, bad debt risk is again reduced and you will get the cash (discounted) quicker, thus minimising forex risk. It is, however, expensive in terms of the discount.

Export factoring

When the invoice to STK is to be settled on open account, rather than via a bill of exchange etc, it may be assigned as collateral for bank financing. RRR will sell the invoice to a factor and receive local currency in return. The factor bears the credit risks, the cost of financing and the cost of covering against exchange risk. This makes this an expensive process for you but brings the additional benefits of the factor's expertise and knowledge in risk assessment, credit management and debt collection.

Answer 67 (Answer 4 of Exam Paper)

CAP plc

(a)   Under CAPM:

k_e (cost of equity) =

R_f (risk free rate) + βg (equity beta) (R_m (expected market return) – R_f)

=   5% + 0.8 (15% - 5%)

=   13%

The beta measure for an investment indicates its level of systematic (undiversifiable) risk relative to that of the market as a whole. A beta of 1 would signify an investment that carried the same level of risk as the average of all securities in the market. A beta of less than 1, as in the case of CAP plc, indicates that CAP plc's equity returns are generally less risky than market average – a change in, say, the economy, will have a lesser effect on the returns to CAP plc's shareholders than that experienced market wide. A 10% downward movement in, say, the FTSE all-share index would only see an 8% downward movement in CAP's share price.

(b) $\quad k_p$ (cost of preference shares) $= \dfrac{d(\text{annual preference dividend})}{P_o(\text{current ex - div MP})} = 9p/90p = 10\%$

The cost of the redeemable debt ($k_{d\ net}$) is the IRR of the related flows represented by r below (assuming no delay on tax relief and redemption at par):

Time	Cash flow	df	PV
0	100.57 market value	1	100.57
1	(8 (0.7) post-tax interest)	1	
	(100.00 redemption)	(1 + r)	(100.57)
			-

$\dfrac{105.6}{1+r} = 100.57 => \dfrac{105.6}{100.57} = 1 + r => r = 0.05$ or 5%

Total market value of equity	=	200m × £3	=	£600m
Total market value of prefs	=	50m × £0.90	=	£45m
Total market value of equity	=	250m × £1.0057	=	£251.425m

WACC

	Cost %	MV £m	Weighted cost
Equity	13	600	8.701
Preference	10	45	0.502
Loan stock	5	251.425	1.402
		896.425	10.605

The weighted average cost of capital is 10.605%.

(c) CAP plc's equity beta measures the risk attached to equity returns. These returns have two elements:

♦ the underlying earnings which are subject to *business risk*; and

♦ the fixed interest charge against those earnings which amplifies the earnings risk in arriving at overall dividend risk – the amplification being known as *gearing risk*.

Any factors that affect either of these two risk elements will affect CAP plc's equity beta. In particular:

♦ the *new project* will carry a different level of business risk in its earnings stream. The low correlation between existing and project earnings will help to diversify unsystematic risk, but this is irrelevant when looking at the beta as this is concerned only with systematic risk. The effect on the overall beta of CAP plc will be determined by the project's own beta which relates the project return risk and market return risk.

♦ The *additional loan stock finance* raised for the project will increase the gearing of the company which will have a knock-on effect on the equity beta, which will rise.

♦ The *redemption of the existing loan stock* and its replacement, if any, may also affect the gearing level and thus the equity beta.

♦ *Other changes* in the economy in general or the farming industry in particular may affect the variability in future equity returns in relation to those of the market. Betas will therefore fluctuate over time even without specific operational or financing changes.

Answer 68 (Answer 5 of Exam Paper)

HRD Ltd

(a)

	£000
Expected cash balance at 30 November 2002	175
Expected cash flow December 2002 ($700 \times 0.7 - 300 \times 0.3$)	400
Expected cash flow January 2003	(900)
Expected cash balance at 31 January 2003	(325)

The expected cash balance at 31 January 2003 is an overdraft of £325,000. This figure should not be used for short-term cash planning as it is not a cash balance that will actually occur. With a 70% probability, the cash balance will be 175 + 700 – 900 = £25,000 overdrawn, or 175 – 300 – 900 = £1,025,000 overdrawn with 30% probability. It is these actual possible balances that should be planned for. The balance calculated above is simply a weighted average of them.

(b) **MEMORANDUM**

To:	Board of Directors, HRD Ltd
From:	Treasury Assistant
Date:	XX/XX/XX
Re:	Investment of short-term cash balances

This memorandum addresses the possibilities for investment of short-term cash balances, if any, in December 2002 and January 2003.

The cash balance at the end of November will be £175,000. During December, whilst we would normally expect a large cash surplus of around £700,000, it is estimated that there is a 30% chance that our rival group will offer discounts that could reduce this significantly to a deficit of £300,000. Taken with our normal negative cash flow in January, the possible cash positions are therefore as follows (excluding interest):

	Cash flow £000	
	Without competition	*With competition*
Balance 30/11/02	175	175
December cash flow	700	(300)
Balance at 31/12/02	875	(125)
January cash flow	(900)	(900)
Balance at 31/1/03	(25)	(1,025)

We should certainly invest the £175,000 surplus at the end of November for at least one month (assuming the monthly cash flows arise at the end of the month).

If the competition does not arise, we would then be able to invest it for a further month along with the £700,000 earned in December. However, in these circumstances, it would have been better to invest the £175,000 for two months up front as this attracts a higher interest rate. The risk with this action, however, is that if the competition does impact on us in December, we will be incurring overdraft rates at 10% whilst only earning interest at 6%.

Taking account of the interest earned/incurred, the various possible actions and outcomes are as follows:

Action 1 – Invest £175,000 for one month initially

		Cash £	
	Without competition		*With competition*
Available at end of:			
December			
- Investment (175,000 × 1.004074)	175,713		175,713
- December cash flow	700,000		(300,000)
	875,713		(124,287)
January			
- Interest on investment (875,713 × 0.004074)	3,568		
- Interest on overdraft (124,287 × 0.007974)			(991)
- January cash flow	(900,000)		(900,000)
	(20,719)		(1,025,278)
Probability	70%		30%
Expected balance end January		£(322,087)	

Action 2 – Invest £175,000 for two months up front

		Cash £	
	Without competition		*With competition*
Available at end of:			
December			
- December cash flow	700,000		(300,000)
January			
- November investment (175,000 × 1.009759)	176,708		176,708
- Interest on Dec investment (700,000 × 0.004074)	2,852		
- Interest on overdraft (300,000 × 0.007974)			(2,392)
- January cash flow	(900,000)		(900,000)
	(20,440)		(1,025,684)
Probability	70%		30%
Expected balance end January		£(322,013)	

On an expected value basis there is very little difference in the final amount of overdraft at the end of January – Action 2, investing the November surplus for two months up front, has a small marginal advantage (£74).

However, it is the actual outcomes which are of greater relevance: if we invest the November surplus for one month only and the competition does not impact on us (70% chance), we will have lost out on £279 against the option of investing for two months up front (20,440 v 20,719). However, if the competition does come into play (30% chance), investing for one month only leaves us with an overdraft which is lower by £406 (1,025,684 v 1,025,278).

Overall, the amounts are not significantly different and since the weightings are in favour of competition not having an impact on us, it is probably advisable to go for the two month investment. However, if the company is getting dangerously near its overdraft limit, investment for one month may be preferable to minimise the potential overdraft at 31 January.

(c)   The Miller-Orr model of cash management has the advantage over more traditional models in the circumstances where cash flows are unpredictable from one month to the next. The model is based upon the setting of three cash levels:

◆   A *return point* – to which cash balances should be restored when it exceeds the limits set out below.

◆   An *upper limit* – above which cash balances should not be allowed to rise; cash should be invested in short-term interest earning securities to bring the balance back to the return point.

◆   A *lower limit* – below which cash balances should not be allowed to fall. Short-term securities must be sold to realise enough cash to bring the balance back to the return point.

The lower limit is set by management from experience and knowledge of the lowest workable cash balance required; the model then computes the upper limit and the return point, based upon the interest rates, transaction costs and variability of the cash flows in each particular case.

On the face of it, the Miller-Orr model would appear to be suitable for use by HRD Ltd as it is facing a 'high degree of uncertainty' in relation to cash surpluses and deficits generated each month from January 2003. The model can also take into account seasonality such as HRD's Christmas and Summer high activity levels. However, it would appear that HRD Ltd is actually likely to have an overdraft for most of the year, leaving little opportunity to apply the model to cash balances. In addition, the model is also based upon the principle that cash takes a 'random walk' between the limits; whilst HRD's cash flows are uncertain, they are not completely unpredictable. The model may not provide as close a control as that afforded by a carefully monitored cash flow forecast with best estimates of sales and costs built into it.

Answer 69 (Answer 6 of Exam Paper)

COE plc

(a)   In a semi-strong efficient market, at any point in time share prices reflect all information that is publicly available at that time.

COE has been testing the new drug kryothin for many years. It is likely that the market will be aware of this; however, in early years of testing it is unlikely that it will have any effect on the share price as the company will always be testing drugs, many of which will not come to the market.

As a positive outcome becomes more likely, investors will start to build their expectations into the share price. Perhaps the first point at which this might happen with kryothin is upon the registration of its patent. However, this will still be some way from successful production and low probabilities will be applied to possible returns when investors predict future expected dividends.

Between patent registration and Government approval, more information about the development of the drug will become available to the market and, depending upon its nature, the share price will move up or down. It will be a period of significant fluctuation.

On 1 March 2002 the drug was given Government approval. Having reached this stage, it is likely that the market has already made some decision about whether approval would be gained or not and the share price will have adjusted accordingly. If approval has been anticipated, its confirmation will have little impact on share price. If this news is unexpected then the share price is likely to rise significantly if good returns from the drug are expected. The same comments will apply regarding the reaction or otherwise to the approval by other countries.

By the time sales commence on 1 January 2003 the expected value of future returns is likely to be already fully reflected in the share price, and this event in itself will have little impact. If sales do not run according to expectations, however, whether for better or worse, this information will be rapidly discounted into the price. As sales decline with increasing competition, the share price will fall back into line with previous levels until the next new drug is developed.

(b)   **Option (1)**

With no extra interest to pay, the total market value of COE plc after the finance is raised is equal to the present value of the dividends as given in the question:

Time	Dividends £m	10% df	PV £m
1 – 5	32.2	3.791	122.07
6 - ∞	19.0	$1/0.1 \times 0.621$	117.99
			240.06

Total market value = £240 million.

Of this, £80m relates to the new shares issued under the offer for sale as they are issued at current market price. Thus, £160m relates to the 20m existing shares giving a market price per share of **£8.**

Option (2)

If the capital is provided by way of the bonds then the dividends will be reduced by the interest payable which is $7\% \times £80m = £5.6m$ (ignoring tax).

In perpetuity, this will reduce the market value of the shares by £5.6m/0.1 = £56m.

Thus, total market value of the shares will now be £240m - £56m = £184m; there will now be just the existing 20m shares in issue giving a share price per share of **£9.20.**

Exam Kit Review Form

CIMA PAPER 4 KIT - FINANCE

We hope that you have found this Kit stimulating and useful and that you now feel confident and well-prepared for your examinations.

We would be grateful if you could take a few moments to complete the questionnaire below, so we can assess how well our material meets your needs. There's a prize for four lucky students who fill in one of these forms from across the Syllabus range and are lucky enough to be selected!

	Excellent	*Adequate*	*Poor*
Depth and breadth of technical coverage			
Appropriateness of coverage to examination			
Presentation			
Level of accuracy			

Did you spot any errors or ambiguities? Please let us have the details below.

Page	**Error**

Thank you for your feedback.

Please return this form to:

Student's name: ....

The Financial Training Company Limited
Unit 22J
Wincombe Business Park
Shaftesbury
Dorset SP7 9QJ

Address: ....

....

....